LANGUAGE ALIVE IN THE CLASSROOM

EDITED BY
REBECCA S. WHEELER

PRAEGER

Westport, Connecticut
London

Library of Congress Cataloging-in-Publication Data

Language alive in the classroom / edited by Rebecca S. Wheeler.
    p. cm.
   Includes bibliographical references and index.
   ISBN 0–275–96055–2 (alk. paper).—ISBN 0–275–96056–0 (pbk. :
alk. paper)
   1. Language and languages—Study and teaching. I. Wheeler,
Rebecca S., 1952– .
   P51.L338   1999
   410'.71—dc21   98–53391

British Library Cataloguing in Publication Data is available.

Library of Congress Catalog Card Number: 98–53391
ISBN: 0–275–96055–2
     0–275–96056–0 (pbk.)

First published in 1999

Praeger Publishers, 88 Post Road West, Westport, CT 06881
An imprint of Greenwood Publishing Group, Inc.
www.praeger.com

Printed in the United States of America

The paper used in this book complies with the
Permanent Paper Standard issued by the National
Information Standards Organization (Z39.48–1984).

10 9 8 7 6 5 4 3 2 1

CONTENTS

III.   Language and Writing

IV.   Language and Literature

V. On Dictionaries and Grammars

INTRODUCTION

This volume is directed to teachers—teachers in preparation and teachers already in practice. It speaks to students in teacher education pursuing certification to teach English in primary or secondary schools as well as seasoned teachers who might appreciate a new, animated vantage on teaching grammar and language structure. The chapters offer material relevant to grades one through twelve and beyond into the college classroom. However, even the higher-gauged materials could be readily reworked for elementary and secondary schools.

This volume assumes that as an English or language arts teacher, you will need to deal with grammar and language in the classroom. It also assumes that you may well feel trepidation at the thought of teaching grammar. Even if you yourself do not view the subject as boring, it is certain that some or even many of your students will. Accordingly, you may be groping for how to engage with grammar so it feels like language structure belongs to you, like it's alive, like it has to do with the world *you* know. *Language Alive in the Classroom* speaks to these concerns.

With Part I, "Beyond Grammar of the Traditional Kind," we begin at our common ground, acknowledging and exploring why we have hard feelings toward traditional grammar. The authors then pull back the curtain on the traditional grammar wizard, showing that the traditional approach doesn't even work as a description of our language.

David B. Umbach, in "Grammar, Tradition, and the Living Language," argues that when we talk about language, what we say can easily be overshadowed by how we say it. He discusses the effects of traditional ways of talking about language on his students' ability and willingness to learn linguistics and finds that the problem is a bit more complicated than the well-known distinction between the descriptive and prescriptive approaches.

Edwin Battistella's chapter on "The Persistence of Traditional Grammar" looks at the nature of traditional grammar and its limitations and at the constituencies that make up its critics and defenders. He goes on to discuss some of the reasons why traditional grammar has remained influential in American society and how linguists can contribute to curriculum discussions.

In "Prestige English Is Not a Natural Language," Nicholas Sobin argues that the nonprestige varieties of English are linguistically sound, viable, natural language, something that linguists have known for a long time. However, he argues further that the constructions characteristic of more prestigious English may be linguistically "unnatural" contrivances—constructions that are characteristically difficult because they do not follow normal linguistic rules and processes available to language learners. Further, the explanations found in traditional grammars of how the prestige constructions work may be inaccurate or completely off base, another factor contributing to their difficulty.

John Myhill, in "Rethinking Prescriptivism," notes that prescriptive norms in most languages, including English, are based upon the native usage of the elite speakers of the language. This results in putting lower-status speakers at a considerable disadvantage; not only do they have more work to do in modifying their native usage, they also have the psychological burden of having to abandon their own everyday usage and adopt someone else's, while elite speakers can to a large extent simply use their everyday language and be declared "correct." There are, however, a few languages, for instance Hebrew, Arabic, and Norwegian, that have a prescriptive norm that is fair in the sense of not being particularly associated with one or another group.

In Part II, "New Ways in the Classroom," the authors offer an alternative model for engaging with language in the school setting. Instead of drills, diagrams, and droning lists, the authors bring us our everyday language, inviting students to become sleuths as they uncover linguistic patterns at work. From discovering that language "errors" may well signal the seismic faults of language change to exploring the complex and subtle patterns of talk in the mountains of Southern Appalachia and on the shores of Ocracoke, students engage with the living language.

In Walt Wolfram's chapter, "Dialect Awareness Programs in the School and Community," we see how dialect awareness curricula have secondary-school children exploring the inner workings of the Ocracoke brogue. Moving inland to Southern Appalachia, schoolchildren discover for themselves the patterns governing sentences like "She was a-building a house" but not *"A-building is hard work" and "They make money a-building houses" but not *"They make money by a-building houses." (The asterisk indicates an unacceptable sentence.) And in doing so, students learn firsthand the falsity of the popular stereotype that vernacular varieties are nothing more than imperfect attempts to speak the standard variety. Students learn that "grammar rules" are about how we actually use natural language, not just prescriptive dicta from books. Wolfram's chapter provides both the rationale and a model for implementing partnerships with communities to share information about dialect diversity. Wolfram demonstrates that dialect awareness programs can be implemented successfully, and that they can involve a range of community agencies and representatives.

In "Linguistics Is for Kids," Jeannine M. Donna urges that the insights of modern cognitive linguistics become the basis for meaningful exploration of language at the K–12 level. Students at any level can explore the properties of words and sentence patterns, she argues, in a way that prepares them for advanced linguistic study or simply to understand and appreciate language more fully. She suggests that we encourage our students to become "miners" and "sleuths"—to discover these patterns themselves, as well as the abstract linguistic principles underlying them, using data from everyday language in an atmosphere where questions and hypothesis testing are encouraged.

Patricia L. MacGregor-Mendoza, in "Looking at Life through Language," reveals how students in an undergraduate sociolinguistics class gained insight into the linguistic principles that shape interaction in their bilingual community in the Southwest. Through focused field assignments, students explored how culture, attitudes, power, and knowledge of school language policies are manifested in an individual's speech or even his or her choice of language. While her course was set in a university venue, one can easily imagine similar approaches extended to the public-school classroom.

Anca M. Nemoianu's chapter, "In Front of Our Eyes: Undergraduates Reflecting on Language Change," offers a look into how students can explore the current status of certain grammatical forms (e.g., *he/she* versus *their*; *who* versus *whom*; *I* versus *me*; and so on). Nemoianu's students explore people's use of these forms, widely employed in the oral mode, but hardly acceptable in the more formal varieties of written English, as instances of contemporary language change, viewed within the larger context of historical language change. The chapter outlines a student project meant to enable undergraduates to understand the mechanism of language change, speakers' attitudes toward change, and the comparatively more resistant nature of written English to any disturbance in the linguistic status quo.

In Richard Hudson's "Grammar Teaching Is Dead–NOT!," we see that grammar teaching can in fact be both systematic and "contextualized," (i.e., relevant to the student's needs and interests). Students can study their own vernacular grammar, they can compare it with other systems (including Standard English where this is different), they can study changes in grammar and geographical variations, they can explore grammatical patterns in texts, and they can even explore the spelling system. All these things can be done in a systematic way, in contrast with the present emphasis on waiting for a student's writing to provide "the right moment" for teaching a grammatical point.

Part III, "Language and Writing," begins by exploring why students often find it so hard to move from fluency in spoken English into comparable fluency in the written language. The authors then offer concrete examples of how attention to language structure can help as we engage with student writing. While this part, as well as the following one, anchors in the university classroom, techniques and insights the authors describe are readily transportable into primary- and secondary-school venues.

Susan K. Heck, in "Writing Standard English IS Acquiring a Second Language," notes that students in the writing classroom often make choices that may baffle a composition teacher. She explains common choices of beginning writing students by comparing them to choices made by students learning a second language. Through this comparison, second-language-acquisition research offers insight into the writing-acquisition process of beginning composition students.

In "Reading, Writing, and Linguistics: Principles from the Little Red Schoolhouse," Gail Brendel Viechnicki describes three linguistically based revision strategies that have worked for students in her composition classes. She argues that using linguistically based suggestions has a number of advantages over more traditional comments. For example, linguistic principles are specific, easy to apply, and applicable to writing that the student will do throughout her or his college career. Linguistic principles also make revision less face-threatening for the student writer and offer her or him a quick way to achieve distance from her or his text.

Todd Oakley's "Copious Reasoning: The Student Writer as an Astute Observer of Language" melds Erasmus's pedagogical theory of copious eloquence with Ronald Langacker's theory of Cognitive Grammar for the purpose of making student writers more astute observers of language. This chapter provides a site where Renaissance humanism meets twentieth-century linguistic science.

Victor Raskin's chapter, "Writing Well in an Unknown Language: Linguistics and Composition in an English Department," establishes a great deal of common ground and modes of mutually beneficial interaction between linguistics, on the one hand, and rhetoric and composition, on the other. At the same time, it attempts to delimit clearly the overlapping but not coinciding domains for each discipline so that they do not expect from each other something the other cannot deliver. Most important, it describes in what ways linguistics can be useful for the other discipline even if it cannot solve or even address some of rhetoric and composition's central issues.

Part IV, "Language and Literature," offers a literary/linguistic sampler ranging from what we can learn about language through science fiction to point of view in literature and on to poetic aspects of everyday conversation. The first two chapters in this part, while directed toward university instructors, provide fertile material for teachers at all levels.

In "Waterships All the Way Down: Using Science Fiction to Teach Linguistics," Suzette Haden Elgin resolves a long-standing problem in teaching linguistic material to students: Instructors who are trying to work basic theoretical concepts regarding language and linguistics into their courses often face serious difficulties because the material, as ordinarily presented, is so intimidating for most students. The chapter shows teachers how to present these concepts using science fiction so that the popular-culture context reduces that intimidation substantially. For example, she shows how students might consider whether *Star Trek*'s "Universal Translator" device is scientifically probable, how they might explore the four most common linguistic myths in science fiction, and how they might learn about word structure by inducing the pluralization rule in Rabbitspeak.

Elizabeth Closs Traugott's "In Fiction, Whose Speech, Whose Vision?" explores the question of how "point of view" is represented in fiction. Starting with the traditional distinction between first- and third-person narratives, she goes on to show why second-person narrative is problematic. She then discusses how various kinds of orienting expressions establish narrative perspective. These include shifters like *come-go, here-there, then-now*, tense, modes of thought representation, and dialect. The focal questions are "Who speaks?" "Who sees?" Traugott explores what clues the reader needs to follow to answer these questions.

In "The Poetics of Everyday Conversation," Deborah Tannen notes that "[m]ost of us tend to think of literature as the artful use of language, and of everyday conversation as a messy, graceless use of it. But the magnetism of stories told in conversation, and the fascination that everyday language holds for so many verbal artists, belies that belief." Tannen shows that forms of language that we think of as "literary" are basic to everyday conversation. She supports this thesis with examples of repetition, dialogue, and details taken from transcripts of everyday conversation, showing how they create not only meaning but also a sense of involvement among participants in the conversation.

Finally, Part V, "On Dictionaries and Grammars," offers another perspective on these reference tools. Sylvia Shaw's "Who Wrote Your Dictionary? Demystifying the Contents and Construction of Dictionaries" reminds us that a dictionary is a type of text, which is (like any other text) constructed by a group of people, by a process of construction, for a particular purpose and readership. It is only by asking simple questions such as "What is 'the dictionary'?" "What is (and isn't) contained within it?" and "How is it made?" that these publications can be demystified and their contents assessed. This chapter considers some of the questions that people don't normally think to ask about dictionaries and their construction.

In "Online Resources for Grammar Teaching and Learning: The Internet Grammar of English," Bas Aarts, Gerald Nelson, and Justin Buckley offer an alternative to traditional teaching tools for presenting grammar to high-school and undergraduate students. Rectifying a deep drawback of traditional grammar (i.e., its heavy use of notional concepts in delimiting language chunks), the authors employ modern understandings of language structure. Here, analysis relies much less on meaning in defining particular grammatical terms; instead, it regards *distribution* (how words and word parts are arranged with regard to each other) as being of paramount importance. Thus, instead of the traditional definition that nouns are words referring to people, places, things, and so forth, modern grammar characterizes nouns distributionally: nouns are the only word class that displays a number contrast (singular versus plural), that can be possessivized, and that can, for example, be preceded by words like *the, every, each,* and *two.* Aarts, Nelson, and Buckley animate this approach clearly and engagingly on the World Wide Web.

Rebecca S. Wheeler

I

BEYOND GRAMMAR OF THE TRADITIONAL KIND

Grammar, Tradition, and the Living Language

David B. Umbach

For the past few years, I have been teaching grammar courses for college English departments. The students in these courses have been mostly English Education majors, future high-school and middle-school English teachers. In teaching these classes, I have found that the biggest obstacle for many of the students is the attitude towards grammar that they bring with them into the class. These people want to be English teachers; they have chosen to spend their professional lives working with the language. Why, then, do they seem so often to hate and fear grammar?

One of the other things that I have been doing for the last few years is teaching writing courses, and, oddly enough, in the process of reviewing textbooks for writing classes, I think that I have found one of the reasons for the problems in the grammar classes. Many of the textbooks I have looked at are "handbooks," with extensive sections on grammar, and being a linguist, I always look for these sections first. Handbooks and textbooks like these represent pretty accurately the kind of exposure to grammar that most of my students would have had before reaching my class, and very early on, I began to notice things about the chapter titles and section headings listed in the tables of contents of these books that made my students' feelings about grammar seem virtually inevitable.

How much can you really tell about a book by looking at the chapter titles? Take a look at the title of this chapter. It is not nearly as informative as the titles of most of the chapters in this volume, and I did that on purpose. The words in the title of this chapter are, all by themselves, pretty harmless. But words don't really exist by themselves, do they? Anyone looking at the table of contents in this book will bring his or her own definitions of words like "grammar" and "tradition," and these definitions will set up expectations in that person's mind that may or may not be met when he or she turns to this page. Chances are very good, in fact, that so far, none of these expectations has been met.

Definitions raise expectations, and in most cases, it is experiences that create definitions. We've seen and heard these words before, understood them, and made connections between them and other words and ideas. The next time we see or hear them, we expect them to make the same connections, and if they don't, we may try to force them. One of the problems that I want to address here is that the students who walk into my grammar classes, on their way to becoming public-school English and language-arts teachers, have expectations that have a lot to do with the ways that grammar has been presented to them in the past. And these expectations tend to hinder them, not help them, because the kind of grammar that I am teaching is not what they expect. What they expect is something like a handbook. What I have been giving them is more like linguistics.

If you look in almost any introductory linguistics textbook, somewhere in the first chapter or two you will find a discussion of the difference between "prescriptive" and "descriptive" grammar, the first associated with "traditional" grammar, the second with linguistics. The students are presumed to be familiar with the traditional prescriptive approach; it is the job of the intro linguistics course to acquaint them with the descriptive approach.

As a linguist, I am expected to be descriptive, to deal with the facts of language as I actually find them. On the other hand, when I teach writing classes, my students expect me to be (at least a little) *pre*scriptive, to tell them how to make their sentences what they *should* be. It is not always easy to reconcile these two situations, and in fact, my experiences with teaching grammar classes have begun to convince me that there are problems here that are not explained by a simple distinction between prescription and description.

Most of the available textbooks that deal with language, whether they are linguistics books, English grammar books or writing handbooks, assume that the students using them will already be familiar with traditional, prescriptive grammar. This is true, up to a point. These students have heard of some of these things, they have seen the red ink on their English papers, and they have, many of them, been required by their past English teachers to use handbooks, on the assumption that they will respond to the red ink by looking things up and fixing them (I have been guilty of making that assumption). They have been exposed to grammar; they know that it exists, but familiarity is not exactly the way to describe their relationship with it. Fear and loathing, maybe, but not familiarity.

Writing handbooks are usually not the only exposure that my grammar students have had to traditional grammar, just the most recent, and while the handbooks are not all alike, most of them do have a lot in common.

They are fairly consistent in WHAT they say about grammar, and more important, they are consistent in HOW they say it. The problems that my students bring with them into the grammar class are more a result of the HOW than the WHAT.

As I said at the beginning, it was the chapter titles and tables of contents of these handbooks that gave me my first insight into my students' problems. Take, for example, two recent, and fairly representative books, both published in 1997; one of them (Hairston, Ruszkiewicz, and Seward 1997) has a section headed "Grammar," and the first chapter in that section is entitled "Sentence Fragments, Comma Splices, and Run-ons." The publishers of this particular book have gone to a great deal of trouble and expense to make the rest of their book "user-friendly," with blue, purple and bright green inks, little pseudocyber icons, and fancy fonts. But grammar, they apparently think, is not friendly; it's about errors and things to avoid.

In the other book (Dodds 1997), which is also made user-friendly, with spiral binding, tabbed section dividers, and three different tables of contents, the grammar section is headed "Sentence Editing" and contains three chapters on identifying grammatical elements and NINE chapters on fixing errors and choosing the "correct" forms. Same message again: grammar is not a friendly thing.

These books are not unique in sending this message. In Kirszner and Mandell (1995), the tab-indexed section entitled "Writing Grammatical Sentences" contains six chapters, with twenty-five subsections between them. Two of the six chapter titles and thirteen of the subsection titles contain the word "revising." Hacker (1995) has a section, also tab indexed, entitled "Grammatical Sentences," in which the first subsection is "Subject-verb agreement," and the second is "Other problems with verbs." O'Hare and Kline (1996) has a section on grammar, with no mention of error or revision in the table of contents, but this section is followed by a section on "Sentence Form," which opens with a chapter on "Fragments."

All of these books have their virtues, as well, and their authors are not to be faulted for the way they treat grammar; they are simply teaching as they were taught, and they may well have been discouraged from making any radical departures from tradition in this area by the textbook publishers, who (I am told by friends with recent experience) are nervous about their ability to sell the unfamiliar. Nevertheless, what the students see when they look for grammar is what they have always seen: problems, errors, red ink, and low grades.

Even if the students never make it past the table of contents, the message is clear. Grammar is what you use to clean up the mess that you make, that you will inevitably make. It has little or nothing to do with creating sentences in the first place, but everything to do with fixing them up afterwards.

There are two points here, I think, that bear further discussion. The first is the impression that grammar is only about revising, about fixing; I see this reflected in the attitudes of many of my students (and, unfortunately, many of my colleagues). They seem to feel that, since they themselves rarely, if ever, make grammatical errors that need fixing, grammar is something that they don't need to learn: as far as they are concerned, "The 'right' form just sounds right, and if you can't hear it, it can't be explained." In extreme cases, this turns into ". . . if you can't hear it, there's something wrong with you."

This leads me to my second point: the students who don't "hear" it come to believe that they are stupid, that error is, for them, inevitable, and there is no hope for them. The predominance of revision and editing in the grammar handbooks seems to confirm this. Apparently, the only reason for knowing any of this stuff is so that, after you've done it wrong, you can redo it until you get it right.

If the students do make it past the table of contents, they may find themselves even more at a loss. The definitions and descriptions they will find are very brief and tend to be written as imperatives, as commands, not as statements or explanations: "Do this, don't do that." The tone is generally very matter-of-fact, if not downright peremptory. Little or no space is given to any explanation of "why" something is as it is said to be (or should be). Apparently, there are no reasons behind any of these orders; just do as you're told. If you don't hear it . . .

Perhaps more importantly, the space and ink devoted to laying out the instructions usually far exceed that devoted to examples. Even if the statement of the rule is very complicated and takes several sentences, one or two examples are considered adequate. "As complex as the rule might be," the traditional handbook seems to say, "it should still be essentially self-evident, once it's been pointed out." If you can't hear it, don't expect the handbook to help you out much. You would need to see a lot of examples to be able to start "hearing" the patterns that most handbook rules refer to, and the handbook does not give them to you.

The passive voice is a good example of these problems. I have found, in my grammar classes, that, for many students, the passive is one of the more difficult nuts to crack. I am sure that this difficulty stems, in part, from their previous experience with the term. I often ask my classes, at the beginning of the semester, how many of them have ever been told to avoid using the passive. Usually, well over half of the students in the class raise their hands. Then I ask how many of them can tell me what the passive is. Usually, no hands are raised. With a little coaxing, it does become clear that at least some of them do know at least some of the distinguishing characteristics of the passive, but it is difficult to say how much difference there is between not knowing and knowing but being so unsure of that knowledge that you are afraid to speak up. And even those who can, when pressed, identify a passive are not entirely sure why they are supposed to avoid it.

Looking closely at the treatment of the passive voice in the handbooks has helped me understand some of their difficulties. Almost every one of them starts from the position that the passive is less emphatic (Rosa and Eschholz 1996), less effective, more complex, and less direct (Hacker 1995), or not as lively (Lunsford and Connors 1997); the primary definition of passive voice is "something to avoid." Only secondarily do we find any mention of what makes a clause passive. But how can you avoid something if you don't know how to recognize it?

Often, where there *is* a discussion of what makes a clause passive, this discussion is of questionable use. For instance, if a student looks up the passive in the index of Lunsford and Connors (1997, 116), he or she will find, in addition to several admonitions against using the form, a reference to the fact that "when the subject is being acted upon, the verb is in the passive voice." But only if the student turns to the section at the back of the book headed "For Multilingual Writers" will he or she find any reference to the "BE + past participle" combination that makes up the passive verb form. The monolingual student is expected either to know this already or to recognize it as self-evident from the four examples provided.

To their credit, Lunsford and Connors (1997, 117) do provide, as an example of an appropriate use of the passive, a one-sentence quote from a newspaper article. Most of the handbooks rely entirely on invented and extremely simple example sentences. The student is left feeling that these things never occur in the writing of *real* writers, and never in the kind of interesting, varied sentences that their teachers seem to want them to use (to avoid sounding "choppy" or immature).

Virtually all of these handbooks do add, almost as an afterthought, some admission that, at times, in some special circumstances, the passive is acceptable. These circumstances are presented almost entirely in terms of "emphasis": the passive shifts emphasis from one thing to another. In contrast, in linguists' discussions of the passive, emphasis is only one factor among many and is not a simple factor, at that. Greenbaum and Quirk (1990, 46) list no fewer than seven reasons for using the passive, only two of which have anything to do with emphasis. Halliday and Martin (1993, 193–94) give a fine example of the way that the emphasis-shifting feature of the passive can be used as an organizational strategy in scientific writing. In this approach to studying grammar, different types of sentences are seen as options, and there are reasons for the existence of these options; the language makes certain resources available to us, and in order to fully understand what those resources are and how to use them, we need to know something about grammar. Here is a reason for studying grammar that has nothing to do with errors, with fixing inevitable mistakes.

Obviously, given my training and predilections, it was inevitable that I would eventually get around to comparing the handbooks to the linguists' descriptive grammars of English that I keep close at hand (Quirk et al. 1985; Greenbaum and Quirk 1990; Leech and Svartvik 1994; Greenbaum 1996), and to some of the linguistically oriented books on writing that I have found useful in both research and teaching (Halliday and Martin 1993; Martin 1989). Their tables of contents say nothing about error, about fixing or avoiding. They are written in the indicative mood; they make statements, rather than giving commands. They make more use of examples, and some (like Greenbaum 1996) depend almost entirely on examples taken from actual speakers and writers, not on examples invented by the grammarian.

This is not to say that the linguists' resources could replace the handbooks. What the student writer usually needs is a quick answer to a simple question, not a complete, in-depth explanation: a reminder, not a lesson. The problem seems to be the number of students who have never had the lessons and thus can't understand the reminder. When the handbook tells you that a comma alone shouldn't join two independent clauses, that's fine, as long as you know what an independent clause is. The linguists' grammars will tell you more than you might need to know about clauses, independent and otherwise, but most have little to say about comma splices.

Although I haven't been able to confirm this scientifically, informal discussion with my students leads me to believe that most of the "grammar" that they have had prior to entering my class has been very similar to what they see in the handbooks: commands and prohibitions that assume a knowledge of and "feel" for language that only a few students have. The kind of systematic description of the language that they might use as a substitute for that "feel" has not been available.

The attitude of fear and loathing that so many of my students bring with them to the grammar class seems to me to stem from the way that they have been taught to view grammar by books and teachers who present grammar and grammatical terms in the traditional ways I have been discussing. The students who don't have that "feel" for the language are presented with things that are apparently supposed to be self-evident but they aren't, so the students feel stupid. They see imperatives that they can't seem to follow, so they feel guilty. They see no alternatives or explanations for the variations that they hear and produce, and they start to feel that, whatever it is they are doing, it isn't English, it isn't really language at all, and so they are afraid to express themselves. Even if they have that "feel," they are nervous about it, because of the absolute terms that they are used to in grammar; what if they start making mistakes now? What if they find out that something they have thought was right all along turns out to be wrong? Add this all up, and it produces students who enter my classes wanting to be given the answers, but convinced, many of them, that they will never understand those answers.

And what kind of grammar have I been teaching them? The kind from the linguists' point of view, the descriptive. I mentioned near the beginning of this chapter that my teaching experiences had convinced me that there are problems here that are not explained by a simple distinction between prescription and description. Linguists, especially those who have never worked in an English department, tend to simply accept the superiority of the descriptive approach; it is, after all, backed up by scientific evidence (whatever that means). For students in an English education program, however, the issue is not so clear-cut. When I started teaching linguistics to future teachers, I would get resistance to the idea of descriptivism on the grounds that prescriptive traditional grammar was what they would be expected to teach, and so I should teach it to them. I would try to explain the sociolinguistics of the Standard Dialect and push them back to descriptivism, and they would respond, essentially, "All this stuff about dialect and Standard and language identity is very interesting, but the school board and the parents will expect me to teach proper English, and if they don't think I'm doing it, I'll be pumping gas instead of teaching, and they won't sit still long enough to hear me explain all this stuff about dialect and Standard."

I began to see that neither the prescriptivism that they were used to, and had been frightened by, nor the extreme, formal descriptivism of much of my linguistic training could meet the needs of these students, the future English teachers. To simply continue with the handbooks' grammar would just reinforce their feelings of exclusion and inadequacy; the language presented by the handbooks belongs to the people who make the rules, and since these students couldn't even manage to understand things that the rule writers consider too obvious to need explanation, these students could never hope to "own" that language.

On the other hand, the students were right in saying that there are consequences to expressing yourself in ways that don't conform to the handbook rules; not only will red ink appear on your English papers, but your job applications will be ignored. And when they become teachers, they will be expected by parents and school boards to provide *their* students with "the rules," the ways of speaking and writing that will lead to high test scores, good colleges, and high-paying jobs.

The students' professional futures will depend upon their ability to at least give the appearance that they are being prescriptive, that they are teaching "the rules." But it is exactly that approach to grammar that is responsible for their fear and loathing of the subject. What I have tried to teach, with linguistics as a guide, is a sort of middle ground, a description of the language that recognizes traditional, prescriptive ideas about grammar as part of the current reality of our language. An accurate description of Modern English should include the very pertinent sociolinguistic fact that educational, economic, and political discourse in this society is carried on primarily in the Standard Dialect, and that using the forms of that dialect has social consequences that are different from the social consequences of using other forms.

I think that this kind of description has a better chance of positive effects than the traditional prescriptivism. The *real* rules are out there where the language is, where people are using it, and I encourage my students to learn (and eventually teach) ways of finding those rules for themselves. As learners, the students need to think, for a while, in a limited way, like linguists. As future teachers, they need to think in terms of "informed advice" rather than commands. The difference is between the teacher telling the students, "You must do it this way," and the teacher telling them, "There are different ways of doing it, and if you want to be understood, you have to figure out how the people you are talking to are used to hearing it, and do it that way; so let's look at what you are trying to do, and see what we can figure out." The first way is traditional grammar, and it takes the language away from the students and puts it in the rule book. The second way uses linguistics, and it makes the language something to be discovered by the student, and what they find on their own will be their own.

REFERENCES

Dodds, Jack. 1997. *The ready reference handbook: Writing, revising, editing.* Boston: Allyn and Bacon.

Greenbaum, Sidney. 1996. *The Oxford English grammar.* Oxford: Oxford University Press.

Greenbaum, Sidney, and Randolph Quirk. 1990. *A student's grammar of the English language.* London: Longman.

Hacker, Diana. 1995. *A writer's reference.* 3rd ed. Boston: Bedford/St. Martin's.

Hairston, Maxine, John J. Ruszkiewicz, and Daniel E. Seward. 1997. *Coretext: A handbook for writers.* New York: Longman.

Halliday, M. A. K., and J. R. Martin. 1993. *Writing science: Literacy and discursive power.* Pittsburgh: University of Pittsburgh Press.

Kirszner, Laurie G., and Stephen R. Mandell. 1995. *The brief Holt handbook.* Rev. ed. Fort Worth: Harcourt Brace.

Leech, Geoffrey, and Jan Svartvik. 1994. *A communicative grammar of the English language.* 2nd ed. London: Longman.

Lunsford, Andrea, and Robert Connors. 1997. *The everyday writer: A brief reference.* New York: St. Martin's.

Martin, J. R. 1989. *Factual writing; Exploring and challenging social reality.* 2nd ed. Oxford: Oxford University Press.

O'Hare, Frank, and Edward A. Kline. 1996. *The modern writer's handbook.* 4th ed. Boston: Allyn and Bacon.

Quirk, Randolph, Sidney Greenbaum, Geoffrey Leech, and Jan Svartvik. 1985. *A comprehensive grammar of the English language*. London: Longman.
Rosa, Alfred, and Paul Eschholz. 1996. *The writer's brief handbook*. 2nd ed. Boston: Allyn and Bacon.
Thompson, Geoff. 1996. *Introducing functional grammar*. London: Edward Arnold.

The Persistence of Traditional Grammar
Edwin Battistella

Recently, I got home in time to see the last few minutes of *Jeopardy*, and I was amused to find that one of the categories—the last category remaining in the "Double Jeopardy" round—was linguistics. I watched as contestants otherwise well informed about mountains, monarchies, and ten-letter words that start with *p* were unable to come up with such responses as "What is a tree diagram?" "What is syntax?" and "Who is Noam Chomsky?"

Watching *Jeopardy* contestants flounder at linguistics brought another game show to mind, this one a *Saturday Night Live* sketch involving a show called *Common Knowledge*. In this spoof, the contestant who offered the correct answers lost points, while those who provided the "common knowledge" won points. All of us who are teachers may sometimes feel like the hapless contestant on *Common Knowledge* who shouted out "1776" as the answer to the question "When was the Declaration of Independence signed?" No doubt there is a body of folk knowledge in any field of study. For language, much of what we take to be traditional grammar is "common knowledge," even though this is what some constituencies think that we ought to be teaching.

WHAT IS TRADITIONAL GRAMMAR?

Traditional grammar is the grammar found in many K–12 English textbooks, college rhetoric manuals, and practical English handbooks and usage guides. Such works typically provide a glossary of vaguely defined grammatical terms as the basis for rules of standard grammar, punctuation, and usage. Traditional grammar embodies both a theory of sentence structure (involving notional parts of speech and unlabelled Reed-Kellogg diagrams) and a purpose for grammar (to indicate how various levels of writing and speech should be expressed). Traditional grammar books vary from works that provide simple definitions of grammatical terms together with advice on grammar, capitalization, punctuation, spelling, and word choice to works of grammatical criticism (such as Fowler's *Dictionary of Modern English Usage*) that assume a robust knowledge of grammatical terminology and provide literate but sometimes misguided suggestions for usage.[1]

Many English educators, composition specialists, and linguists have noted problems with traditional grammar and for over half a century have been chipping away at its use in the classroom, largely unsuccessfully. There are three main objections to traditional grammar:

- Traditional grammar does not work as a theory of English structure.
- Traditional grammar does not work as a set of conventions for describing educated usage.
- Time spent teaching grammar is better spent on other things.

As an account of English structure, traditional terminology is hopelessly imprecise. Even basic things, such as the definition of subject as "the person, object, or idea being described," fail if they are applied with any seriousness. Sentences such as "It was raining" or "There was a book on the table" illustrate the weakness of the definition: in the first case the weather is being described, but the subject is a placeholder, *it*, which does not refer to either the weather or the sky; in the second case the book (or perhaps the table) is being described, but the grammatical subject is again a placeholder, *there*. Problems in defining subjects are not restricted only to sentences with *it* and *there*. Even in applying the definition to an example as pedestrian as "Mary saw John," one can ask whether the sentence is not as much a description of John (or of an act of seeing) as it is of Mary.[2]

As a prescriptive system, traditional rules are also inadequate in that many are either inconsistent or not followed. Consider the proscription against sentence fragments, which is widely ignored by writers of fiction. What is someone to make of dialogue like the following, from Robert B. Parker's *Small Vices* (1997, 11)?

> Jackson shrugged, "Probably was. Happens a lot. Because he's black. Because he's poor. Either one is bad, the combination is very bad."

Such dialogue, complete with fragments and a comma splice, is not uncommon in fiction and is entirely effective in capturing the rhythm of normal speech both in dialogue and in narrative.

While much more could be said about each of these examples, the point is clear. Teaching students oversimplified rules of structure and correctness is like teaching them oversimplified biology or history. Patriotic fictions about Washington and Jefferson are fine, but they are not the sort of myths appropriate for high-school or college students. Similarly, grammatical oversimplifications have no place in an advanced academic curriculum. Inquisitive students will spot the inconsistencies of traditional grammar and may come to see grammar as irrelevant and arbitrary (particularly when their teacher cannot provide a good explanation for the inconsistencies). In addition, students who are struggling with grammar may find the vagueness and inconsistency of traditional grammar a further source of confusion and frustration in learning the conventions of writing. Teachers themselves, especially new teachers, are apt to be frustrated when trying to teach traditional grammar.[3]

The third set of objections to traditional grammar has to do with its place in secondary-school and college classes. Research on English education, while not unequivocal, has supported the view that teaching grammar in isolation does little to improve writing. Work published by the National Council of Teachers of English as early as 1963 had already concluded that "the teaching of formal grammar has a negligible or, because it usually displaces some instruction and practice in composition, even a harmful effect on improvement in writing" (Braddock, Lloyd-Jones, and Schoer 1963, 37–38).[4] The objection is not so much to traditional grammar per se, but to including grammar in the English curriculum as a separate subject. On this view, grammar is best taught in the context of writing assignments and targeted to actual problems in students' writing.

Still, English majors, especially those pursuing teaching certificates, often feel that they should be familiar with the canon of traditional grammar, since they will be viewed as English experts and will most likely be required to teach grammar. One English student wrote in her self-assessment that "the area in which I am most weak in English is grammar. As a junior high and high school student I excelled in grammar. Years of being away from the rules and regulations have taken a toll on my grammar knowledge." Another wrote that "I have had relatively little experience with grammar in college and feel somewhat unprepared to teach it in high school." Students do report that the linguistics classes they take are useful, but they do not see them as addressing their grammar insecurities. One wrote, "I must say that while I believe the linguistics classes are of benefit, they do little, if anything, to improve or teach grammar to students." Another added that the linguistics courses "have taught me a great deal about the developmental process. . . . [However,] I didn't get much preparation to teach grammar."

What is interesting about these perceptions is that the students are exposed to grammar in their linguistics courses, but do not recognize it as such. At my institution, English education students take two semesters of English linguistics, the first a descriptive survey of English (covering syntax, phonology, morphology, and history) and the second an introduction to the field (covering prescriptivism, the diversity of the world's languages, the regularity of change, dialects, social stratification, language acquisition, and the psychology and physiology of language). But to many students, grammar means traditional grammar—time spent on fragments and commas and correctness, not on syntactic argumentation, adverb classes, complement types, and noun-phrase modifiers.

THE ATTRACTIONS OF TRADITIONAL GRAMMAR

Student opinion is but one indication of the way in which traditional grammar, despite its intellectual thinness, remains influential in American society. Why has traditional grammar remained so influential? A friend of mine has suggested that schools persist in traditional grammar for the same reason that people continue to press an elevator button—because they are not getting the results they want (competent student writing) and they do not know what else to do.[5]

But there is more to the influence of traditional grammar than results. Traditional grammar is also to a great extent a surrogate for traditional values and morality. In its most unsophisticated version, it assumes that simple definitions and rules handed down from earlier generations ("the basics") have some inherent cultural priority and that those who do not follow the rules of correct usage have failed to learn English due to classlessness, stupidity, laziness, or obstinence. So when theatre critic John Simon writes about "corruptions based on ignorance" and promulgated by "ignoramuses" (1980, 194), he makes his attack ad hominem rather than addressing usage issues or the history of the language.[6] There is sometimes a dose of hypocrisy involved in the moralistic approach as well, in that it is the mistakes of other social groups that are uneducated, while one's own grammatical lapses may be seen as a healthy measure of rugged anti-intellectualism.

Also, as Constance Weaver (1996a) has noted, traditional grammar, in its practice-makes-perfect mode, reflects a behaviorist view of learning in which repetition and mastery of a discrete skill (doing grammar exercises) is assumed to underlie a more complex holistic one (writing well). Weaver argues that "the traditional approach has been to teach concepts and skills from a grammar handbook or language arts series, where the primary method of teaching has been to assign grammar, revision and editing exercises and to give tests on the material" (148). However, this approach to traditional grammar—in terms of identification and correction exercises that attempt to build applicable knowledge of a complex system like language—fails to take into account what psychologists have learned about the nature of language development.[7]

Another reason that English educators and linguists have made surprisingly little headway in supplanting traditional grammar and traditional attitudes is that linguistics often seems unnecessarily complex.[8] When I was growing up, I remember a series of books that included *Trigonometry Made Easy, Physics Made Easy*, and of course *English Made Easy*. For many, however, linguistics is English made hard: abstruse, overly technical, and without clear application. Linguistics brings with it new terms and diagrams, funny names (like Noam Chomsky), and counterintuitive notions (that all dialects are rule governed and that language is innate).

So there are several things at play in the persistence of traditional grammar:

- The belief that an explicit course of instruction and practice in traditional grammar is a good way to learn to use and understand language
- The folk sentiment that correct grammar is a moral issue and ought to be inculcated by a course of instruction in schools
- The feeling that linguistics is too academic and hence irrelevant

WHAT TO DO

One way to begin to address these issues is to point out the parallels between the grammar debate and curriculum debates in other fields. The distinction between traditional grammar and linguistics parallels the distinction between folk history and real history (history that takes into account actual social and political forces and the complexities and ambiguities of individuals' and nations' roles). The objection that linguistics is too hard and unfamiliar has the same response as the objection that British literature is too hard and unfamiliar. Literary works are worthwhile in part because they have the complexity to withstand sustained analysis and appreciation. The same holds for grammar. Like literature, language is complex, and approaches to language that oversimplify its structure and nature are just as unworthy of consideration in the classroom as simplistic approaches to literature. We teach linguistics rather than traditional grammar for the same reason that we require students to defend their interpretations of literature rather than just memorizing a list of great works and plot summaries, and for the same reason that we teach Shakespeare and Jane Austen rather than Stephen King and Jackie Collins.

It is also important for educators to take the lead in presenting the case against moralistic traditional grammar, while at the same time recognizing the extensiveness of that view and the expectations that will be placed on our students. Certainly we must acknowledge, even embrace, the idea that students need to master certain norms in writing. But we must also connect an academically sound descriptivist approach to the future needs and interests of students.

One way to address the debate is to spend some time teaching the controversy in the English major. The fact that students are anxious about grammar suggests that they will be attentive to the question of grammatical correctness, and there is a fairly extensive body of literature on how and whether grammar should be taught.[9] Turning students' concerns about grammar into a teachable moment has some risks, of course: it is easy to be misunderstood in a classroom, and when students are told that traditional grammar is inadequate and that no varieties of language are linguistically right or wrong, they may hear that grammar does not matter.

So what do students need to hear? Coursework in linguistics needs to provide a commonsense reconciliation of descriptive linguistics with realistic linguistics by addressing issues of usage and standard. There are two aspects to this, I think. The first is to make it clear that the virtue-and-value theory of grammar is simply incorrect. To accomplish this, we must ground students in the history of English, demonstrating that dialects are regular and rule governed and that correctness is a convention placed on dialect by society and history.

The second aspect is to acknowledge the common truth that we all make grammatical choices and judgments and to encourage students to reflect on their own usage. For example, I maintain the distinction between *infer* and *imply*, use *ain't* only for stylistic effect (and rarely at that), and never use perfectives like *have went* or the reflexive *hisself*. However, I also split infinitives, strand prepositions, use *who* rather than *whom*, and use *hopefully* to modify an entire sentence (as in "Hopefully, it won't snow"). All of this usage is second nature to me, but I can reflect on it and explain it, drawing on both social and linguistic considerations. Thus I recognize that I do not use *hisself* because (a) the dialect I grew up speaking uses *himself* instead, and (b) I have not felt a social need to adopt *hisself*. I also recognize that the form *hisself* is entirely logical and analogical to *myself, yourself*, and other reflexives. So my choice follows my early usage and social logic rather than any structural logic of English. Similarly with *hopefully*. Here again my usage follows long habit that I have had no social reason to change. In addition, I recognize the structural logic of English—that the use of *hopefully* in "Hopefully, it won't rain" is parallel with other sentence adverbs like *frankly* (as in "Frankly, I don't care"). I see this parallelism as having priority over the etymology of *hopefully* as meaning "full of hope," which some commentators take as evidence that *hopefully* is illogical when used to modify a sentence. Thus my understanding of grammatical parallelism and adverb classes allows me to understand and feel secure in my usage.

So when Mark Halpern, writing in the *Atlantic Monthly* (1997, 20) says that "what linguistic scientists have been doing . . . has absolutely no relevance to the constellation of literary-philosophical-social-moral issues that we are talking about when we discuss usage," he is wrong on two counts. First, the issues are never moral ones. Second, linguistics is indeed relevant to literary-philosophical-social issues of usage. What sociolinguists have been doing for decades (and dialectologists before that) has established that much so-called error has a basis in dialect usage and is not a failure to learn English but rather the learning of something different. What is learned in studying syntax, semantics, and the history of English makes it possible to discuss the literary and philosophical issues surrounding usage in a way that those who only understand traditional grammar as "correct English" cannot.

The role of linguistics in the English curriculum should be to counterbalance unreflective traditionalism and the popular moralizing that often goes along with it. More broadly, the role of service linguistics courses should be positive: they should provide an accurate and comprehensible view of the structure of English and the methods of its study; and they should give a robust and up-to-date view of the nature of language, its history, and its acquisition. In this way students can relate linguistics to issues that are relevant to their lives and careers and can avoid relying on "common knowledge" about language and language use.

NOTES

1. See Nunberg (1982) for a discussion of the range of traditional grammar approaches. For accounts of the history of grammar, see also Leonard (1962), Finegan (1980), and Baron (1982).

2. For more on the weaknesses of traditional approaches, see Fries (1952, chap. 13), Levin (1960), Allen (1972), Haussamen (1993), and Pinker (1994, chap. 12), among others.

3. See Maxwell and Meiser (1997, chap. 10), who write that traditional grammar also persists because of teachers' self-perceptions that their own language skills came from studying grammar. Maxwell and Meiser also suggest that another factor is the way grammar is packaged in textbooks and associated curriculum material to make it easy to teach. The self-organizing nature of the grammar (beginning with the parts of speech and moving to larger units and then to sentence faults) and the apparently objective nature of grammar tests may appeal to teachers and school administrators. Cleary and Lund (1993) also point out other folk beliefs about traditional grammar—that it aids the learning of foreign languages, raises Scholastic Aptitude Test (SAT) scores, and disciplines the mind.

4. See Kolln (1981) for a critical discussion of early studies and Noguchi (1991) for an overview of research on grammar and writing.

5. Related to this may be the naïve assumption that a college composition class or two will eradicate any grammatical infelicities in writing. Interestingly, the same does not apply to other general-education disciplines: speech, music, and physical education, for example, are not assumed to produce dialect-free speakers, competent singers or athletes.

6. There is as well a homiletic tradition in traditional grammar that sees English

grammar as wishing to promote virtue through grammar. Thus Lindley Murray and other grammarians who followed in this tradition often chose examples that had moral and religous overtones. As Baron (1982, 166) notes, the "pietistic tone [of nineteenth-century school grammars] reinforced the authority of the rules of grammar as they were presented and contributed to the aura of reverence and fear that surrounds grammatical study in schools to this day." Constance Weaver (1996b) shows that the idea that grammar disciplines the soul remains today when she points to Home School Catalog (1996), a home schooling book catalog that asserts that "grammar is taught with a purpose of making clear to students the orderly structure of their language, a picture of God's orderly plan for the world and for their lives."

7. In particular, it glosses over the fact that some deviations from standard adult expectations are due to the way in which complex language develops, while others may be due to students' unfamiliarity with writing (agreement errors that occur in writing but not speech) or due to their speaking a nonstandard dialect. See Murdick (1996), Weaver (1996a, 1996b), Shaughnessy (1977), Hunt (1977), and Harris and Rowan (1989), among others.

8. The changing and sometimes fragmented nature of linguistics has doubtless made it hard for English education specialists and K–12 teachers to find a received approach to apply to the classroom, and the failure of both structuralist and generative applications to grammar to provide a magic bullet for writing instruction has doubtless caused frustration and perhaps contributed to a call for a return to "the basics" (see Lester 1990, 339–40). In addition, in some quarters linguistics may continue to be associated with permissiveness due to misunderstandings surrounding *Webster's Third New International Dictionary of the English Language*; see Morton (1994).

9. The National Council of Teachers of English's publication *English Journal* devoted a special issue to "The grammar controversy" in November 1996; other useful references include Baron (1982), Nunberg (1982), Weaver (1979, 1996a), Kolln (1996), Noguchi (1991), and Finegan (1980).

REFERENCES

Allen, Robert. 1972. *English grammars and English grammar*. New York: Scribner's.

Baron, Dennis. 1982. *Grammar and good taste: Reforming the American language.* New Haven: Yale University Press.

Braddock, Richard, Richard Lloyd-Jones; and Lowell Schoer. 1963. *Research in written composition*. Urbana, IL: National Council of Teachers of English.

Cleary, Linda Miller, and Nancy Lund. 1993. Debunking some myths about traditional grammar. *Linguistics for teachers*, ed. by Linda Miller Cleary and Michael D. Linn, 483–90. New York: McGraw-Hill.

Davis, Frederica. 1993. In defense of grammar. *Teaching secondary English: Readings and applications*, ed. by Daniel Sheridan, 251–60. London: Longman.

Finegan, Edward. 1980. *Attitudes toward English usage: The history of a war of words*. New York: Teachers College Press.

Fowler, Henry. 1926. *A dictionary of modern English usage.* Oxford: Clarendon Press.

Fries, Charles Carpenter. 1952. *The structure of English.* New York: Harcourt, Brace.

Halpern, Mark. 1997. A war that never ends. *Atlantic Monthly* (March): 19–22.

Harris, Muriel, and Katherine E. Rowan. 1989. Explaining grammatical concepts. *Journal of Basic Writing* 8.2: 21–41.

Haussamen, Brock. 1993. *Revising the rules: Traditional grammar and modern linguistics.* Dubuque, IA: Kendall/Hunt.

Home School Catalog. 1996. Pensacola, FL: A Beka Book.

Hunt, Kellogg. 1977. Early blooming and late blooming syntactic structures. *Evaluating writing: Describing, measuring, judging,* ed. by Charles R. Cooper and Lee Odell, 91–106. Urbana, IL: National Council of Teachers of English.

Kolln, Martha. 1981. Closing the books on alchemy. *College Composition and Communication* 32: 139–51.

———. 1996. Rhetorical grammar: A modification lesson. *English Journal* 85.7 (November): 25–31.

Leonard, Sterling. 1962. *The doctrine of correctness in English usage, 1700–1800.* New York: Russell and Russell.

Lester, Mark. 1990. Grammar in the classroom. New York: Macmillan.

Levin, Samuel R. 1960. Comparing traditional and structural grammar. *College English* 21: 26–65.

Maxwell, Rhoda J., and Mary Jordan Meiser. 1997. *Teaching English in middle and secondary schools.* Upper Saddle River, NJ: Prentice Hall.

McQuade, Finlay. 1980. Examining a grammar course: The rationale and the result. *English Journal* 69.7 (October): 26–30.

Morton, Herbert C. 1994. *The story of Webster's Third: Philip Gove's controversial dictionary and its critics.* Cambridge: Cambridge University Press.

Murdick, William. 1996. What English teachers need to know about grammar. *English Journal* 85.7 (November): 38–45.

Noguchi, Rei. 1991. *Grammar and the teaching of writing.* Urbana, IL: National Council of Teachers of English.

Nunberg, Geoffrey. 1982. The decline of grammar. *Atlantic Monthly* (December): 31–46.

Parker, Robert B. 1997. *Small vices.* New York: G. P. Putnam's Sons.

Pinker, Steven. 1994. *The language instinct.* New York: William Morrow.

Shaughnessy, Mina. 1977. *Errors and expectations.* New York: Oxford University Press.

Simon, John. 1980. *Paradigms lost.* New York: C. N. Potter.

Small, Robert. 1985. Why I'll never teach grammar again. *English Education* 17.3: 174–79.

Weaver, Constance. 1979. *Grammar for teachers: Perspectives and definitions.* Urbana, IL: NCTE.

———. 1996a. *Teaching grammar in context.* Portsmouth, NH: Heinemann.

———. 1996b. Teaching grammar in the context of writing. *English Journal* 85.7 (November): 15–24.

3

PRESTIGE ENGLISH IS NOT A NATURAL LANGUAGE

Nicholas Sobin

People are heavily exposed to standard English, English involving prestige constructions, every day. They hear it on television and radio. They read it in publications of all sorts. They hear religious services conducted in it. They are enticed to buy all sorts of things, both useful and useless, in it. It is the only variety of English taught in schools (the feeling of many being that this variety must be taught or it will cease to exist). Even the attempts on popular television to mimic nonstandard speech varieties (such imitations hardly exist in any other medium) are often thinly veiled versions of standard English. Nonetheless, true nonstandard dialects persist, and they persist strongly, though they are frequently condemned (even by their own speakers!). They are almost never the object of formal instruction and evidently don't need to be. Do the persistence and apparent easy learning of the nonstandard and the learning-resistant nature of the standard tell us something about the linguistic character of these various dialects?

It has been known among linguists for some time that nonstandard varieties are not the degenerate forms of language that many assume them to be, but are instead natural, full-fledged languages. However, beyond this, work is emerging that suggests that prestige language may not be the "pure" form of the language that it is so often assumed to be, but rather a form of language that can only be produced with a considerable amount of "abnormal" tinkering and adjustment. Where nonstandard language varieties are natural and "low-maintenance," formal prestige varieties involve unnatural gimmicks for superficially creating constructions, some of which the language may have allowed naturally and easily at an earlier time in its history, but which are no longer supportable by the real underlying grammar of the language. Such a situation begs for a reassessment of the teaching of formal grammar to native speakers of English.

WHAT IS A NATURAL LANGUAGE?

Human languages like English are frequently referred to as "natural languages" because they are "naturally" occurring in human beings—that is, all normal human children learn a first language. No normal human child fails to do this, and no other species accomplishes this feat. Learning a human language is no trivial matter. These languages all show a formidable complexity.

NO "PRIMITIVE" LANGUAGES OR "DEGENERATE" DIALECTS EXIST

Those who we may call "language purists" (including most of the public) hold the view that the most prestigious variety of a language is (somehow) the "best" or "purest" form of that language, and the dialects that differ from it are only degenerate forms of that language. Along such lines, even other languages (usually spoken by groups whose assets other groups covet) such as the languages of various Native Americans have been incorrectly characterized by some as primitive. Much work in the linguistics of this century has gone toward demonstrating that there is no such thing as a primitive or a degenerate human language.[1] Linguistic research clearly shows that all human languages (including the nonstandard dialects) utilize very comparable linguistic rules and devices. No one who has seriously looked has ever discovered a human language of less complexity than, or lacking the grammatical machinery to express the propositions and ideas expressible in, other human languages.

THE COMPLEXITY OF NORMAL LANGUAGE

Normal language is quite complex, and its speakers handle this complexity with a natural ease. Consider the fact (well established in language-acquisition circles) that a 4-year-old English speaker (of any dialect of English) can routinely deal with a complex structure such as "What do you think that Ernie said that Big Bird lost?" Such a question involves three sentences (or clauses, in more formal parlance): the highest one, the one containing the others, is "What do you think" (cf. "you think [something]"); the middle one, the one that is immediately contained in the highest sentence, and that itself contains another, is "that Ernie said" (cf. "Ernie said [something]"); and the lowest one is "that Big Bird lost" (cf. "Big Bird lost [something]"). Here, the question in the highest sentence is formed on the object (*what*) of the verb (*lost*) in the lowest sentence, a complex phenomenon that a 4-year-old can readily process and produce.

The average speaker of English may have a hard time seeing that such facts are of any interest or that they might pose any difficulty because speakers, given their natural ability to learn and to use language, take this ability for granted. (In the same vein, a bee "takes for granted" the ability to fly, even though a physical explanation of this ability had proved quite elusive.) Though they are "easy" for the speaker, such linguistic constructions looked at in detail are of sufficient complexity that theoretical linguistics still seeks full explanation of them. Why, for example, does the question word not simply remain in place, yielding the (impossible) form "Do you think that Ernie said that Big Bird lost what?" which seems in certain respects a simpler structure to process, with *do* signaling the question high up, and with the object *what* simply following its verb, as it would in a statement? Quite interestingly, in studies of language acquisition, children learning English do not even produce such constructions as errors.[2] Further, no grammar text ever instructs a student in how to move question words such as *what*. It is a complex operation that English learners acquire and execute early and naturally, and that they do not need to be told about.

Another illustration of the complexity of normal language comes from what most people think of as a simple phenomenon: pronouns. I have yet to encounter a college grammar student who is unfamiliar with the characterization of a pronoun as "something that takes the place of a noun." However, absolutely no one who speaks English actually follows this characterization, a fact that is easy to demonstrate. Consider the sentences in (1):

(1) a. [$_{NP}$ The tall [$_N$ girl] in blue jeans] is an MIT student.

    b. *The tall she in blue jeans is an MIT student.

    c. She is an MIT student.

    d. [$_{NP}$ Mary] is an MIT student.

Anyone actually following the traditional characterization of pronouns given above would produce sentence (1b) and would not produce (1c) as a pronominalized version of (1a), but no English speaker does this. The facts of English are the reverse: a pronoun such as *she* always targets the noun and all of its attached modifiers—a piece of structure that linguists call noun phrase (or NP; in sentence [1a], *the tall girl in blue jeans* is an NP). Thus it is (1c) that is the pronominalized version of (1a), and (1b) is not an option. Traditional grammars usually cite examples for pronoun substitution such as (1d/1c) to support the traditional definition; however,

---

* The asterisk marks a sentence that sounds odd or impossible to a native speaker.

expressions such as *Mary* are also NPs, ones consisting of a noun with no modification. The NP characterization works in all cases.

These examples clearly illustrate two important ideas about normal human language: (i) normal language involves an abstract and complex structure that children learn very readily, and (ii) some of the most widely known characterizations in traditional classroom grammar (such as the above characterization of pronoun) are not at all accurate and have little effect on how the people who know them speak. The consideration of pronouns here provides a good example of how extremely divorced people's conscious ideas about language can be from the real, operative, subconscious grammatical system that they use to speak the language (and must use, because there is no other "language machine" in one's head). Real linguistic knowledge—knowledge of how to construct and understand the sentences of one's language (Noam Chomsky's [1965] *linguistic competence*)—is by its very nature subconscious knowledge. It is obvious that no one has learned to speak English based on such grammar-book characterizations as the one of pronoun.

ARE SIGNATURE CONSTRUCTIONS OF PRESTIGE ENGLISH "NATURAL"?

With this brief sketch of the character of normal language in mind, let us now turn to the central question concerning the linguistic character of prestige English—English with constructions signaling prestige and formality. Are such constructions (and hence the language variety containing them) "natural"? That is, are these constructions a genuine, straightforward product of the basic underlying grammar of English (what we earlier called linguistic competence, the real grammar machine in one's head), so that speakers who do not produce these constructions "correctly" are ignoring or misapplying rules of this grammar (approximating the "purist" position)?[3] Alternatively, are these prestige constructions contrived ("fake") constructions, ones that speakers must somehow patch together, contrary to the rules of the real, underlying grammar of English, to effect higher social status? As we shall see, considerable linguistic evidence points to the latter conclusion.

The constructions that we will look at here involve an aspect of the grammatical system called *case*.[4] In English, case is seen largely as the form that a pronoun assumes depending on its location in a sentence. For instance, in simple sentences like "She saw them" or "They talked to her," the pronouns *she* and *they* are *nominative* case forms, and the pronouns *them* and *her* are *objective* case forms.

SOME SIGNATURE FEATURES OF PRESTIGE ENGLISH

The constructions of prestige English that we will consider here include

(i) a nominative object of comparison, such as *I* in "Mary is smarter than I";

(ii) a nominative predicate of *be*, such as *I* in "It was I";

(iii) the objective interrogative pronoun referring to objects, such as *whom* in "Whom did you see?" and

(iv) a nominative subject in coordination, such as *I* in "Mary and I left."

Each construction is supported by some rationale, which often serves as the heuristic for learning and operating it.[5] In the case of (i), the rationale offered centers on analogy to another structure: there is another sentence that has the same meaning ("Mary is smarter than I/*me am") in which the pronoun in question is necessarily nominative in a partial clause. Since there are some such sentences in which normal (nonprestige) English uses an objective pronoun (e.g., "Mary sees movies more than me") that are ambiguous ("Mary sees movies more than I do" or "Mary sees movies more than she sees me"), a simple appeal is made to "be careful to choose the pronoun form that fits your meaning" (Fowler 1983, 165).

In the case of (ii), not much is said in traditional grammars about these constructions beyond the fact that *I* is a subject complement (in some sense it refers to the subject), so the reasoning goes that it should bear the case of the subject (here, nominative). As for (iii), traditional grammars say that *whom* should be used when questioning the object of a verb, following the form that pronouns take when they are objects (e.g., *him* or *them*). Regarding (iv), the rationale for saying *I* here is that the pronoun is a part of the subject and hence should show nominative form, just as if it alone were the subject.

DOUBTS ABOUT THE "NATURALNESS" OF PRESTIGE CONSTRUCTIONS

A red flag common to all of these constructions is that English speakers do not "naturally" and easily produce them (hence the attention to them in grammar books), quite a surprising result in light of the fact that children learning English (all dialects, not just standard English) have command of the case forms of pronouns (the common forms, as in "She saw them," and the normal, nonprestige forms) and the "targeting" properties of pronouns (e.g, they target NPs), as well as of other complex aspects of language, at a very early age.[6] A significant question surrounding the prestige constructions is this: why, when children are known to acquire complex aspects of language early and easily, do these seemingly simple constructions (in fact, exceedingly simple if the rationales offered for them are correct) not emerge in acquisition as normal, basic case usage? Why do these formal constructions pose any difficulties at all?

The answer may involve a mismatch between these constructions and the real, operative grammar of the language, the speaker's naturally acquired linguistic competence, as discussed earlier. For convenience, I shall refer to this naturally acquired grammatical system as *the operative grammar.* Closer consideration of each of these constructions shows that each of them may indeed be at odds with apparent norms of the operative grammar.[7] Consider first *than I* in (i). The rationale offered here (that the pronoun form should reflect meaning) is quite suspect. If in the operative grammar (the mental repository of grammatical structure, the only language machine in the speaker's head) there did exist the mechanism presupposed here, then it would be generally true that NPs with a subject meaning would simply be nominative, and NPs with an object meaning would be objective. But what of the sentences in (2) and (3)?

(2) a. I believe her to be innocent.

    b. I believe that she is innocent.

(3) She was seen in Berlin.

In sentence (2b), *she* is the subject of the lower clause ("that she is innocent"), playing no other role in the sentence overall. Sentences (2a) and (2b) are paraphrases, and hence in (2a), *her* is only the subject of the lower clause. In sentence (2a), we have an example of what is clearly a subject showing objective case. This example shows that the case of a subject can vary for structural reasons: subjects are not simply nominative. In sentence (3), *she* only has an object meaning (someone saw her), and the logical subject is unspecified. This is an instance of a logical object in nominative case; logical objects are not always in objective case. Taken together, what such sentences illustrate very clearly is that the operative grammar has no mechanism or rule that directly relates the case of a pronoun to its meaning as a subject or object. Case is decided on different (structural) grounds. Thus an appeal to a putative rule for determining case by meaning is an appeal to a nonexistent device, a device not present in the operative grammar.

Further, justifying a nominative pronoun in *than I* by appeal to analogy with a partial clause (e.g., "Mary is smarter than I am") also does not hold up. Consider the sentences in (4) and (5):

(4) a. ??Mary is as smart as I.

    b. Mary is as smart as I (*me) am.

(5) a. *Mary baits her hook like I.

   b. Mary baits her hook like I (*me) do.

Sentence (4a) clearly sounds strained, and no one would ever say sentence (5a).[8] There is a clear degradation of how natural or plausible the isolated nominative pronouns in (4a) and (5a) are, though in each instance, there is a supporting "tacit" clause, as in (4b) and (5b). Obviously, the operative grammar shows no clear or consistent evidence of utilizing such tacit clauses to facilitate nominative pronouns in isolation.

Similar problems accompany the *it is/was I* construction. The rationale for the nominative *I* here too is that it follows a linking verb and refers to ("renames") the subject. However, what of sentences like (6), with a subject complement that no one would ever render as *I*, even though the same conditions hold?

(6) *In this picture, the person in the purple shorts is I.

The rationale collapses quickly, lacking any generality. Further, as argued in connection with sentences like (2) and (3), there is in the operative grammar no simple, general connection between subject meaning or reference and nominative case.

Rather than being the normal product of the operative grammar, this construction has more the appearance of a memorized expression—a sort of idiom divorced from the grammatical norm. One thing pointing in this direction is how "fragile" this construction is—how quickly it becomes implausible, while its normal (nonprestige) counterpart does not. To see this, consider the sentences in (7) and (8):

(7) a. It was I.

   b. ??It was just I.

   c. ??It was we.

   d. *It was just we.

(8) a. It was me.

   b. It was just me.

   c. It was us.

   d. It was just us.

Adding expressions or changing to plural pronouns, as in (7b–7c), quickly strains the viability of this construction, and the combination of the two is worse yet, as in (7d). However, the same alterations to (8a), with its normal, productive objective pronoun, have no such effect. Whereas (8) is behaving like a normal, productive syntactic construction, easily admitting modification, (7) is behaving quite oddly, as if it were not a productive construction but a memorized expression that does not as readily admit deviation (any more than an idiom does; cf. "That's life!" but not ??"That's really life!" or *"That's not life!"; also, "That's how it goes!" but not *"That's how they go!")[9]

As for the use of *whom* in (iii),[10] grammars talk about this form as though the "problem" with it had arisen only recently. In fact, Otto Jespersen (1970, 482) notes that "from about 1500, *who* came to be used instead of *whom*," and "in many cases modern editors print *whom* where the old editions of Sh[akespeare] have *who*." *Whom* appears to be an example of something that the earlier language (or, more accurately, the operative grammar of that language; it was arguably a different language with a different grammar) did produce normally at one time, but that has since lost its support in the evolved operative grammar of the modern language.

As for the traditional claim that *who* and *whom* are supposed to be treated as pronouns such as *they/them* when determining which form to select, it is doubtful that such question words have (or ever had) any relation to pronouns in the operative grammar. For example, pronouns have antecedents, referents that precede them. Question words do not, but are instead involved with attempts to elicit a reference. Historically, the objective form *whom* seems to have been dropped from the language closer to the time that English stopped showing nominative/objective case differences on normal noun phrases (as modern German still does, e.g., *der Hund* 'the dog' [nominative]; *den Hund* 'the dog' [accusative]). Real pronouns did not lose their case forms at that time and still display case distinctions.

Another clear indication of the separation between question words like *who* and *whom* and pronouns can be seen in a comparison of the sentences in (9):

(9) a. It was him.

  b. *Whom was it?

In normal, productive (nonprestige) English, the objective pronoun form (here, *him*) appears easily in a construction like (9a). If, in the operative grammar, question words were simply pronouns (like *him*), then (9b) should also be an easy, normal form. However, it is not viable in any variety of English, even the most formal. Such a striking difference suggests that question words simply have no connection to pronouns in the operative grammar, and hence the rationale offered in (iii) connecting *who/whom* to pronouns does not correspond to any existing grammatical device. One cannot operate a part of grammar that does not exist.

According to Emonds (1986), another indicator that a construction does not follow a claimed grammatical norm is hypercorrection—speakers using a construction where it shouldn't be used (if the construction were the sort of grammatical product that it is claimed to be). Regarding *whom*, Otto Jespersen (1965, appendix) notes numerous hypercorrections like those in (10), where "reputable writers" have used *whom* in reference to a subject:

(10) a. We feed children whom we believe are hungry.

     b. Writers whom we must all admit are honest in their intentions have treated unpleasant subjects.

In (10a), *whom* is the subject of "are hungry," and in (10b), it is the subject of "are honest" Such uses occur because they have a ring of naturalness about them. They sound much better than other, more obvious "misuses" of *whom*, such as "*Whom saw Mary?". Now, consider that the only reason that any construction can sound good or plausible is that some rule of the operative grammar allows or "licenses" the construction. Constructions sound good or natural if there exist the subconscious rules to produce them, and they sound odd or unnatural if these rules cannot produce them. Thus the apparent relative "naturalness" of the sentences in (10) suggests that the subconscious rule or rules dictating the use of *whom* in modern English, whatever it might be, is not one that can be reduced simply to following the normal system of pronominal case (cf. "*Them are hungry" or "*Them are honest").

Finally, the *and I* construction of (iv) (e.g., "Mary and I left") poses an interesting puzzle. At first blush, it is not at all clear why there should be any problem making a pronoun in a coordinated subject nominative when this is done quite easily with a single pronoun subject (e.g., "I/*me left"). However, the tendency in normal nonprestige speech is to use an objective form such as *me* in (11):

(11) Me and Mary left.

One can roughly characterize what may be going on here as follows. Many linguists agree that a case such as nominative or objective is assigned to a pronoun (really to any noun phrase) by what is called a "governor," for example, a verb or a preposition that has that pronoun (or NP) as its object. Also, a finite verb (a verb with a tense suffix on it) such as *walks* or *walked* governs its subject NP, giving it nominative case.[11] Each subject or object must be sufficiently "close" to its governor for the governor to give it a case. It is quite possible (Emonds 1986; Chomsky 1993; Sobin 1997) that the members of a coordinated subject are structurally too far from their governor, so that the governor cannot reach them to assign nominative case in the normal way; instead, a "default" objective (accusative) case may appear, as in (11).[12]

Quattlebaum (1994) shows something crucial to further understanding the appearance of the nominative case in these constructions: speakers prefer the nominative pronoun *I* in them over other nominative pronouns (e.g., *she*). Further, speakers who say *and I* in subjects also frequently say this in object positions as well, for example, "just between you and I" (cf. *"just between we").[13] These facts support the following picture: as suggested earlier, the governor that would assign nominative to a subject cannot "reach" coordinated subject pronouns; they are too distant. Thus the speaker must use either the default case (e.g., *me*) or some contrived strategy for making the coordinated subject pronoun nominative, perhaps something as simple as a memorized formula such as saying *I* after *and*, a sort of idiom.[14]

If this is what speakers are doing, then it might explain not only why nominative pronouns other than *I* are less favored, as Quattlebaum shows, but also why the nominative case (especially *I*) is easily extended to certain object pronouns, as in (12), another hypercorrection:

(12) Jane saw Mary and I/me.

Objects may also be coordinated, and such coordinated pronouns are also too distant from their verb or preposition governors. So the speaker must employ either the default-case strategy or the "idiom" strategy. The "idiom" strategy ("say *I* after *and*") is a very limited one that simply cannot "see" whether it is looking at a subject or object, and this explains why both coordinated subjects and coordinated objects show case fluctuation.

What we have just seen may be summarized as follows. Not one of the four prestige constructions discussed here appears to follow from rules of the operative grammar, the "normal" subconscious rules of sentence production. Further, not one of these prestige constructions shows evidence of working in the way that traditional grammars claim them to work. For example, *whom* clearly does not work along the lines of normal personal objective pronouns like *them*. Each prestige construction behaves not like a normal, productive construction, but more like a structural "idiom," a virtually memorized word combination that is (in effect) imposed on what would otherwise be a normal construction.

PRESTIGE CONSTRUCTIONS MAY BE UNNECESSARILY COMPLEX

These observations suggest the following interesting and surprising picture of the prestige constructions and their relation to the operative grammar. If the prestige constructions discussed here were normal, productive constructions that worked, as traditional grammar claims them to, along the same lines that (in some instances) other productive constructions do work, then we would not expect to see the surprising limitations on them that we have just seen. If we assume, as we have, that the operative grammar is the core mechanism responsible for what a speaker of a language can (or cannot) produce easily and straightforwardly, it appears that the operative grammar does not (and very likely cannot) accommodate these prestige constructions as productive constructions; consequently, standard English with the full set of prestige forms predicted by the traditional description of them is evidently not a natural language.

The prestige constructions themselves are unnecessary, since there is a productive, nonprestige counterpart to each. Thus prestige constructions represent unnecessary complexity in the operative grammar that may, in fact, be the basis of their perceived prestige.

These findings are not all that surprising in light of one line of work on the linguistic character of prestige dialects that argues that prestige dialects seem generally to prefer "difficulty." Kroch (1982), noting Zwicky's observation (1972, 608) that "casual speech processes [as opposed to those of formal speech] seem to be constrained to be phonetically natural," offers a close look at various pronunciation features of prestige dialects in a variety of languages. His work argues that the speakers of prestige dialects "mark their distinctness in a negative way— . . . by inhibiting many of the low level, variable processes of phonetic conditioning that characterize spoken language and that underlie regular phonological change" (1982, 228). That is, prestige speech varieties tend to seek out more laborious pronunciation features rather than utilize the more natural and economical ones of less prestigious varieties, introducing a factor of "unnecessary difficulty" into prestige pronunciation. Since change in the pronunciation system of a language frequently involves innovations toward economy, prestige varieties resist change. Thus in this view, prestige dialects have a general tendency to select and preserve more difficult (unnecessarily difficult) features. We may also be seeing this phenomenon in syntax, where certain prestige constructions appear to have no basis in the normal operative grammatical system, but appear to need "special" rules that by their nature are still incapable of yielding complete prestige paradigms.

IMPLICATIONS

The question of the "naturalness" of prestige English is not a question about whether it is "good" or "bad." It is a question of how learnable the hallmark constructions of this variety are, and to what extent they actually require conscious instruction (which normal language does not, as noted earlier). This question, along with the frequently offered reasons for learning prestige English, still needs serious attention and further clarification.

A couple of the major reasons frequently offered for learning and using prestige English are (i) that it is the "correct" way to speak, and (ii) that it is more logical or communicative. However, these motivations are both compromised. Regarding (i), if what we mean by "correct" is operating the grammar the way that it should most naturally and optimally operate, then we have shown here that this is precisely what prestige English does not do. The alternative is to simply equate "correct" with using the prestige variety, a trivialization of the notion. As regards (ii), nearly anyone who has ever taught writing will know that clarity of expression involves strategies other than invoking prestige constructions; it has never been shown that a prestige construction is more "logical" than its nonprestige counterpart.[15]

Humans appear to use language for two major purposes: communication and identification, including indications of social status. The identification use is as universal among humans as language itself. As discussed in considerable detail by Emonds (1986), there emerges the very interesting possibility that humans contrive statusful language by complicating particular aspects of it unnecessarily so that it is not easily learnable via natural-language acquisition, and people have to be "schooled" in it, the entry into this schooling being controlled by the prestige group itself. The study of the prestige variety is rationalized in various ways (e.g., "correctness"), but these rationalizations collapse quickly under scrutiny.

If the work discussed here is on the right track, then it is the unusual complexity, the linguistically perverse character, of prestige constructions that explains why they are problematic, and that suggests that, unlike normal language, these constructions do in all likelihood require instruction, as Emonds (1986) and Chomsky (Olson and Faigley 1991) argue. And here is where other major problems lie. It is well documented that traditional grammar instruction is ineffective (e.g., Braddock, Lloyd-Jones, and Schoer 1963). This ineffectiveness is not at all surprising, given the typically incorrect explanations involved, as sketched out above. Yet there is no widely recognized pedagogical alternative. If it is agreed that students should learn prestige English, including constructions such as those discussed here,[16] then we have a rather large, serious problem on our hands, a problem in applied linguistics. Following Emonds, the most likely solution is to develop an effective grammar pedagogy that has linguistic viability, one that deals with English as it actually works. That means dealing accurately with the prestige constructions as the archaic and "quirky" things that they are in Modern English. It also means giving the nonprestige constructions their due as viable linguistic products.[17]

NOTES

My sincere thanks to Michel DeGraff, Byrd Gibbens, James Levernier, and Anne Marie Sobin for a variety of contributions to this chapter. Any errors are solely the responsibility of the author.

1. A classic work on a Native American language in this vein is Whorf (1964). A more recent classic on nonstandard English is Labov (1969).

2. A couple of acquisition classics that deal with this issue are Menyuk (1969) and Dale (1976).

3. In fact, it is not clear what the language purists mean by "grammar," beyond the characterizations of prestige constructions that one finds in grammar and usage books.

4. Emonds (1986) was the first to observe that case was systematically problematic in the respects discussed here. Much of what follows here is based on his insights.

5. The rationales discussed here can be found in Fowler (1983, 160–66), a very typical classroom grammar text.

6. For example, see Schütze (1997) for a recent, comprehensive consideration of the acquisition of case forms.

7. The following observations are based on Emonds (1986), Quattlebaum (1994), and Sobin (1997). In addition, see Olson and Faigley (1991) for Chomsky's comments on the linguistically contrary character of such features.

8. Fowler (1983, 164–65) mentions only *than* and *as* and only gives examples with *than*, suggesting tacit recognition of this hierarchy. While he recognizes the use of *like* as a conjunction in informal speech, as in sentence 5b, he cautions against this in formal usage (1983, 267).

9. For an elaboration of this position, see Sobin (1997).

10. Thanks to Howard Lasnik for his collaboration on the ideas put forth here on *whom*. More detailed discussion of *whom* appears in Lasnik and Sobin (manuscript).

11. Actually, Chomsky's proposal (1993 and earlier) is that it is the tense affix itself that governs the subject, but we won't pursue this further here.

12. A default case is one that would be used by convention when there is no governor present or close enough to assign a case to a pronoun (or NP). As Emonds (1986) points out, that the default case form in English is objective case (e.g., *me*) is indicated by the fact that in constructions where no governor appears, as in (ii–iii) following, native speakers of English say (ii) in response to (i) and not (iii), even though the answer involves a subject:

(i) Who wants to go to the movies?

(ii) Me!

(iii) *I!

13. Emonds (1986) also observes that nominative case appears on coordinated objects.

14. This strategy is often disguised as "politeness," but an assertion that the first-person pronoun being placed last is more polite has no generality; that is, there is no like politeness difference with first-person *me* in the sentences "Mary saw Max and me" and "Mary saw me and Max."

15. Labov (1969) addresses the logic rationale extensively.

16. This is by no means a universal assumption. See, for example, O'Neil (1972), Sledd (1972), and Emonds (1986).

17. Quattlebaum (1994) shows the potential for success of this approach.

REFERENCES

Braddock, Richard, Richard Lloyd-Jones, and Lowell Schoer. 1963. *Research in written composition.* Urbana, IL: NCTE.

Chomsky, Noam. 1965. Aspects of the theory of syntax. Cambridge, MA: MIT Press.

———. 1993. A minimalist program for linguistic theory. *The view from Building 20: Essays in linguistics in honor of Sylvain Bromberger,* ed. by Kenneth Hale and Samuel Jay Keyser, 1–52. Cambridge, MA: MIT Press.

Dale, Philip S. 1976. *Language development.* 2nd ed. New York: Holt, Rinehart and Winston.

Emonds, Joseph E. 1986. Grammatically deviant prestige constructions. *A festschrift for Sol Saporta,* ed. by Michael Brame, Heles Contreras, and Frederick Newmeyer, 93–129. Seattle, WA: Noit Amrofer.

Fowler, H. Ramsey. 1983. *The Little, Brown handbook.* 2nd ed. Boston: Little, Brown.

Jespersen, Otto. 1965. *The philosophy of grammar.* New York: Norton.

———. 1970. *A modern English grammar on historical principles.* Vol. 5. London: George Allen and Unwin.

Kroch, Anthony S. 1982. Toward a theory of social dialect variation. *Readings in applied English linguistics,* 3rd ed., ed. by Harold B. Allen and Michael D. Linn, 227–244. New York: Alfred A. Knopf.

Labov, William. 1969. The logic of nonstandard English. *Georgetown monograph series on languages and linguistics* no. 22, ed. by James E. Alatis, 1–43. Washington, DC: Georgetown University.

Lasnik, Howard, and Nicholas Sobin. The *who/whom* puzzle: On the preservation of an archaic feature. Unpublished manuscript (available upon request), University of Connecticut and University of Arkansas at Little Rock.

Menyuk, Paula. 1969. *Sentences children use.* Cambridge, MA: MIT Press.

Olson, Gary A., and Lester Faigley. 1991. Language, politics, and composition: A conversation with Noam Chomsky. *Journal of Advanced Composition* 11: 1–35.

O'Neil, Wayne. 1972. The politics of bidialectalism. *College English* 33: 433–38.

Quattlebaum, Judith. 1994. A study of case assignment in coordinate noun phrases. *Language Quarterly* 32: 131–47.

Schütze, Carson T. 1997. INFL in child and adult language: Agreement, case, and licensing. Ph.D. dissertation, Massachusetts Institute of Technology.

Sledd, James. 1972. Doublespeak: Dialectology in the service of Big Brother. *College English* 33: 439–56.

Sobin, Nicholas. 1997. Agreement, default rules, and grammatical viruses. *Linguistic Inquiry* 28: 318–43.

Whorf, Benjamin Lee. 1964. A linguistic consideration of thinking in primitive communities. *Language in Culture and Society,* ed. by Dell Hymes, 129–41. New York: Harper and Row.

Zwicky, Arnold M. 1972. On casual speech. *Papers from the Eighth Regional Meeting of the Chicago Linguistic Society,* ed. by P. Peranteau, J. Levi, and G. Phares, 607–615. Chicago: Chicago Linguistic Society.

4

RETHINKING PRESCRIPTIVISM
John Myhill

In the English-speaking world, and indeed in most languages throughout the world, the overwhelming majority of choices concerning which form is declared to be prescriptively "correct" and which is declared to be "incorrect" are based upon a single simple principle: Whenever different groups use different forms in their everyday language, the form used by the group with more power (economic and political) is considered to be "correct" while the form used by the group with less power is considered to be "incorrect" (e.g., Milroy and Milroy 1985; Joseph 1987). Thus, for example, in American English, the prescriptive norm is based upon the everyday usage of White middle-class Midwesterners (which has spread to varying degrees to the elite in other sections of the country), because these people have been admired while other people have been, for one reason or another, stigmatized. For example, African Americans have been stigmatized because of their race and poverty, Southerners have been stigmatized since their side lost the Civil War, and the inhabitants of East Coast cities have been stigmatized because they are more likely to be poor immigrants or the immediate descendants of poor immigrants.

Thus in every single case where the typical everyday usage of White middle-class Midwesterners differs from the typical everyday usage of African Americans, it is the usage of White middle-class Midwesterners that is judged "correct" while African American Vernacular English (AAVE) is judged to be "incorrect" (in a general sense, we can say the same for higher-status Whites versus lower-status Whites, but the situation in this case is less serious because there are fewer differences between the dialects). Consider, for example, the following pairs of sentences, having the same meanings, corresponding to typical usages of White Americans and Black

Americans (this is not to say that all Whites always use the "White" forms or that all Blacks always use the "Black" forms, but linguistic research has shown a clear and very strong statistical trend in this direction):[1]

(1a) White: He says he's hungry now.

(1b) Black: He say he hungry now.

(2a) White: He's at Mary's house every afternoon.

(2b) Black: He be at Mary house every afternoon.

(3a) White: I didn't tell him anything.

(3b) Black: I ain't tell him nothing.

As shown by Labov (1972), among others, from a logical point of view, neither characteristic "White" usages nor characteristic "Black" usages are superior to the other; White usage follows a system, but Black usage also follows a system, although this system may not be apparent to someone not familiar with it. For example, consider how Black usage represents *is* or its contracted form *'s*. In (1), White *'s* is simply omitted in the Black version (*he hungry*), while in (2), White *'s* corresponds to *be* in the Black version. Is this just random variation in AAVE? It only appears that way to someone who does not understand it: *Be* is used in (2b) because the event is repeated (every afternoon), while it is not used in (1b) because the event is not repeated; this alternation in AAVE is therefore governed by a rule that has no parallel in White usage (in other cases the reverse is true).

The use of the terms "correct" and "incorrect" to describe the (a) and (b) sentences, respectively, is in fact strictly speaking inappropriate, because "correctness" normally implies a logical or factual quality, and there is nothing more logical or factual about the White usages as opposed to the Black usages here. Although pseudoscientific explanations might be invented to justify the preference for the (a) sentences over the (b) sentences, they are easily refuted by linguists with a more extensive knowledge of different languages who can point to languages where the "correct" usage is parallel to the (b) sentences; for example, many languages (e.g., Hebrew, Arabic, Russian, Chinese, and Hungarian) do not use a verb like *to be* in the present (as in [1b]), many languages (e.g., Danish, Norwegian, Chinese, and Japanese) have no subject-verb agreement (as in [1b]), and in many languages (e.g., Spanish and Italian) two negatives make a negative (as in [3b]), not a positive. When someone in a position of authority such as a teacher inappropriately uses the word "incorrect" to describe constructions such as those in the (b) sentences here, it conveys to students an inaccurate message about the (lack of) logical value of the Black usages, which has a powerful psychological impact upon both Whites and Blacks in the sense that White behavior is seen as "right" and Black behavior is seen as "wrong" without any logical justification, purely as a result of the imposition of authority. In my discussion here, I am concerned with the psychological effect of the use of these terms, so I will use the words "correct" and "incorrect," but put them in scare quotes so as to convey the idea that these terms do not have their normal meaning relating to logical value but rather to the social effect of condemnation without justification.

It is unfair to base the prescriptive norm upon White usage in the sense that this means that Black people have to do more work to learn the "Standard language." More significantly, it also means that, for Black people who speak AAVE, learning the "Standard language," rather than being an intellectual and objective process, amounts to simply imitating the usage of White people. By advocating this standard, the educational establishment is essentially saying that the way to evaluate the English ability of Black people is to give higher ratings to Blacks whose English is more like that of Whites and lower ratings to Blacks whose English is less like that of Whites, to reward Blacks to the extent that they imitate White language usage rather than for intelligence, logical thinking, and hard work.

This situation is reflected in the comments made by African Americans in a discussion on an episode of the *Oprah Winfrey Show* in 1987. African Americans are well aware that the prescriptive norm is unfair, for example, "Why is it when White people use slang i's okay but when Blacks use slang i's Black language?" (said by a Black woman in her early 20s who is identifiably Black but with more or less standard grammar) and "Why is it that we're always wrong?" (said by a Black man, about 45, identifiably Black in pronunciation, who switches between standard and nonstandard grammar). Since Blacks are aware that the situation is unfair, they commonly express the feeling that this puts them in a dilemma: an individual African American can have a more materially comfortable lifestyle by adopting Standard White English, but by doing this s/he explicitly endorses and supports a system that Black society in general correctly views as unfair, and it assumes considerable moral blindness on the part of Black people to expect them to take advantage of such a system without feeling very uncomfortable about this. Therefore, speakers of AAVE who learn Standard (White) English often do not feel good about it. For example, Oprah says, "For Ronny Carter [an African American], though, the way he speaks is causing a personal conflict. He has a good job in a major corporation but he says he was surprised when his bosses sent him to Dr. Anderson [a speech therapist] for training. Ronny says he wants to advance so he's working on his language, but he says, inside there is some resentment because his identity is being changed." Such African Americans are often the target of hostile feelings from other Blacks, who see them as opportunistic and unprincipled, for example, "People suggested I come here because they say I speak White. It wasn't a compliment" (said by a Black woman on the show, in her early 30s, identifiably Black in her speech; her grammar is more or less standard, which is presumably why people think that she "speaks White").

Not surprisingly, under these circumstances, most speakers of AAVE do not learn and use Standard English[2]; this is reflected in their generally low scores on standardized English tests. For example, African Americans average about 90 points lower than Whites on English Scholastic Aptitude Tests (SATs) and are on the average four years behind in reading and writing level by the time they are 17 years old. They are aware that they can ingratiate themselves with White people by trying to use language like White people, but they feel that this would be opportunistic and unprincipled. They correctly perceive that middle-class Whites are successful without having to change their speech to accommodate anyone else, so they do not see why they should have to change themselves: "I say Black English is cool, ain't nuttin' wrong wit it. I's da fact dat you speak whatever you feel okay, dose who can't undestan', i's dey problem" (said by a Black male on the *Oprah Winfrey Show*, about 18, with very strong AAVE pronunciation and grammar). In fact, of the eleven African Americans who speak on the episode who are capable of speaking AAVE and express an opinion regarding the requirement to use Standard English in mainstream society, only two of them think that this is reasonable, and these are Oprah herself and another woman who hosts a less-known talk show (a would-be Oprah); the other nine either explicitly refuse to even try to talk like a White person (i.e., use Standard English) or make some effort but express discomfort at the situation.

We find similar sentiments expressed by academic African Americans:

One factor [in Black psychological vulnerability, stigma, and poor school performance] is the basic assimilationist offer that schools make to blacks: You can be valued and rewarded in school (and society), the school says to these students, but you must first master the culture and ways of the American mainstream, and since that mainstream (as it is represented) is essentially white, this means you must give up many particulars of being black—styles of speech and appearance—at least in mainstream settings. This is asking a lot. But it has been the "color-blind" offer to every immigrant and minority group in our nation's history, the core of the melting-pot ideal, and so I think it strikes most of us as fair. Yet non-immigrant minorities like blacks and Native-Americans have always been here, and thus are entitled, more than new immigrants, to participate in the defining image of society projected in school. More important, their exclusion from these images denies their contributive history and presence in society. Thus, whereas immigrants can tilt toward assimilation in pursuit of the opportunities for which they came, American blacks may find it harder to assimilate. For them, the offer of acceptance in return for assimilation carries a primal insult; it asks them to join in something that has made them invisible. (Steele 1994, 286)

Similarly, according to a study by the *Washington Post*, young Black students generally believe that "Black kids who do their schoolwork and behave must want to be White" (reported in Brown 1995, 122; see also Labov 1972, 255–92); since schooling is perceived as teaching Black children how to behave like Whites (and this perception is entirely correct with regards to language), this means that Black children have to choose between being educated and maintaining their own identity. Under these circumstances, it is hardly surprising that many African Americans are not learning Standard English and are consequently performing very poorly in subjects and standardized tests requiring Standard English, with disastrous economic consequences.

While the present English prescriptive norm is unfair and is related to serious social inequalities, this need not be the case. There are a number of languages where the idea of "correctness" is more egalitarian, fair, and inclusive. In such languages, sometimes the "correct" usage corresponds to the everyday usage of one group and sometimes it corresponds to the everyday usage of another group; there are no groups like American middle-class Whites whose general usage is always declared "correct" or American Blacks whose general usage is always declared "wrong."

In Hebrew and Arabic, for example, the "Standard language" is based, in theory, upon linguists' interpretations of the language of a particular text (the Bible/Mishna and the Koran, respectively). The "correct" language, therefore, is not associated with the everyday usage of any particular group, and no one speaks it natively. This means that, in cases where higher-status people and lower-status people differ in their everyday usage, the "correct" form is as likely to correspond to the everyday lower-class usage as to the everyday higher-class usage. I will discuss Hebrew here, but the situation is more or less the same in Arabic (see Ibrahim 1986). (4) gives three Hebrew sentences with the same meaning: (4a) has usages that are generally associated with speakers of a higher social status (particularly Ashkenazic Jews), (4b) has usages that are generally associated with speakers of a lower social status (particularly Sephardic Jews), while (4c) has the prescriptively "correct" usages (I use the phonetic symbols ʁ and ɾ in [4] to distinguish two pronunciations of the letter *resh*, as a voiced uvular fricative [like French *r*] and as an alveolar tap [like *tt* in American English *butter*]):[3]

(4a) Higher-status: hu lo mekiʁ otax.

(4b) Lower-status: hu lo makiɾ otex.

(4c) "Correct":   hu lo makiɾ otax.

                    he not know you (female)

"He doesn't know you."

In (4) we find three differences, two involving the choice of *a* or *e* as the vowel and the third involving the use of ʁ or ɾ. Here the everyday higher-status usage is "correct" once (otax), and the everyday lower-status usage is "correct" twice (makiɾ). Another example is (5):

(5a) Higher-status: militi oto vnisiti   leharim   oto.

(5b) Lower-status: mileti oto vniseti   leharim   oto.

(5c) "Correct":   mileti oto vnisiti   leharim   oto.

                 I-filled it and-I-tried to-pick-up it

"I filled it and I tried to pick it up."

Example (5) shows two differences, and in one case the everyday lower-status usage is "correct" (mileti), while in the other the everyday higher-status usage is "correct" (nisiti). This is a general pattern in Hebrew and Arabic: The "correct" usage is not particularly associated with any status group, so that there is no group whose members are always "right" or "wrong" in their everyday usage. Learning the "Standard language" therefore consists of learning an abstract linguistic system rather than simply learning how to imitate the everyday usage of certain high-status people, as it does in English.

Hebrew and Arabic are not alone in having a fair "Standard language" system. Icelandic and Sinhala (the language of Sri Lanka) similarly use standards based on a specific set of texts rather than the usage of a particular social class, and there are other possible types of fair standards. Standard Shona (spoken in Botswana) is an artificial combination of different dialects (Ansre 1970). Norwegian has two standards, Bokmål and Nynorsk; Bokmål is based upon the speech of the high-prestige group, while Nynorsk is based upon the usage of poorer rural areas. Here is an example of the variation allowed:

(6) B: Hun/Ho tar   fram/frem boka/boken selv/sjøl.

    N: Ho   tek/tar fram   boka/boki sjøv.

       she   takes out   book-the herself

"She takes the book out herself." (Jahr and Janicki 1995)

In writing Norwegian, people can choose which standard to write, and for some words in each there are even alternative forms that are both considered correct for a given dialect (e.g., *hun* or *ho* for "she" in Bokmål, and *tek* or *tar* for "take" in Nynorsk). Norwegian scholars have been attempting to gradually unify these two into a single Standard Norwegian (Samnorsk), combining various features of the two standards.

In Hebrew, Arabic, Shona, and Norwegian, people are not called upon to give up their distinctive everyday usages in casual speech (in fact, in Norway it is explicitly forbidden for teachers to correct pupils' speech, though there is of course a standardized writing system). On the other hand, in the written language and more formal speech (e.g., news broadcasts), the common prescriptive norm should be used. Thus the purpose of the prescriptive norm is to give the various groups a common language; it is not intended to force the assimilation of one group to norms established at the convenience of a different group.

If we consider the situation in such languages, we see that there is no reason why Standard English should necessarily be based upon whatever people in the prestige group (White middle-class people) happen to do naturally; it is not superior to or more logical than the everyday language of other people, and setting the standard in this way penalizes people who naturally speak in other ways for being different. Such a standard divides the society by distinguishing between those who are to be emulated and entitled to speak naturally and those who cannot speak naturally and must emulate or fail. On the other hand, a standard language such as is used in Hebrew, Arabic, Icelandic, Sinhala, Shona, and Norwegian ties the society together, because it takes elements from each of their natural usages and fuses them into a whole; it unites the society rather than dividing it.

NOTES

I thank Rebecca Wheeler for the unusually large number of helpful comments she gave on earlier drafts of this chapter.

1. See, for example, Labov (1972, 201–40) for discussion of this. There are Whites who use *ain't* for standard *am not/aren't/isn't/haven't/hasn't*, but the use of *ain't* for *didn't* is basically restricted to Blacks.

2. I know of no systematically gathered data on the number of Blacks who do not use Standard English; at the Ann Arbor Black English trial, Joe Dillard estimated that 80 percent of the Blacks in the United States use AAVE as their everyday language (William Labov, personal communication), which seems about right to me. Clearly AAVE speakers constitute the great majority of Blacks, as is apparent from a brief trip to any of the numerous urban ghettoes where Blacks are most likely to live.

3. See Ravid (1995) for a discussion of these general patterns in higher-class usage and lower-class usage.

REFERENCES

Ansre, G. 1970. Language standardisation in sub-Saharan Africa. *Current Trends in Linguistics* 7: 680–98.

Brown, Tony. 1995. *Black lies, White lies: The truth according to Tony Brown*. New York: William Morrow and Co.

Ibrahim, Muhammad H. 1986. Standard and prestige language: A problem in Arabic sociolinguistics. *Anthropological Linguistics* 28.1: 115–27.

Jahr, Ernst Håkon, and Karol Janicki. 1995. The function of the standard variety: A contrastive study of Norwegian and Polish. *International Journal of the Sociology of Language* 115: 25–46.

Joseph, John Earl. 1987. *Eloquence and power: The rise of language standards and standard languages*. London: Frances Pinter.

Labov, William. 1972. *Language in the inner city*. Philadelphia: University of Pennsylvania Press.

Milroy, James, and Lesley Milroy. 1985. *Authority in language: Investigating language prescriptivism and standardisation*. London: Routledge.

Ravid, Dorit Diskin. 1995. *Language change in child and adult Hebrew: A psycholinguistic perspective*. New York: Oxford University Press.

Steele, Claude M. 1994. Race and the schooling of Black Americans. *Morality in practice*, 4th ed., ed. by J. P. Sterba, 279–88. Belmont, CA: Wadsworth.

II

NEW WAYS IN THE CLASSROOM

Dialect Awareness Programs in the School and Community

Walt Wolfram

One of the ironies of language arts education in the United States today is the movement away from the study of language as a topic in its own right at the same time that the language arts classroom has become increasingly multicultural and multilingual. Thus Cleary and Lund (1993) report that a focus on language per se in language arts is of questionable educational value, and the National Council of Teachers of English (NCTE) has gone so far as to resolve that a focus on grammar is a "deterrent to the improvement of students' speaking and writing" ("NCTE to You" 1986, 103). Meanwhile, the increasingly multicultural composition of the classroom exhibits more linguistic diversity than ever before as students use a wide range of nonmainstream English language structures to reflect their sociolinguistic identities.

Public controversies such as those related to the resolution of the Oakland School Board on Ebonics in 1996 and 1997 (Wolfram 1998a), have indicated once again that (*a*) beliefs and attitudes about language diversity are intense and entrenched; (*b*) there is widespread misinformation and "miseducation" about dialects that pervade the understanding of this topic in American society; and (*c*) there is a critical need for informed knowledge about language diversity and its role in education and in public life. The need for education about language diversity was highlighted in the resolution passed by the American Association for Applied Linguistics (1997) that noted that "all students and teachers should learn scientifically-based information about linguistic diversity," that "education should systematically incorporate information about language variation," and that linguists and other language professionals "should seek ways and means to better communicate the theories and principles of the field to the general public on a continuing basis" (resolution of the American Association for Applied Linguistics, March 11, 1997).

In this chapter, I discuss the role of dialect awareness programs in raising the level of understanding about dialect diversity in American society.[1] The term *dialect awareness* is used here to refer to activities that promote an understanding of and appreciation for language variation. The term *dialect awareness* is an obvious derivative of *language awareness*, which is defined as "a person's sensitivity to and conscious awareness of the nature of language and its role in human life" (Donmall 1985, 7). Such programs may center on the *cognitive parameter*, in which the focus is on the patterns of language, an *affective parameter*, in which the focus is on attitudes of language, or a *social parameter*, in which the focus is on the role of language in effective communication. In the United Kingdom and other European countries, a number of language awareness curricular programs now exist (e.g., Hawkins 1984, 1985; Edwards 1990), although considerable controversy remains surrounding the nature and goals of such curricula (Clark et al. 1990). In the United States, there have been no wide-scale curricula related to language awareness, although there is an obvious need for such programs. Furthermore, some of the central notions about language found in these programs have certainly been applied in sociolinguistic education for several decades now.

A RATIONALE FOR DIALECT AWARENESS PROGRAMS

In this section, I set forth a rationale for dialect awareness programs, and in the following one I offer some themes that should be part of such a program. My focus is upon the affective and cognitive goals of such programs rather than the social parameter as set forth earlier. Thus the types of programs I discuss are clearly different from, though not in opposition to, programs designed to teach proficiency in Standard English. In fact, I would argue that the most effective program for teaching Standard English is one that necessarily couples this teaching with dialect awareness as discussed here.

To begin with, dialect awareness programs should be justified on the basis of a commitment to search for fundamental truth about laws of nature and matter. With respect to language differences, there is an educational and societal tolerance of misinformation and folklore that is matched in few subject areas. Myths about the basis of language variation, the linguistic status of dialect structures, and the socioeducational implications of dialect divergence are deeply rooted in our educational system and society at large, and they need to be confronted as honestly as any other unjustified set of beliefs in other disciplines (Bauer and Trudgill 1998). At the very least, then, dialect awareness programs are justified on the basis of a need to provide factual information about language variation to counter the entrenched mythology about language differences.

Issues of social and educational equity are also tied in with the need for accurate information about language differences. If one operates on erroneous assumptions about language differences, it is easy to fall prey to misguided assessments about language capability as it relates to class, race, and region. The potential for dialect discrimination cannot be taken more lightly than any other type of discrimination. As Milroy and Milroy (1985, 3) note, "Although public discrimination on the grounds of race, religion and social class is not now publicly acceptable, it appears that discrimination on linguistic grounds is publicly acceptable, even though linguistic differences may themselves be associated with ethnic, religious and class differences." An educational and social system that takes on the responsibility to educate students concerning the truth about racial and social differences and the effects of this discrimination in other areas certainly should feel obliged to extend this discussion to language as well.

The equity issue also extends to the impartial representation of sociolinguistic history at the same time that it points to a sociohistorical rationale for dialect awareness programs. As history and social studies texts strive to represent more fairly the contributions of various sociocultural and ethnic groups to the development of the United States, it seems only reasonable to extend this requirement to language representation as well. A variety of vernacular dialects have had an important influence on the development of American English, but there is little or no acknowledgment of this role. Nor is there any discussion of how different varieties have arisen and developed over time. Studying dialects formally and informally provides a wealth of information for examining the dynamic nature of language and the historical and cultural contribution of various groups to American society.

From a humanistic perspective, the reasons for endorsing dialect awareness programs given thus far are probably a sufficient basis for promoting such programs. There is, however, another, cognitive rationale for these programs related to the nature of intellectual inquiry. The study of dialects affords us a fascinating window through which we can see how language works. Furthermore, the inner workings of language are just as readily observed in examining dialects and their patterning as they are through the exclusive study of a unitary standard variety. Language, including dialects, is a unique form of knowledge in that speakers know a language simply by virtue of the fact that they speak it. Much of this knowledge is not on a conscious level, but it is still open to systematic investigation. Looking at dialect differences thus provides a natural laboratory for making generalizations drawn from carefully described sets of data. We can hypothesize about the patterning of language features and then check our hypotheses on the basis of actual usage patterns. This, of course, is a type of scientific inquiry.

Hypothesizing about and then testing language patterns is quite within the grasp of a wide age range of formal and informal learners. I have led classes of students in the middle elementary grades, ages 9 through 11, through the steps of hypothesis formation and testing about language patterning by using exercises involving dialect features. At the same time, I have also led informal groups of adult learners, such as participants at civic-group meetings, church-group meetings, and continuing-education groups of all ages, through the same steps of inquiry. For example, the exercise on the *a*-prefixing dialect pattern (e.g., "She was a-hunting") illustrated in the next section comes from an eighth-grade curriculum on dialects that we have taught in North Carolina for several years now, but it is also part of a curriculum we developed for an elderhostel curriculum on dialects as well (Wolfram and Schilling-Estes 1996).

Finally, there is a utilitarian reason for studying dialects. Information about dialects should prove helpful to students and citizens of all ages as they work to develop the language skills required for success in mainstream education and formal social interaction, including the use of the standard variety. Vernacular-dialect speakers may, for example, apply knowledge about dialect features to composing and editing skills in writing. I have personally witnessed students who studied particular structural features of vernacular dialects such as -*s* third-person absence (e.g., "She go to the store") transfer this knowledge to their writing when called upon to write Standard English. As mentioned at the outset of this section, the study of various dialects hardly endangers the sovereignty of Standard English in the classroom. If anything, it enhances the learning of the standard variety through heightened sensitivity to language variation. It also places the learning of a standard variety in a more honest and realistic context by stressing the fundamental social and economic advantages of a standard variety rather than a mythical linguistic rationale for learning the standard variety.

THEMES IN A DIALECT AWARENESS PROGRAM

Although it is beyond the scope of this chapter to offer an extensive set of activities and exercises that might be incorporated into a dialect awareness curriculum (cf. Wolfram, Schilling-Estes, and Hazen 1996; Wolfram and Creech 1996; Wolfram, Dannenberg, Anderson, and Messner 1996), it is reasonable to suggest some of the major themes that should be included in such programs, especially since they are still relatively novel in formal and informal education in American society. Our own experimentation with dialect awareness programs in formal education has focused on the design of a middle-school curriculum, but similar units can be developed for an upper-level elementary language arts curriculum and for the secondary level as well. In informal education, we have worked with a full spectrum of groups and organizations and have designed programs that range from one-time, special-topic seminars and workshops to ongoing, community-based partnerships in continuing education.

One theme that needs to be included in virtually all dialect awareness programs focuses on the fundamental naturalness of dialect variation in American society. Participants in these programs at all levels of formal and informal education need to confront stereotypes and misconceptions about dialects, but this is probably best done inductively. An easy method of doing this involves having participants listen to representative speech samples of regional, class, and ethnic varieties. Participants need to hear how native Standard English speakers in New England, the rural South, and the urban North compare with each other and with the dialect of their own community to appreciate the reality of diverse regional spoken standards, just as they need to recognize different vernacular varieties in these regions. Students in "Standard"-speaking regions need to consider some of the features of their own dialect as it compares with others in order to understand that everyone really does speak a dialect.

Although most tape-recorded collections of dialect samples are personal ones that are not commercially available, video productions like *American Tongues* (Alvarez and Kolker 1987) can be used to provide an entertaining introduction to dialects while, at the same time, exposing basic prejudices and myths about language differences. For example, in one activity (Wolfram, Schilling-Estes, and Hazen 1996, 3), we have participants view real-life vignettes that expose raw prejudices about dialects from the video *American Tongues*. Participants are then asked to reflect on the justness of the attitudes reflected by those reacting stereotypically in the video vignettes (taken from spontaneous video footage) to the different dialects. Such reflective interaction often causes participants to confront the unjustified stereotypes and prejudices that often accompany our recognition of dialects. It is not surprising that an evaluative summary of one of our dialect awareness curricula (Messner 1997) indicated that the learning experience most often cited from the program concerned knowledge about prejudice and human relations related to dialect differences.

It is also important to involve participants in examining cases of dialect variation from their own community as a basis for seeing how natural and inevitable dialects are. For example, virtually all communities have some local and regional lexical items that can be used as a starting point in examining dialect diversity. In some of our dialect awareness materials (Wolfram, Schilling-Estes, and Hazen 1996; Wolfram and Creech 1996: Wolfram, Dannenberg, Anderson, and Messner 1996), we have developed activities and exercises on local lexical items such as the following, taken from our dialect curriculum titled *Dialects and the Ocracoke Brogue* (Wolfram, Schilling-Estes, and Hazen 1996).

Ocracoke Dialect Vocabulary Game: How to Tell an O'cocker
from a Dingbatter

Fill in the blanks to the sentences below, choosing your answer from the list provided. You only have five minutes to complete the worksheet, and you may not look at the lexicon or share answers. At the end of five minutes, you will swap your book with a neighbor to check each other's work. For each correct answer, you will receive 1 point, and for each question missed, you will receive no points. Good luck.

WORD LIST: *across the beach, buck, call the mail over, dingbatter, doast, goaty, goodsome, meehonkey, miserable 'n the wind, mommuck, O'cocker, pizer, quamish, Russian rat, say a word, scud, smidget, slick cam, to, up the beach, yaupon, young 'uns*

1. They went _____ to Hatteras to do some shopping.
2. That _____ is from New Jersey.
3. That place sure was smelling _____ .
4. Elizabeth is _____ the restaurant right now.
5. I put a _____ of salt on my apple.
6. We took a _____ around the island in the car.
7. They're always together because he's his _____ .
8. At night we used to play _____ .
9. The ocean was so rough today I felt _____ in the gut.
10. Last night she came down with a _____ .
11. I saw a big _____ in the road.
12. They sat on the _____ in the evening.
13. When Rex and James Barrie get together, they sure can _____ .
14. You can't be an _____ unless you were born on the island.
15. The sea was real rough today; it was _____ out there.
16. When they _____ , I hope I get my letter.
17. She used to _____ him when he was a child.
18. There was no wind at all today and it was a _____ out there on the sound.
19. There was a big, dead shark that they found _____ .
20. _____ don't act like they used to back then.

Put a 1 by all the correct answers and an X by all the incorrect answers. Add up all of the correct answers and place the total in the blank. Hand the workbook back to its owner.

[Answers: 1. up the beach; 2. dingbatter; 3. goaty; 4. to; 5. smidget; 6. scud; 7. buck; 8. meehonkey; 9. quamished; 10. doast; 11. Russian rat; 12. pizer; 13. say a word; 14. O'cocker; 15. miserable 'n the wind; 16. call the mail over; 17. mommuck; 18. slick cam; 19. across the beach; 20. young 'uns]

Activities such as this simple vocabulary exercise underscore the dialect resources that reside in all speech communities regardless of social status. Learners themselves can even take an active role in the construction of dialect vocabulary exercises by helping to collect local lexical items. In the process, they learn to document and compile dialect items and determine the ways in which their local dialect is similar to and different from other varieties. In our dialect studies of lexical items, community members have often taken leading roles in the collection and compilation of community-based lexical inventories (e.g., Locklear et al. 1996).

Another essential theme in dialect awareness concerns the acquisition of knowledge about the patterning of dialect. It is essential for dialect awareness programs to combat the popular stereotype that vernacular varieties are nothing more than imperfect attempts to speak the standard variety. Furthermore, people tend to think of "grammar rules" as prescriptive dicta that come from books rather than from natural language usage. An inductive exercise on the systematic nature of dialects can thus go a long way toward dispelling such notions. It also can set the stage for generating a nonpatronizing respect for the complexity of systematic differences among dialects. Over the years, I have used the following exercise on the patterning of *a-* prefixing hundreds of times in all types of formal and informal discussions of dialect patterning to demonstrate the fundamental patterning of all dialects regardless of social position. The advantage of this particular exercise is that it involves a form whose patterning is intuitively accessible to both those who use the form in their own dialect and those who do not (Wolfram 1982). This fact makes the exercise appropriate for participants regardless of their native dialect. This exercise is reprinted from one of our curricula designed for middle-school students (Wolfram, Schilling-Estes, and Hazen 1996), but I have used it for diverse groups at all age levels.

An Exercise in Dialect Patterning

In historically isolated rural dialects of the United States, particularly in Southern Appalachia, some words that end in *-ing* can take an *a-*, pronounced as *uh*, attached to the beginning of the word. We call this the *a-* prefix because it attaches to the front of the *-ing* word. The language pattern or "rule" for this form allows the *a-* to attach to some words but not to others. In this exercise, you will figure out this fairly complicated rule by looking at the kinds of *-ing* words *a-* can and cannot attach to. You will do this using your inner feelings about language. These inner feelings, called *intuitions*, tell us where we can and cannot use certain features. As linguists trying to describe this dialect, our task is to figure out the reason for these inner feelings and to state the exact patterns that characterize the dialect.

Look at the sentence pairs in List A and decide which sentence in each pair sounds better with an *a-* prefix. For example, in the first sentence pair, does it sound better to say, *A-building is hard work* or *She was a-building a house*? For each sentence pair, just choose one sentence that sounds better with the *a-*.

List A: Sentence Pairs for *A-* Prefixing

1. a. __ Building is hard work.
   b. __ She was building a house.

2. a. __ He likes hunting.
   b. __ He went hunting.

3. a. __ The child was charming the adults.
   b. __ The child was very charming.

4. a. __ He kept shocking the children.
   b. __ The store was shocking.

5. a. __ They thought fishing was easy.
   b. __ They were fishing this morning.

6. a. __ The fishing is still good here.
   b. __ They go fishing less now.

Examine each of the sentence pairs in terms of the choices for the *a-* prefix and answer the following questions:

- Do you think there is some pattern that guided your choice of an answer? You can tell if there is a definite pattern by checking with other people who did the same exercise on their own.
- Do you think that the pattern might be related to parts of speech? To answer this, see if there are any parts of speech where you cannot use the *a-* prefix. Look at *-ing* forms that function as verbs and compare those with *-ing* forms that operate as nouns or adjectives. For example, look at the use of *charming* as a verb and adjective in sentence pair 3.

The first step in figuring out the pattern for the *a-* prefix is related to the part of speech of the *-ing* word. Now let's look at another difference related to prepositions such as *from* and *by*. Based on the sentence pairs in List B, say whether or not the *a-* form can be used after a preposition. Use the same technique you used for List A. Select the sentence that sounds better for each sentence pair and say whether it is the sentence with or without the preposition.

List B: A Further Detail for *A-* Patterning

1. a. __ They make money by building houses.
   b. __ They make money building houses.

2. a. __ People can't make enough money fishing.
   b. __ People can't make enough money from fishing.

3. a. __ People destroy the beauty of the island through littering.
   b. __ People destroy the beauty of the island littering.

We now have another detail for figuring out the pattern for *a-* prefix use related to prepositions. But there is still another part to the pattern for *a-* prefix use. This time, however, it is related to pronunciation. For the following *-ing* words, try to figure out what it is about the pronunciation that makes one sentence sound better than the other. To help you figure out the pronunciation trait that is critical for this pattern, the stressed or accented syllable of each word is marked with the symbol ´. Follow the same procedure that you did in choosing the sentence in each sentence pair that sounds better.

List C: Figuring out a Pronunciation Pattern for the *A-* Prefix

1. a. __ She was discóvering a trail.
   b. __ She was fóllowing a trail.

2. a. __ She was repéating the chant.
   b. __ She was hóllering the chant.

3. a. __ They were fíguring the change.

   b. __ They were forgétting the change.

4. a. __ The baby was recognízing the mother.

   b. __ The baby was wrécking everything.

5. a. __ They were décorating the room.

   b. __ They were demánding more time off.

Say exactly how the pattern for attaching the *a-* prefix works. Be sure to include the three different details from your examination of the examples in Lists A, B, and C.

In List D, say which of the sentences may take an *a-* prefix. Use your understanding of the rule to explain why the *-ing* form may or may not take the *a-* prefix.

List D: Applying the A- Prefix Rule

1. She kept handing me more work.
2. The team was remémbering the game.
3. The team won by playing great defense.
4. The team was playing real hard.
5. The coach was charming. (from Wolfram, Schilling-Estes, and Hazen 1996, 23–26)

Exercises of this type are an effective way of confronting the myth that dialects have no rules of their own. At the same time, such exercises effectively demonstrate the underlying cognitive patterning of language, in keeping with the cognitive goal of language awareness programs. We have found that these exercises can appropriately be undertaken by a wide range of learners in a variety of settings. The most effective exercises in dialect patterning typically include examples taken from local, community-based dialects as well as exercises that represent the dialects of other regional and ethnic groups. For example, we often use the *a-* prefixing exercise illustrated here along with the following exercise on the habitual *be* construction of African American Vernacular English in dialect awareness programs for both Northern inner-city groups that are predominantly African American and Southern rural groups that are predominantly Anglo American.

Be in African American English

Now we're going to look at a form that's used in a dialect that is sometimes used by young African American speakers in large cities. The form *be* is used where other dialects use *am, is,* or *are,* except that it has a special meaning. People who use this dialect can tell where it may be used and where it may not be used, just as you did for the *a-* prefix. In the sentences given here, choose one of the sentences in each pair where *be* fits better. Choose only one sentence for each pair. If you're not sure of the answer, simply make your best guess. Put a check next to the answer you think is right. *Do this work by yourself.*

1. __ a. They usually be tired when they come home.
   __ b. They be tired right now.

2. __ a. When we play basketball, she be on my team.
   __ b. The girl in the picture be my sister.

3. __ a. James be coming to school right now.
   __ b. James always be coming to school.

4. __ a. Wanda don't usually be in school.
   __ b. Wanda don't be in school today.

5. __ a. My ankle be broken from the fall.
   __ b. Sometimes my ears be itching.

Now that you've given your answers, you'll see a video of some speakers of this dialect doing the same exercise. How well did you do on the exercise compared to these students in the video who regularly use the *be* form?

Following the Patterns for *be* Use

Now that you know how the form *be* is used, predict which of the sentences below follow the rule for *be* use in the African American English dialect and which do not. Write (*Y*)es if the sentence follows the dialect pattern and (*N*)o if it doesn't.

1. __ The students always be talking in class.
2. __ The students don't be talking right now.
3. __ Sometimes the teacher be early for class.
4. __ At the moment the teacher be in the lounge.

5. ___ Linguists always be asking silly questions about language. (from Wolfram, Schilling-Estes, and Hazen 1996, 26)

We also use examples of dialect patterning from primary regional varieties to complement the focus on the vernacular-standard distinction highlighted in the preceding exercises. Students are therefore exposed to the
interaction of region, class, and ethnicity in understanding the distribution
of dialect patterns. For example, following is an exercise on the patterning
of postvocalic *r* in Eastern New England, where it is defined as a primary
though not exclusively regional phenomenon. The following activity is used
with an audio recording of a native speaker from an Eastern New England
dialect pronouncing the words in the lists.

How Pronunciation Differences Work: Dropping *R* in New England Speech

In New England and some other dialects of English, the *r* sound of words
like *car* or *poor* can be dropped. In these words, the *r* is not pronounced,
so that these words sound like *cah* and *poo*. However, not all *r* sounds can
be dropped. In some places in a word the *r* sound may be dropped, and in
other places it may not be dropped. By comparing lists of words where the
r may be dropped with lists of words where it may not be dropped, we
can figure out a pattern for *r* dropping.

List A gives words where the *r* may be dropped.

List A

1. ca*r*
2. fathe*r*
3. ca*r*d
4. bigge*r*
5. ca*r*dboard
6. bee*r*
7. cou*r*t

List B gives words where the *r* sound may not be dropped. In other words,
speakers who drop their *r*'s in List A pronounce the *r* in the words in
List B.

List B

1. *r*un
2. bring
3. p*r*incipal
4. st*r*ing
5. ok*r*a
6. app*r*oach
7. Ap*r*il

To find a pattern for dropping the *r*, look at the type of sound that comes before the *r* in List A and in List B. Does a vowel or a consonant come before the *r* in List A? What comes before the *r* in List B? How can you predict where an *r* may or may not be dropped?

In List C, pick those words that may drop their *r* and those that may not drop their *r*. Use your knowledge of the *r*-dropping pattern that you learned by comparing Lists A and B.

List C

__ 1. bea*r*
__ 2. p*r*ogram
__ 3. fea*r*ful
__ 4. *r*ight
__ 5. compute*r*
__ 6. pa*r*ty
__ 7. fou*r*teen

Think of two new words that may drop an *r* and two new words that may not drop an *r*.

More about *R*-dropping Patterns

In the last exercise we saw that *r* dropping only takes place when the *r* comes after a vowel. Now we are going to look at the kinds of sounds that may come after the *r* in some dialects of English. This pattern goes along with the one you already learned. Let's see if we can figure out the pattern.

Here are some words where the *r* may not be dropped even when it comes after a vowel.

List A: Words That Do Not Drop R

1. bea*r* in the field
2. ca*r over* at the house
3. ga*r*age
4. ca*r*ing
5. take fou*r* apples
6. pea*r* on the tree
7. fa*r* enough

What kinds of sounds come after the *r* in List A? Are they vowels or consonants?

In List B the *r* may be dropped. What kind of sounds come after the *r* in this list?

List B: Words That Drop R

1. bea*r* by the woods
2. ca*r* pa*r*ked by the house
3. pa*r*king the bus
4. fea*r*ful
5. take fou*r* peaches
6. pea*r* by the house
7. fa*r* behind

How does this pattern or rule for *r* dropping work in terms of sounds that come after *r*? Use your knowledge of the rule for *r* dropping to pick the *r*'s that may and may not be dropped in the sentences given below.

1. The teache*r* picked on th*r*ee students fo*r* an answe*r*.
2. Fou*r* ca*r*s pa*r*ked fa*r* away f*r*om the fai*r*. (from Wolfram, Schilling-Estes, and Hazen 1996, 16–18)

The advantages of these types of exercises should be obvious, as learners see how linguists collect and organize data to formulate the "rules" that describe language patterning. More important, students come to appreciate fully the intricate details of patterning that apply to language variation. Such exercises may also provide students with a model for analyzing data that they might collect from their own community. In the best-case scenario, learners record language data, extract particular examples from the data, and formulate linguistic rules themselves. In this way, they experience on a firsthand basis the examination of language in a rigorous, scientific way.

In addition to viewing dialect study as a kind of scientific investigation, learners should be encouraged to see how dialect study merges with the social sciences and the humanities. Dialect study can be viewed from the perspective of geography, history, or sociology; it also can be linked with ethnic or gender studies. Thus the examination of dialect differences offers great potential for learners of all ages and positions in life to probe the linguistic manifestations of other types of sociocultural differences.

In examining the role of dialect as a dimension of social history, it is important to provide a general perspective on language change as well as a local, community, or regional vantage point. For example, we often use the following activity to demonstrate how the English language in general is naturally evolving over time. At the same time, we include for particular curricula a section that highlights the historical development of the predominant dialect of the speech community, such as African-American English in inner-city Baltimore, Maryland (Wolfram, Detwyler, and Adger 1992), Outer Banks English dialects in Ocracoke Island and in Harkers Island in coastal North Carolina (Wolfram, Schilling-Estes, and Hazen 1996; Wolfram and Creech 1996), and Appalachian English in the mountains of Western North Carolina (Wolfram, Dannenberg, Anderson, and Messner 1996).

The Changing of the English Language

English has changed quite dramatically over the centuries. In fact, if we go back far enough, we can barely recognize the language as English. Compare the versions of English at various stages in its history, as found in the first verse of the Lord's Prayer.

Old English (about 950 A.D.)
 Fader urer ðu bist in heofnas, sie gehalgad noma ðin
Middle English (about 1350 A.D.)
 Oure fadir þat art in heuenes, halwid be þi name
Early Modern English (about 1550 A.D.)
 O oure father which arte in heven, hallowed be thy name
Modern English (about 1985 A.D.)
 Our father, who is in heaven, may your name be sacred
 or
 Our father, who art in heaven, hallowed be your name

1. Try pronouncing the different versions of English. In the older versions (Old and Middle English), "silent letters" do not exist, so you'll need to pronounce all the letters. The symbol ð is pronounced something like the *th* of *this*, and the þ is pronounced like the *th* of *think*.

2. Try to identify some of the older versions of modern words. For example, trace the words that became the current words *father, heaven, name,*

is, and *our*. What modern English word, besides *sacred*, did *hallow* become?

3. What does this comparison tell you about the way the English language has changed over the centuries?

One of the greatest advantages of the examination of dialects is its potential for tapping the language resources of learners' indigenous communities. Participants can learn by going into the community to collect live dialect data. In most cases, the language characteristics of the local community should make dialects come alive in a way that is unmatched by textbook knowledge. Educational models that treat the local community as a resource to be tapped rather than a liability to be overcome have been shown to be quite effective in other areas of education, and there is no reason why this model cannot be applied in an analogous fashion to the study of community dialects. A model that builds upon community strengths in language, even when the language is different from the norm of the mainstream educational system, seems to hold much greater potential for success than one that focuses exclusively upon language conflicts between the community and the school. The study of dialects can indeed become a vibrant, relevant topic of study for all learners on a formal and informal level, not just for those who choose to take an optional course on this topic at a postsecondary level of education.

COMMUNITY-BASED COLLABORATION: THE OCRACOKE MODEL

Our own efforts to promote dialect awareness in recent years have included the K–12 classroom, but we also have moved beyond it as we have established community-based programs that involve informal education for broadly based audiences as well as in-school programs. These include television and video documentaries (e.g., Alvarez and Kolker 1987; Blanton and Waters 1995; Creech and Creech 1996), trade books on dialects for general audiences (Wolfram and Schilling-Estes 1997), museum exhibits (Gruendler et al. 1997), and presentations to a wide range of community organizations such as civic groups, churches, preservation societies, and other local institutions and agencies. Our personal involvement with local communities on the Outer Banks of North Carolina, whose dialects are in a moribund or dying state (Wolfram and Schilling-Estes 1995), includes work with local institutions and a variety of community agents. For example, a summary of products we have produced and the activities we have undertaken with the Ocracoke community follows. Also included is a partial listing of the media coverage that the programs have received.

- *Hoi Toide on the Outer Banks: The Story of the Ocracoke Brogue* (Wolfram and Schilling-Estes 1997). A book for nonexperts made available at tourist sites on the Outer Banks, museums, and general-interest bookstores throughout North Carolina.
- *Ocracoke Dialect Vocabulary* (North Carolina Language and Life Project). A popular booklet for visitors to Ocracoke.
- *Dialects and the Ocracoke Brogue* (Wolfram, Schilling-Estes, and Hazen 1996). A student text used for an eighth-grade social studies curriculum taught at the Ocracoke School.
- *Ocracoke Live.* An archival compact disc of select community speech samples.
- *The Ocracoke Brogue* (Blanton and Waters 1995). A video documentary on the history and state of the Ocracoke brogue.
- Presentations to the Ocracoke Preservation Society and to visitors' groups on the state of the Ocracoke brogue; book signings and presentations at popular bookstores.
- Design and distribution of "Save the Brogue" T-shirts in the community, at local stores, and at the museum operated by the Ocracoke Preservation Society.
- An issue of the Ocracoke School newspaper dedicated to dialect awareness efforts, including articles and poems about the Ocracoke brogue.
- Construction of a permanent exhibit on the Ocracoke brogue at the museum operated by the Ocracoke Preservation Society.
- Grant writing on behalf of the community to raise funds for establishing programs and exhibits related to the Ocracoke dialect.
- News articles on endangered dialects and dialect awareness distributed by the Associated Press, including some with accompanying sound samples that readers may access by phone.
- International television and radio press coverage, including spots on BBC television and radio and articles in London newspapers such as the *London Times* and the *Evening Standard.*

As indicated in the list, our involvement has included a broad range of products and activities. We have written a book for nonexperts, compiled archival tapes, developed a dialect awareness program for the school, and produced a couple of documentary videos on Outer Banks sites where we have conducted research. We even designed a commemorative "Save the Brogue" T-shirt that we have given to many members of the Ocracoke community and now sell through the Ocracoke Preservation Society. Involved local institutions include the Ocracoke Preservation Society, the Ocracoke School, and various North Carolina museums. Key community members, including the president of the Ocracoke Preservation Society, community leaders, and students and teachers in the school, have also served as active participants in various phases of our program.

The venues we use to disseminate information include both traditional and nontraditional agencies. For example, we have instituted experimental programs in the Ocracoke School and have made presentations to the Ocracoke Preservation Society and to various visitors' groups on Ocracoke. Along with these institutional efforts, we have even shown our documentary several times on the big-screen television monitor at the local bar and grill, Howard's Pub, where both residents and tourists typically congregate for informal socializing. These showings resulted in animated, positive discussions about the dialect by both Ocracoke residents and tourists. The endangered status of the Ocracoke brogue has also been the subject of several local, regional, and even international television and radio news programs, and there were at least a dozen major feature articles in local and regional newspapers from 1992 to 1998 that focused on the state of the dialect and the threats to its survival. As noted in the list, several of these stories were accompanied by sound bites; readers were invited to call an advertised telephone number and listen to a recorded sample of the brogue for themselves.

Although I have presented our community-based dialect awareness programs as a model for working with communities, I must admit that community-based collaboration raises deeper issues about the roles of sociolinguistic researchers in local communities (Rickford 1997). In principle, probably few sociolinguists would be opposed to working with local communities in dialect awareness programs, but working out the everyday details of this relationship and the exact nature of community-based partnerships can often be complicated and controversial. There are ideological, sociopolitical, and ethical matters that need to be confronted squarely by linguists and sociolinguists who engage in such programs (cf. Wolfram 1993, 1998b). These include issues of authority, power, representation, presentation, and profit. Nonetheless, the concept of working with communities and returning linguistic favors in some form, including dialect awareness programs, seems to be a good and proper thing. It also seems to be the least that linguists and sociolinguists can do when we consider how we have mined so many of the speech community's linguistic resources to our linguistic advantage.

NOTE

1. To a large extent, this chapter is an amalgam of several different discussions on dialect awareness, including Wolfram (1998a), Wolfram (forthcoming), and portions of chapter 11 in Wolfram and Schilling-Estes (1998). The curricular activities included here are reproduced from materials such as Wolfram, Schilling-

Estes, and Hazen (1996), Wolfram and Creech (1996), and Wolfram, Dannenberg, Anderson, and Messner (1996).

REFERENCES

Alvarez, Louis, and Andrew Kolker, producers. 1987. *American tongues*. New York: Center for New American Media.

American Association for Applied Linguistics. 1997. Resolution on the application of dialect knowledge to education. Annual Meeting of AAAL, Orlando, Fl.

Bauer, Laurie, and Peter Trudgill, eds. 1998. *Language myths*. New York: Penguin.

Blanton, Phyllis, and Karen Waters, producers. 1995. *The Ocracoke brogue*. Raleigh: North Carolina Language and Life Project.

Clark, Robert, Norman Fairclough, N. Ivanic, and Marilyn Martin-Jones. 1990. Critical language awareness, Part I: A critical review of three current approaches to language awareness. *Language and Education* 4: 249–60.

Cleary, Linda Miller, and Nancy Lund. 1993. Debunking some myths about traditional grammar. *Linguistics for teachers*, ed. by Linda Miller Cleary and Michael D. Linn, 483–90. New York: McGraw-Hill.

Creech, Kevyn, and John Creech, producers. 1996. *That island talk: Harkers Island dialect*. Raleigh: American Media Productions and North Carolina Language and Life Project.

Donmall, B. G., ed. 1985. *Language awareness*. NCLE Papers and Reports 6. London: Centre for Information on Language Teaching and Research.

Edwards, Viv. 1990. *A directory of English dialect resources*. London: Economic and Social Research Council.

Gruendler, Shelley, Charles Holden, Walt Wolfram, and Natalie Schilling-Estes. 1997. *An exhibit on the Ocracoke brogue*. Ocracoke, NC: Museum of the Ocracoke Preservation Society.

Hawkins, Eric. 1984. *Awareness of language: An introduction*. Cambridge: Cambridge University Press.

———, ed. 1985. Awareness of language series. Cambridge: Cambridge University Press.

Locklear, Hayes Allen, Natalie Schilling-Estes, Walt Wolfram, and Clare Dannenberg. 1996. *A dialect dictionary of Lumbee English*. Raleigh: North Carolina Language and Life.

Messner, Kyle. 1997. Evaluative summary of Appalachian Dialect Awareness Program. Unpublished report, Appalachian State University, Boone, NC.

Milroy, James, and Lesley Milroy. 1985. *Authority in language: Investigating language prescriptivism and standardisation*. London: Routledge and Kegan Paul.

NCTE to you: Issues, news, and announcements. 1986. *Language Arts* 63: 103.

Rickford, John R. 1997. Unequal partnership: Sociolinguistics and the African American speech community. *Language in Society* 26: 161–97.

Wolfram, Walt. 1980. A-prefixing in Appalachian English. *Locating language in time and space*, ed. by William Labov, 107–43. New York: Academic Press.

———. 1982. Language knowledge and other dialects. *American Speech* 57: 3–17.

———. 1993. Ethical considerations in language awareness programs. *Issues in Applied Linguistics* 4: 225–55.

———. 1997. Dialect awareness and the study of language. *Students as ethnographers of language*, ed. by Ann Egan Robertson and David Bloome, 167–90. Cresskill, NJ: Hampton Press.

———. 1998a. Language ideology and dialect: Understanding the Ebonics controversy. *Journal of English Linguistics* 26: 108–21.

———. 1998b. Scrutinizing linguistic gratuity. *Journal of Sociolinguistics.* 2: 271–79.

———. Forthcoming. Repercussions from the Oakland Ebonics controversy: The critical role of dialect awareness programs. *Language Diversity and Academic Achievement in the Education of African American Students*, ed. by Carolyn Adger, Donna Christian, and Orlando Taylor. Washington, DC: Center for Applied Linguistics.

Wolfram, Walt, Carolyn Adger, and Donna Christian. Forthcoming. *Dialects in the school and community*. Mahweh, NJ: Erlbaum.

Wolfram, Walt, and Kevyn Creech. 1996. *Harkers Island speech and dialects.* Eighth-grade curriculum, Harkers Island School, Carteret County, NC. Raleigh: North Carolina Language and Life Project.

Wolfram, Walt, Clare Dannenberg, Bridget Anderson, and Kyle Messner. 1996. *Dialects and Appalachian English.* Eighth-grade curriculum, Mabel School, Watauga County, NC. Raleigh: North Carolina Language and Life Project.

Wolfram, Walt, Jennifer Detwyler, and Carolyn Adger. 1992. *All about dialects* (instructor's manual). Washington, DC: Center for Applied Linguistics.

Wolfram, Walt, and Natalie Schilling-Estes. 1995. Moribund dialects and the endangerment canon: The case of the Ocracoke brogue. *Language* 71: 696–721.

———. 1996. Speech at the beach: Dialects and Outer Banks English. An elderhostel course of study at the Trinity Center, Salter Path, NC.

———. 1997. *Hoi toide on the Outer Banks: The story of the Ocracoke brogue.* Chapel Hill: University of North Carolina Press.

———. 1998. *American English: Dialects and variation.* Cambridge: Basil Blackwell.

Wolfram, Walt, Natalie Schilling-Estes, and Kirk Hazen. 1996. *Dialects and the Ocracoke brogue.* Eighth-grade curriculum, Ocracoke School, Hyde County, NC. Raleigh: North Carolina Language and Life Project.

Linguistics Is for Kids

Jeannine M. Donna

THE PROBLEM

Suppose you walked into Miss Fraction's elementary math class in your neighborhood school and saw the students quietly engrossed in hanging number-shaped cutouts from the light fixtures or sewing them into random colorful designs on miniature quilts. "Looks like fun," you might remark. But you would look for something beyond the fun: you would expect applications of mathematical concepts in the activity. Finding none, you would be puzzled, or possibly downright critical, of Miss Fraction's wisdom in providing for her students.

We take it for granted that, at its best, K–12 mathematics (or history or geography) is accomplishing four broad goals: (*a*) exposing learners to the discipline's basic concepts; (*b*) inspiring fascination with its discoveries and dilemmas; (*c*) teaching skills that adult nonspecialists need; and (*d*) laying the groundwork for advanced study. Thus we expect our math scholars to be adding, learning to use a calculator, or plotting parabolas. Likewise, young artists learn shading, color chemistry, and brush techniques, while history students explore functions of government or causes and effects of war.

The one glaring counterexample is language. In stark contrast to other disciplines, the formal study of language in our schools too often ignores these four goals, doing little to establish basics, inspire wonder, train useful skills, or support advanced study. Traditionally, English classroom forces have been marshaled by weathered veterans, matronly figures whose mission was to stamp out sins of improper usage and guard the bastions of "good" grammar, rather than to inspire deeper understandings of how language works. As for linguistic analysis, too many of us have memories of old-style parsing and diagraming, memories which cause us to smile when we read of James Thurber's Miss Groby, taking a demented delight in "[t]he shape of a sentence crucified on a blackboard" (Thurber 1964, 52).

Needless to say, Miss Groby's grim manner would have provided a poor role model for the modern generation of teachers in any field. But being in the crucial area of language, she has unwittingly left her successors doubly dispossessed, in that the subject matter she championed, with its traditional, Latin-based grammar, prescriptive rules, memorized lists, and inadequate definitions, is now viewed as no more acceptable than the sentence crucifixion that came with it.

Forced to trudge on, Miss Groby's modern heirs have had no choice but to turn to "modern" materials, whose creators have bravely avoided the traditional, but have often had virtually nowhere else to turn for meaningful ideas on language, and whose content has certainly not been guided by our four criteria. I can think of no serious nonschool activity, for instance, that corresponds to the "word searches" engaged in by elementary students, cryptic matrices in which the seeker must find decontextualized words embedded backwards and forwards on unpredictable planes—or to writing assignments asking students to "use" random isolated linguistic elements: "Write a letter to your Aunt Emily in which you use the words *democratic, license,* and *federation*"; "Write a story in which you use all the four sentence types."

Grammatical exercises in the new mode fare little better. While shying away from some of the prescriptive rules Miss Groby might have championed, they too often preserve the repressive spirit behind such rules, applying them to meaningless forms—for instance, asking students to "correct errors" which I, for one, have never seen in over two decades of student writing ("*Me* came home late"). In short, the newer language arts curricula sometimes totter precariously on the edge of the cutouts-and-quilts scenario imagined for Miss Fraction's math class, keeping students occupied without discernible purpose—and quite often with little trace of the fun of the cutouts scenario.

In this seeming chaos, the "whole language" approach seems at first sight to offer an attractive alternative, dismissing grammar altogether as fragmented, abstract, and simply useless. But the result, if comforting to the teacher, is sadly ironic for the students: the formal study of language, arguably our most crucially defining human behavior, has often disappeared altogether as a conscious focus of their study by the secondary level. Anyone who has taught Linguistics 101 at a university has met students who lack the basis for even an elementary underpinning to a thoughtful study of language.

Our schools have never been able to benefit from a curriculum designed within the spirit of a lively, challenging discipline. In fact, it has been assumed that the study of "grammar," intrinsically dry and boring, has no such tradition to draw on. It is the goal of this chapter to show that we do indeed have precisely such a tradition in modern cognitive linguistics, although to embrace that tradition fully, we will have to discard a common view of "grammar" that has reigned unchallenged for centuries. We will have to reject Miss Groby's dedication to grammar as remedial medicine for petty linguistic misdemeanors in favor of a much bolder view of grammar as the place where patterns are discovered, explored, and wondered at—a place where answers are never memorized, and where the oldest of questions can always find a new form and a novel set of answers.

HOW DID WE GET WHERE WE ARE?

Recently, English teachers and their students have come through some confusing times. For hundreds of years, and especially since the eighteenth century, the study of the English language had been grounded in the classical grammars of Latin and Greek; word-class definitions were memorized ("a noun is a word that names"); verbs were conjugated ("I speak, you speak, they speak"); sentences were "parsed" in much the way Cicero might have done. Linguistics quietly wormed its way into the academic establishment in the nineteenth and the early twentieth centuries; but by 1950, the discipline was still virtually unknown to English programs, preferring, it seems, to lurk in college anthropology departments, or on the borders of psychology, where early- and mid-twentieth-century linguistics supported behaviorist ideas. The common view was that children "learned" language by imitation, repetition, and reward from their parents.

But a little blue paperback published in the mid-1950s and bearing the unassuming title *Syntactic Structures* changed all that. This early work by an unknown linguist named Noam Chomsky was to usher in a major paradigm shift in linguistics, one which moved the discipline away from both traditional grammar and behaviorist views of language into a new era where language can be seen as creative, rule-governed activity. Previously thought of as "blank slates," learning language through imitation and practice, children could now be seen as active constructors of language who begin their task with a major boost from nature in the form of the cognitive brain structures that process and deal with language. Previously seen as a string of words to be parsed (or crucified, if you prefer), a sentence could now be analyzed as the dynamic output of a very few general principles which speakers use quite unconsciously, provided they have acquired some basic information about the verbs of their language.

The nature of this shift remains a mystery to many educators, and the spirit underlying it remains hidden. Though Steven Pinker's best-selling *The Language Instinct* (1995) gives an excellent overview of new paradigm thinking for the educated layperson, the so-called Chomskyan revolution has been all too often represented outside linguistics journals via misinformation and distortions. To make matters worse, the sole linguistics course available to many teachers in their undergraduate curriculum during the tumultuous period of change typically represented the newborn leading the blind. Often taught by professors themselves only vaguely aware of the depths of the new field's soul, these courses often stressed only mechanical rules, rather than the probing questions about language that had inspired the fledgling field's birth.

But now, finally, after half a century, modern Chomskyan-inspired linguistics has begun to write its own history and to develop its own rich traditions in a line reaching back to Aristotle. We are beginning to see what the revolution was about, and how deeply the discipline it produced is able to "see into" the workings of language. It is time to share that understanding with teachers, who can in turn open the door to its benefits for their students. This chapter represents a plea for such a move and a tentative glimpse at what it might involve.

DISCOVERING LANGUAGE

Some years ago, my then-sixth-grade daughter came back from school with a sad tale. It seems a "troublesome" boy—let's call him Jim—had asked a question on grammar. "If *very* is an adverb," he had mused, "and *quickly* is an adverb, why is it that you can say, 'John runs quickly,' but you can't say, 'John runs very'?" The teacher—let us call her Mrs. Adams— clearly threatened by this challenge to her authority, had answered, in what I gather was a disparaging tone, "It's just not that *kind* of adverb!"

The sad thing about such stories is that nobody ends up happy. Jim is presumably unhappy because his question has been rejected. Mrs. Adams is unhappy because she has been pressed for an answer she does not have and has been (mis)led to believe that she should have. Most important, the students are unhappy because they still have no grasp of what an adverb is. They are set for a lifetime of trembling when the ugly term—or for that matter any of its grammatical kin—so much as dares to rear its mocking head, evoking as it does a discipline where one memorizes definitions that do not work and cannot be applied systematically to the language one knows as natural.

I, too, am unhappy, because Jim may never know that he was right on target: he was asking a sophisticated linguistic question and using the right kind of evidence to justify it. His question could have led to the generation of more examples and to an exciting, teacher-guided but student-driven conclusion. Yes, Jim. This kind of word does seem to be different. Words like *very*, in *very crafty*, seem like *mere*, in *a mere child*; or again like *right*, in *right around the corner*. Unlike other adverbs, they tend to give some indication of the extent to which the next word or phrase (*crafty, child, around the corner*) is true. Linguists typically make exactly this distinction, using the term *intensifiers* to talk about this special class of terms.

This chapter envisions a classroom where teachers will be delighted to have questions they cannot answer, for these teachers will be trying to convey to their students, from the start, the secret linguists have been sitting on for at least four decades: that language is teasingly infinite and infinitely delightful, both in its mysteries and in the hints it allows us to ferret out in trying to solve them. Millions of students like Jim are willing to take the first step to discovery; we need only encourage them to view language as I believe they naturally would if we did not constrain them to do otherwise: as a dynamic territory, its caves, lakes, and forests beckoning to the young explorer. The following sections provide the beginnings of a roughly sketched map to guide the expedition.

I take it as given that the basics of map reading will have to come first. Concepts like *noun* and *verb* need to be taught if one is to talk about language at all. In the framework I envision, such concepts will be worked out by students, using structural as well as semantic properties and in a way that respects the inherent flexibility of categories. The suggestions in this chapter largely presuppose such a discovery-based foundation and are meant to show some of the ideas that can rest on its solid footing.

WORDBEAT: MINING AND REFINING LINGUISTIC ORE

This week, my graduate psycholinguistics students have spent some class time playing the popular games Taboo and Pictionary. In the first, a player must cue a word, such as *check*, to her teammates without using related words such as *bill* or *write*. In the second, the active player must draw a picture to cue the word, without speaking or using any recognizable symbol. In both games, gestures are outlawed. For the students who chose these activities, themselves experienced English teachers, the games were an ideal way to illustrate how the mental lexicon (the store of words speakers carry in memory) works. In playing Taboo, for instance, they were able to experience firsthand a research finding that they had been reading about. If we think of our mental word store as a set of electrical terminals connected by imaginary wires, once a word is "activated" in a speaker's mind, a whole network of other, closely related words also become "charged," as it were, and ready for use. The game helps one to sense this on a personal level, since players will time and again violate the rules and use the very words they are trying to avoid.

I, too, learned something—or, rather, reinforced an important belief of mine: that a game can be linked to a meaningful, important insight. People at any age love wordplay; and, by extension, they love words. How fortunate this is; for the latest trends in linguistic theory today are placing the power of language right at the heart of information about the individual word. Thus the would-be linguist wishing to start students off right can do no better than to exploit their natural love of words and to encourage them to learn as much as they can about these complex entities, their workings, relationships, and uses. What my graduate students did in class this week, students at any level can do; and like my students, they can learn valuable lessons in the process about the connections between words and about the relationships between words and images.

Ray Jackendoff unwittingly inspires another enjoyable word-based set of activities in *The Architecture of the Language Faculty* (1997a). Jackendoff wanted to ask what kinds of language bits are listed in the mental lexicon of a native speaker. To find out, he asked his daughter Beth to compile what he calls the "Wheel of Fortune Corpus," consisting of solutions from the popular television show, solutions which, since they come readily to the minds of the players, must be stored in memory as part of our mental store of words. As Jackendoff points out, the list yields some surprising information. We generally think of words as individual units, like *cow, dog,* or *chair*. But interestingly, only 10 percent of Beth's list consisted of individual words like this. *Compounds,* or word combinations, like *peanut butter* and *piano bench* were three times as frequent; and a host of other kinds of stock phrases were at least as prevalent.

What Beth did, any group of students could collaboratively enjoy doing. Once the resulting list arrives in the classroom, some pretty sophisticated categorization can happen. By the middle school years, students should be able to distinguish the compounds given here from such forms as *idioms* (phrases like *red herring* or *raining cats and dogs*) and *clichés* (overworked phrases like *smart as a whip,* which are often also idiomatic). Later, these might be further subdivided: compounds might be analyzed into their component parts, for instance, ranging from noun-verb units to what Jackendoff calls "odds and ends compounds" (*bed-and-breakfast, lost-and-found column*).

Working further on meaning, students could be encouraged to discern three kinds of idiomatic meaning according to how easily a hearer can predict or figure out the idiom's meaning from that of its parts: to note, for instance, that in *pay one's respects,* the individual words each have independent meaning (*pay* means "give, convey"; *respects* means "greetings"). Contrast this with *shoot the breeze,* whose generalized meaning resists such analysis, and with a third type, exemplified by *pull strings,* which falls somewhere in between.

This is a seemingly simple activity; yet students working on it will nevertheless be doing some of what linguists Geoffrey Nunberg and two of his colleagues do in a 1994 publication. They will have done linguistics hands-on, collecting and dealing with raw data, grappling with recalcitrant forms—and inevitably having a few hearty laughs in the process. They will end up with a grasp of *semantic compositionality*; and if they have not used the linguist's term, they will be primed to learn it when the time comes.

In fact, these students will probably become curious about where these linguistic chunks come from. If so, they may discover another professional concept, which Nunberg and his colleagues call *opacity*. Do speakers know that *to pan out* comes from the gold rush, or *getting sidetracked* from the days of the steam engine? If so, the idiom is said to be *transparent*; if not, it is *opaque*. By any name, flexible young minds should enjoy playing with *conventionality*, the ease with which one can distort an idiom, for instance, by replacing one of its parts. What would it mean to *take the sheep by the horns* (instead of *the bull*), or *find one's cool* (rather than *losing* it), or to *pick only political bones* with one's congressman (cf. "I have a bone to pick with you")? In this last activity, it is easy to see where linguistic analysis blends into inspiration for creative writing.

Of course, other data mines abound. Science fiction character names might launch lessons on sound structures. (If you read James Hogan's *Code of the Lifemaker*, how do you know that the characters Giraud and Zambendorf are human, while Thirg, Groork, and Methgark are aliens? Do some aliens, like Lofbayel and Rekashoba, sound a little more like earthly foreigners than aliens, and why?) The possibilities are endless. Advertising texts, book titles, and Internet lingo are all mines from which precious linguistic metals can be mined. In the course of sorting the ore, important insights about the nature of language can be derived.

SYNTAX: PLAYING WITH WORD STRINGS

In the 1991 issue of *Linguistic Inquiry*, C. L. Baker examines the syntax of the negative form *not* in English. To the uninitiated, the article might as well be in secret code. Baker peppers his article with such mind-boggling concepts as core and peripheral grammar, verb raising, affix lowering, the ominous ECP (empty category principle), and dual adverb positions, just for starters. Theta-assigning verbs attach to a mysterious entity called Agr, we are told, which might as well, to the uninitiated, mean that golden Martian mushrooms are settling on Mount Vesuvius. It is as difficult, abstract, and theoretical a linguistic article as you will find anywhere in the literature. Should we consign it to the fate of being appreciated only by linguists? At the risk of surprising many readers here, my answer is a resounding "No!"

Often, even the most abstract of studies contains data that can be made highly accessible to virtually any speaker—easily elicited data that can help a young mind begin to explore *grammaticality patterns* and use the valuable skill of *introspection*; data that ultimately address a crucial question: what is English? What, exactly, does our language contain, and what does it exclude? How clearly can the linguistic boundary be drawn between the two?

Take the two words *not* and *never*, discussed by Baker. Both are negative, and the meaning of one tends to contain the meaning of the other (*never* meaning "not at any time"). But they sometimes act in intriguing ways, one showing up in a position where the other would be unacceptable (the asterisk on [b] signifies an ungrammatical sentence):

(1) a. Jane never works.

   b. *Jane not works.

Older forms of English, as Baker shows, introduce still more questions. In these, the proper form would be "Jane works not."

Likewise for *enough* and *very*. Both mean similar things; yet they sit on opposite sides of their host word (*clever enough, very clever*). If students are encouraged to become aware of these kinds of contrasts, they will be taking the first step toward advanced linguistics, doing what Baker himself must have done in beginning his research. There will be time for formal analysis later; at the early stages, students will be taking a major step if they simply sharpen their powers of observation and wonder—if they develop the skill to describe the linguistic patterns we normally take for granted. If the K–12 teacher can provide this kind of observational work as grounding, the Linguistics 101 professor will have no trouble adding the theoretical notions later. Whether or not our students take Linguistics 101, they will be linguistically aware and awake, with all that suggests for their abilities in areas as different as writing and scientific work.

CONTRASTS ANONYMOUS

Human beings are drawn by contrasts—intrigued, almost addicted, one might say. William Lederer's popular books, which bear titles like *Anguished English* and *Crazy English*, make readers listen and laugh as he entertains with lighthearted linguistic pairs, repeated so often as to quite obscure their original source: "Why do we park in a driveway and drive on a parkway?"

A teacher can harness that same fascination, leading her students to explore linguistically meaningful pairs that are not so popular. Take the twosome given here, involving what Jackendoff (1997b) calls "time-away" constructions. Why can we say (a), but not (b)?

(2) a. Mabel slept the afternoon away.

   b. *Mabel read a book the afternoon away.

Meaning does not seem to be the problem. Mabel is presumably able to waste her time either sleeping or reading books. And one observation leads to another: note that, without *a book*, (b) becomes much better. Armed with this, and after testing other examples, students may be able to come up with some equivalent of Jackendoff's own observation, that the construction only "works" with intransitive verbs like *sleep, swim,* or *read* (without an object). In fact, this construction is a gem among English linguistic oddities; one does not "sleep" afternoons or read them. In using these forms, the speaker makes a kind of "fake" object of some time expression (*the afternoon, half his life*), which cannot occur as object of *sleep* without the special form *away*. Again, working on generalizations of this kind, without the formality of theoretical analysis, will alert the students to the important patterns in their language, patterns that we ignore as we use them every day, but that form the backbone of human language and make it a unique code. It is just patterns like this that make up the true "grammar" of English, in its deepest sense.

Contrasts may also involve meaning difference. The five kinds of sentences given here look structurally identical at first sight; and they are all fine English, though they are not usually mentioned or even listed in traditional grammars. Each sentence consists of a noun phrase (*Jennifer, George*, and so on) followed by a verb (*roasted, wrote*, and so on), another noun phrase (*fish*), then some kind of modifying adjective (*whole, angry*).

(3) a. Jennifer   roasted   the fish   whole.
    b. George   wrote   the letter   angry.
    c. Eulette   wore   her coat   threadbare.
    d. Roger   walked   his shoes   thin.
    e. The boys   laughed   themselves   silly.

But the sentence types are actually quite different. First, the patterns express quite different action patterns. In (a), it is the fish, and not Jennifer, that is whole. But in (b), in contrast, it is George, and not the letter, who is angry. In (c–e), nothing starts out threadbare, thin, or silly; the verbal objects (*coat, shoes, boys*) simply become so. Making distinctions like this can greatly sharpen students' language awareness, whether or not they realize that they have discovered the difference between *depictives* (a and b), *transitive* and *intransitive resultatives* (c and d), and the sort of odd fake *reflexive* in (e), all of which have received close attention in recent research (e.g., Carrier and Randall 1992). Again, the labels are not important, and the formal linguistic theory can come later; hands-on skill with fine meaning distinctions is what matters at this stage.

Interestingly, some formal kinship cuts across the semantic diversity here; that is, though these five sentences express subtly different meanings, there are similar restrictions on the form they can take. If the teacher is willing to prime the pump with a question or two, students can doubtless discover that prepositional phrases can replace the final word in all types (*in a bad mood* for *angry* in [b]). But in no case will they be able to replace the final descriptive word with a noun phrase (try *an eyesore*, for instance, in [c]).

As in the "time-away" examples, also, something is odd here about the basic sentence pattern. Speakers seem to be inventing grammatical objects for these verbs in some of these cases, even when the verbs would not normally allow such objects. True, we do roast fish, write letters, and wear coats, though perceptive students should be urged to see an ambiguity in this last one—we wear coats, but not in the sense of "causing to become thin." But we cannot claim, under normal circumstances, to *?walk our shoes* (as compared with our dog), or *laugh ourselves*.

Once again, if students are encouraged to play with patterns like these, at any appropriate level, they will have come in contact with real English grammar. Of course, this one extended example barely scratches the surface. English provides patterns rich and abundant enough to fill the K–12 language-arts hour with delightful explorations in every year of our young scholars' grammatical development. The possibilities are as prolific as language itself, the activities as endless as the imagination of energetic teachers and their linguist curriculum-designer partners. In the ideal situation, teachers might find the raw material for contrasts like these in popular songs, stories, or poems, combining the best of whole-language contextualization with state-of-the-art linguistics.

MISSING THINGS: *X* MARKS THE SPOT

Until now, I have been proposing that we let our students play, alternatively, the roles of miner or detective, digging out and probing the patterns of English grammar, using words and then strings of words as their raw material. But the sleuth in all of us loves to search for what is not at hand, as well as what is clearly there for easy finding. And the grammars of every human language provide plenty of hidden treasure, right alongside the "real" words we have been looking at so far.

Everybody knows that when we say, "Go buy me a coke," we are leaving something out. There is a sort of empty spot before *go* where the word *you* belongs. Traditional grammar called this the "understood" *you*. But we seldom think of the many mysterious missing things elsewhere in language. What is left unsaid in the places marked X in (4)?

(4) The doll is easy X to see X.

Linguists have found that when we process this sentence, we are actually inserting a fully specified sentence "around" the second verb, *see*. To paraphrase, our mind registers something like "it is easy for *anyone/someone* to see *the doll.*" When Carol Chomsky carried out a now-famous experiment with preschool children, however, she found that five-year-olds responded to such sentences in a strange way by adult standards. Given a blindfolded doll and asked, "Is the doll easy to see or hard to see?" they tended to respond "hard to see." Why? Well, where adults substitute the meaning "doll" for the *second X*, these children seem to have been equating the *first X* with "doll" instead. Their translation, in contrast to our adult reading, was "it is hard for *the doll* to see (*something/anything*)."

Again, in making this part of English grammar explicitly conscious for students, we encourage them to have fun with language, and we teach them something significant at the same time: that grammars typically feature "missing" elements. Again, the possibilities for linguistic detective work are too many to elaborate here. Imagine, for instance, asking our young explorers to decide what the Xs in these sentences represent:

(5) Jeremiah ordered wonton soup, Sally X fried rice, and Harita X shrimp lo mein.

(6) What's wrong, Joe? X X Lose the game or something?

(7) My friends are eager X to see Disneyland. (Hint: compare "My friends are eager for Lucy to see Disneyland"—this one is like the "doll" sentence of example 4.)

I would expect middle school learners to enjoy guessing games with such examples and to watch with interest videos of 5-year-olds having trouble with the doll experiment described earlier. Linguists label the blank spaces with symbols like *PRO* for (roughly) "invisible pronoun," or *t* for "trace" of something missing, or simply *e* for "empty" position. Our students need not worry about these labels, though in this case they are probably easy enough (X) to learn (X) (i.e., for our students to learn them). Whether they do or not, they will have been trained to recognize an important feature of English grammar.

GENERALIZATIONS

So far, I have claimed that the K–12 curriculum should be training observational powers: the ability to recognize, categorize, identify, and find the characteristics of linguistic patterns. This much seems unproblematic, since we are simply giving students the underpinnings of advanced college-level study. We are asking them to see and recognize the kinds of things that make our language what it is, things that we would never think about without training, but that any theory of language or model of grammar ultimately has to deal with in this new cognitive linguistic era.

But I think that we can do even more. By the middle-school years, when students are learning generalizations about natural and physical laws in science, they can also be led beyond the level of data observation and description to discover generalizations in language. In fact, any student who has grasped the notion of missing elements just discussed has mastered the very abstract notion of *null elements* in syntax. Other theoretical notions are likewise eminently accessible, and I would argue that these need not all be "saved" until the college years.

Language can be shown to be *infinite*, for instance, at almost any level. Imagine a game in which one student begins with a sentence, and each player repeats, adding a little, until memories crumble, laughter springs forth, and the point is made. Likewise, the idea of *recursiveness*, or the infinite ability for linguistic phrases to embed inside each other, almost flows in the rhythms of "The House That Jack Built," a nursery rhyme that my college students have normally forgotten, but that should be readily available in the fresh minds of schoolchildren.

The well-known *right-head rule* of modern generative morphology, originally proposed by Edwin Williams (1981), can be taught by yet another simple game. Each student in a sixth-grade class writes a word, unknown to anyone else, on a file card. The cards are collected, drawn in random pairs by a student volunteer, and written on the board. Then players write fanciful definitions for the concoctions that result. Sure enough, a *piano-bicycle* will always turn out to be a bicycle, not a piano. *Snake-silly* will denote a kind of silliness, not a species of snake. Elegant and abstract as it is, the generalization is sure to emerge in the students' own direct and untutored words.

Semantic concepts, too, can be explored by the youngest of learners. *Thematic roles*, for instance, can be the basis for games and discussions, again, provided complex jargon and abstraction are not made central. What is an *agent*? A thinking individual who does an action on purpose, of course, like *Joyce* in "Joyce picked the violets." There is no reason, beyond perhaps habit, for seeing such a concept as too complex or difficult for our students. With a few well-placed cartoons, the youngest learner can be intrigued by the difference between "The prince turned into a frog" and "The witch turned into a beautiful maiden." The prince, I think our little sleuths will agree, has a good deal less choice in his transformation than his powerful companion, at least in most stories. Older students might explore the thematic difference between the italicized subjects in "*My father* threatened to ground me" and "*The storm* threatened to destroy the village."

Possibilities range into areas hitherto seen as among the most abstract. Can students distinguish between what we can do *in an hour* (solve a math problem) as opposed to *for an hour* (drive a van)? If so, they can understand the basis of the notions *telic* and *atelic*, often used in current generative semantics. Can they play with word association, likeness and difference in meaning, and occurrence pairs like *lions* and *the lions*, or ask why we order *rice* (no preceding word) but *a steak*? If so, they can explore the notions that classify nouns into semantic fields, and they can label them with terms like *generic* or *specific, count* or *mass.*

Pragmatics might prove the most interesting area of all. Why does what we say so often differ from what we mean? Why does "I saw the doctor" typically convey more than a fact about my visual experience? When a prospective traveler asks, "Let's see, have I forgotten anything?" why does no one answer, "Well, you probably don't remember the capital of Alabama"? I picture students composing humorous skits to illustrate the absurd in the ordinary stuff of everyday language. I leave it to your ingenuity, and theirs, to structure the activity; I can only guarantee that it will be fun—and that it will yield a wealth of insight into the real use of language in context.

SOME PRACTICAL CONSIDERATIONS

In all this talk, have we forgotten Mrs. Adams, the teacher who, trained only in traditional grammar, did not have the resources to respond to student demands for discovery? Have we simply increased her work load—or left her no choice but frantic midnight flights to MIT for night courses on the latest in generative theory?

Certainly not. Obviously, our new language curriculum will need developing over time, and with many minds at work; in my contact with our teacher graduate students, I have found brave souls already "doing" linguistics with kids, at least at the high-school level, simply by encouraging questions, discovery, and open wonder.

Some texts for teachers have already begun to reflect the spirit of modern linguistics; Kolln (1994), Sedley (1990), Jacobs (1995), and Teschner and Evans (1993) come to mind. But many more materials will be needed before a full, linguistically meaningful K–12 program can emerge. Nevertheless, as a teacher who still remembers the bright, enthusiastic faces of my sixth-graders from thirty years ago, I think we should give it our best try.

REFERENCES

Baker, C. L. 1991. The syntax of English *not*: The limits of core grammar. *Linguistic Inquiry* 22: 387–429.

Carrier, Jill, and Janet Randall. 1992. The argument structure and syntactic structure of resultatives. *Linguistic Inquiry* 23: 173–234.

Chomsky, Noam. 1957. *Syntactic structures.* Mouton: The Hague.

Hogan, James. 1983. *Code of the lifemaker.* New York: Ballantine Books.

Jackendoff, Ray. 1997a. *The architecture of the language faculty*. Cambridge, MA: MIT Press.

———. 1997b. Twistin' the night away. *Language* 73: 534–59.

Jacobs, Roderick A. 1995. *English syntax*. New York: Oxford University Press.

Kolln, Martha. 1994. *Understanding English grammar*. 4th ed. New York: Macmillan.

Lederer, Richard. 1987. *Anguished English*. Charleston, SC: Wyrick and Co.

———. 1989. *Crazy English*. New York: Pocket Books.

Nunberg, Geoffrey, Ivan Sag, and Thomas Wasow. 1994. Idioms. *Language* 70: 491–538.

Pinker, Steven. 1995. *The language instinct*. New York: HarperPerennial.

Sedley, Dorothy. 1990. *Anatomy of English*. New York: St. Martin's Press.

Teschner, Richard V., and Eston Evans. 1993. *Analyzing the grammar of English*. Washington, DC: Georgetown University Press.

Thurber, James. 1964. *The Thurber carnival*. New York: Dell.

Williams, Edwin. 1981. On the notions "lexically related" and "head of a word." *Linguistic Inquiry* 12: 245–74.

LOOKING AT LIFE THROUGH LANGUAGE
Patricia L. MacGregor-Mendoza

Many instructors take great care in designing courses that are rigorous and complete, yet also provide knowledge and skills that students will be able to carry on into future endeavors. In order to roughly evaluate my success toward this end, I asked the students of the first introductory sociolinguistics course I taught, "Now that you've learned and discussed about how language and society relate around the world, what are you going to do with this knowledge? How are you going to use it in your lives and in your careers?" After a lot of blank stares and a long, uncomfortable silence, I began to call on a few people to encourage them to share their views. How could they not help but be enriched after spending a semester reading from an excellent book written by an established scholar that exposed them to a host of sociolinguistic nuances from around the globe? When called upon to give his opinion, one young man stated, "Uh, I dunno, I'm in Professional Golf Management, I just took this course to fulfill my 'Viewing the Wider World' requirement." I must admit that at that moment I, too, was stymied as to how to relate his chosen field to gender inflection in Japanese, Spanish-Quechua diglossia, or any number of other topics that we had discussed over the semester. I was further struck by the irony in his statement. The course had succeeded in fulfilling a college requirement designed to provide cultural enrichment, but yet had obviously failed to fulfill its promise to the student in that regard. I reasoned that my students' experiences that semester had been similar to that of looking at their Aunt Milly's vacation pictures. The linguistic snapshots they had viewed from around the world had been interesting in their exoticness, but they were so far removed from the students' own reality in Southern New Mexico that it was unlikely that they would leave any lasting impression. For sixteen weeks my students had remained politely interested in what was revealed to them, but had not developed any meaningful understanding of the subtleties of language and its functions as applied to their own lives.

In reworking my approach to the course, I decided to break with tradition by replacing the book with a coursepack of readings that centered around common sociolinguistic themes such as Culture, Power, and Attitudes. Additionally, I prepared tasks that would aid them in exploring how these themes were manifested in language within their own community. Also, since many of the students who enroll in the class are preservice teachers, I felt it appropriate for them to examine what present and historic relationships exist(ed) between language and school. Their keen observations in the field assignments not only revealed to them a variety of subtle sociolinguistic phenomena that mediate the formal and informal social interactions in their community, but the fact that they actively participated in the discovery of these phenomena further grounded their awareness of linguistic issues and honed their analytical skills.

To undertake their field assignments, the students have a fertile ground with which to work. Southern New Mexico boasts a particularly rich cultural and linguistic heritage and is an excellent area for sociolinguistic discovery. Over the course of time the cultural and linguistic landscape has been molded by numerous Native American tribes, Spanish colonists, Mexican mestizos, and Anglo and African American immigrants from the nation's more easterly regions. Language is as much etched in the history of the Southwest as it is in the rough geography of mesas and arroyos. Nonetheless, while the mix of individuals who have influenced the present-day community may be unique to this area, an equally diverse blending of peoples can be found in other regions of the country. Thus, exploring the relationship between language and society in any community can render an equally rich sociolinguistic tapestry.

In order to begin examining how culture and language are linked, the students first needed to define what culture is. Goodenough (1957, 167) explains that culture "consists of whatever it is one has to know or believe in order to operate in a manner acceptable to its members, and to do so in any role that they accept for any one of themselves" (as cited in Wardhaugh 1992, 216). Such a broad definition implies that not only is culture a concept based on a collective decision, it is also one that can vary greatly among different groups of people. By extension, our cultural knowledge is derived from our constant interaction with the various members of our community. Language, then, is both a tool of facilitating the transmission of cultural knowledge as well as an element within culture constrained by its norms. The verbal interaction that we engage in, therefore, implies a great deal of knowledge about who comprises our community at any given moment (family members, neighborhood, city, and so on) and what our shared norms are.

To begin to discern the cultural elements found within the conversations of family and friends, the students in my class were asked to select someone who they thought was "just like" themselves. Next, they were to engage in and/or observe that individual in a casual conversation, note whatever features of the person's speech stood out to them, and explain what these conversational features revealed about the individual and/or how conversations are structured between family and friends. In one instance a student noted that a shift from English to Spanish, as well as a change in the pace and volume of her sister's speech, provided clues to the background knowledge that was common to both, signaled the intimacy of the topic, and revealed a pattern of speech common to her family:

> As if a flip of a switch, once the topic focused on our family, she began to speak in Spanish. . . . I also noticed that her voice became louder, and she spoke faster. I feel that this stems from the unwritten rule in our family that states, "the louder and faster you talk, the more people will listen." Furthermore, I also noticed that she used more gestures and that she interrupted me to finish my statements more often than during any other one of our topics of conversation. There was a greater use of pronouns, and many things were left implicit because she knew her audience (me) understood who and what she was talking about without the need for much explanation and background information. (Sandra L., Assignment 1, p. 2)

Thus the student was able to identify several linguistic devices employed by her sister and recognize the functions each occupied. She was further able to determine that the interruptions, heightened volume, and accelerated pace of the conversation were efforts commonly employed in her family to retain control of the discourse. The information revealed in this example not only reflects the speech norms within a particular family, but also informs us that conversations can also represent power struggles between speakers.

Relatively few of our daily conversations place speakers on equal footing. More often than not we find ourselves in situations where we are requesting a favor, dictating a preference, providing knowledge to those who lack it, or receiving information from those who possess it. Each of these situations, at some level, places one or more speakers in a more powerful position than others. Establishing conversational status among speakers involves "powerful participants *controlling and constraining the contributions of non-powerful participants*" (Fairclough 1989, 46; emphasis in original). The linguistic behaviors used to establish the relative power of the persons engaged in conversation can be employed overtly, as in the previous example by the speaker verbally signaling her wish to assert her control of the conversation, or can appear in rather understated ways in which the less powerful participants willingly cede control of the conversation through no effort on the part of the more powerful speaker. One student found this to be true while reflecting on an amiable chat with a coworker. She wrote:

> Another thing that stood out was that she and I do a lot of code-switching. I noticed that we speak a few sentences in English and then a few in Spanish. I never really noticed that before. A few people walked up and spoke to us throughout the course of our conversation. At one point a supervisor joined our conversation. My friend and I spoke English the entire time and did not switch to Spanish once. After the supervisor left we went back to speaking both languages. . . . I am not sure exactly why we only spoke English, because the supervisor is also someone who speaks Spanish. I thought about it afterwards and realized that my friend and I speak English with all supervisors. It is [sic] just always seemed more appropriate. (Lisa B., Assignment 1, pp. 1–2)

Our perception of the conversational partner before us is one factor that works to structure our interaction with that person. In the preceding example the student and her coworker viewed the third member of the conversation as a supervisor rather than as a member of the Spanish-speaking community and chose to verbally recognize his authority by interacting with him in English. Furthermore, she acknowledges that such interaction is standard practice, implying that to have addressed him in Spanish might have been perceived as demonstrating less respect for him than for other supervisors.

Similar to our perceptions of others' status, our attitudes about how others speak guide our conversations and further influence our judgment of them. Generally, those who "speak like us" are broadly accepted, while reactions to those whose speech is different from our own may range from novelty to suspicion to anger. To poll the reactions of the students' community to a different language variety, an option on one assignment was to survey three to five people on their reactions to the Ebonics controversy. Students were surprised to be able to find informants who held strong opinions about the topic, despite the fact that many of their interviewees readily admitted that they had not really researched the topic beyond hearing thirty-second excerpts from the news. One of the strongest opinions was expressed by a woman who has worked with migrant populations through Health and Human Services for several years. The student who interviewed her quoted her as saying:

> People come here from other countries—Italy, Greece, Germany, Mexico— and they learn English within a generation or two. Why are the blacks given "special dispensation"? Why should people who came from Africa 10 or 15 generations ago be allowed to bastardize our language? . . .
>
> In accounts in the newspaper after drive-by shootings, interviews sound

like, "There be no reasons them be goin' down him like this. He be a good boy!" Who's going to be in control when we get older? If they can't talk, can they add? Can they read? Are they honest? (Donna B., Assignment 3, pp. 3–4)

Clearly, opinions people express regarding different language varieties also often reflect opinions about the speakers of that language. In this case, the informant regards African American Vernacular English as a substandard form of English and is quick to characterize its speakers as victims or perpetrators of violent crimes and individuals who possess questionable literacy and math skills and are of dubious moral standing. Although from a purely linguistic standpoint, all varieties of language are equally expressive, complex, and bound by rules, what cannot be adequately measured or controlled is the value or prestige each variety of language is afforded by various members of society.

Societal attitudes about language often collide in school environments. The attitudes held by individuals in positions of power in academic circles (teachers, principals, school boards) can profoundly affect decisions made regarding the educational development and outcomes of the children in their care. The far-reaching effects of such decisions are strongly felt in communities that employ multiple languages or multiple varieties of the same language. If the school language differs from that of the student's home environment, there lies a potential for conflict.

An option to the third assignment explored an area of conflict particularly prevalent in the Southwest. For many years schools advocated "No Spanish" rules. Children who spoke Spanish in class, on the playground, and in the lunch room were subjected to a variety of penalties ranging from verbal admonishments to physical punishments. To document this community history and recognize the immediate and long-term effects of such treatment, one option to the third field assignment called upon students to interview three to five informants over the age of 35. Informants were to reflect on their experiences in school as Spanish speakers and recount what events, if any, they experienced or witnessed that exemplified their school's language policy. To be fair, not all informants reported suffering physically or emotionally as a result of speaking Spanish in school; however, several informants did admit to being punished, particularly in the early grades. Surprisingly, even after three decades or more these informants were able to recall vivid, often painful memories of being mistreated for speaking Spanish:

The last interview was that of a 40 year old man who attended a school in El Paso. He preferred not to disclose the name of the school. As he spoke I could sense the anger and hurt in his voice. He was definitely not allowed to speak any Spanish in school. . . . The consequences for speaking Spanish were unbelievable to me. He told me that if they spoke in Spanish the teacher would trim the finger nails of a hand down low, almost making them bleed, and if that wasn't enough the teacher would hit the students with a ruler right on the tips of these fingers. (Sylvia G., Assignment 3, p. 3)

In the first grade if anyone got caught speaking Spanish, their teacher, Mrs. Veeder, pulled the student by the ear and put them in a corner. They also got hit on the knuckles with a ruler if they got caught speaking Spanish. (Lydia S., Assignment 3, p. 1)

If they were caught speaking Spanish [in High School], they would get detention, have their mouths washed out with soap, have to run around the track for hours and/or be sent home until they were ready to be a "true Tiger" (which was the school mascot). There was one punishment that left a lasting impression for both my aunt and my mom. To understand the seriousness of this punishment, you need to be familiar with the architecture of the school. The school was built to resemble a Roman Coliesium [sic], with many steep steps leading into a pit in the very bottom. It was not strange to see ten to twenty Mexican students running up and down those stairs at all hours of the day, and in whatever weather. Needless to say, both my aunt and my mom as well as the other Spanish speaking students cringed at the sight of the much admired architectural style. (Sandra L., Assignment 3, pp. 1–2)

The consequences of such linguistic discrimination can be long-lasting. One student reported that her 48-year-old informant felt ashamed of her home language and of her parents due to the school punishments. "She always kept to herself and seldom spoke up in class. Now she has a hard time expressing herself verbally" (Maggie S., Assignment 3, pp. 3–4). Similar sentiments were expressed by another student's informant. "For fear of getting punished my husband chose not to participate in class. He was embarrassed to speak English and he wasn't allowed to speak Spanish. So, his only other choice was to sit quietly and avoid shame or punishment" (Lydia S., Assignment 3, pp. 1–2). Perhaps even more revealing, however, is the internal conflict such rules forbidding Spanish to be spoken at school created in the young minds of the students. Such was evident in Albert's dilemma:

Albert was not allowed to speak Spanish during school. He never witnessed anyone getting disciplined for speaking Spanish. "It was just understood that while in school we spoke English and at home we spoke Spanish." Though, [sic] Albert spoke English prior to entering school he was very aware of the no Spanish speaking rule during school. He remembers one incident when he was in first grade that he was asked what his mother's name was, that his fear of knowing the rule and yet not knowing the consequences for breaking it, prompted him to respond "Betty" instead of his mom's Spanish name Carlota. (Lidia T., Assignment 3, p. 2)

It is easy to feel Albert's inner struggle. So strong was his desire to comply with the school's unwritten yet well-understood rules that he felt it easier to invent an anglicized name that bore no resemblance to his mother's true name than to suffer the unknown consequences for speaking Spanish. Thus, 6-year-old Albert willingly erased even the smallest indication of his Spanish-speaking heritage in order to save face and get along in school.

It is evident that even young children recognize the dramatic influence that Culture, Power, and Attitudes have on daily linguistic interaction and can display a sensitivity toward implicit opinions about language, recognize and willingly acquiesce to the desires of the powerful participants in their conversations, and respond to the members of the culture (e.g., school) in a manner they feel is expected or appropriate, even if their response conflicts with reality. As adults, we continue to possess these skills, but we can also probe the meaning behind this knowledge. By examining our lives through the lens of language we can identify unconscious patterns of thinking, hidden biases, and latent assumptions. A heightened awareness of the linguistic practices and behaviors displayed by ourselves and those around us not only can aid us in appreciating the rich tapestry of language, but can also steer us away from the trap of prejudging another based on his or her style of speech.

From a pedagogical standpoint, the students' linguistic explorations in their own community have served them better than the previous erudite discussions of linguistic curiosities from around the world. Far from the hesitant "Uh, I dunno" reply of several semesters ago, students in the current course clearly articulate—without prompting—how the knowledge they gained in each assignment has had an impact on their lives and relationships with family and friends. They are further able to state how the information learned through the course will aid them in their professional and personal lives. Thus, rather than simply fulfill a college requirement, the course truly does prepare them for viewing the wider world.

REFERENCES

Fairclough, Norman. 1989. *Language and power*. Essex, England: Longman Group UK.

Goodenough, W. H. 1957. Cultural anthropology and linguistics. *Report of the Seventh Round Table Meeting on Linguistics and Language Study*, ed. by P. I. Garvin. Washington, DC: Georgetown University Press.

Wardhaugh, Ronald. 1992. *An introduction to sociolinguistics*. 2nd ed. Oxford: Blackwell.

In Front of Our Eyes: Undergraduates Reflecting on Language Change

Anca M. Nemoianu

Lately, ever more students have been approaching me with embarrassed smiles on their faces and the confession that they have "problems" with such language arcana as the apostrophe, the choice of *who* over *whom*, *lie* over *lay*, and *as* over *like*, or the plural of words such as *syllabus* or *vertebra*. They are caught between their teachers' editing marks on their papers and their own spirited conversations, between the style manuals they are asked to consult in order to "cleanse" their writing of these many nagging problems and what they see on public billboards and in prestigious publications. They feel betrayed by the seemingly friendly spellcheck and the style manuals that seem to proffer grandparently pedantic advice that makes their linguistic fluency flounder. They are asking me, the grammarian, to help them get rid of what they call the "slang" that permeates their speech and written work. Their incredulous looks tell me that praising slang as "ordinary people's poetry" is not what they expect. I could also tell them that slang is used to signal group belonging, to create intimacy, to make one sound different and funny, or to play with language and thus enrich it—to mention just a few of the many admirable uses of slang (Partridge 1970). But that would hardly put their fears to rest.

What I need to make them understand is that the problems they bring up are not slang, but simply symptoms of language change happening right in front of our eyes. In other words, I need to redirect their search toward change, in a planned process of discovery. I start this process with a not-too-distant television vignette, a humorous treatment of language change and speakers' attitudes to it, and follow it with time-honored examples of change in different language areas. By the time the lessons of history have been laid down, the students are ready to look again at their urgent language queries, put them under the microscope, understand their true nature, and then investigate how other speakers deal with them. The new direction for discovery thus leads them to a new understanding of how language works.

CIGARETTES AND CONJUNCTIONS

We start by going back to an almost mythical time, the 1960s, when cigarette advertising was not yet banned from television, to the story of a Winston ad. In my memory of the ad, a young smoker's declaration that "Winston tastes good like a cigarette should" prompts the glaring condemnation of a group of prim schoolmarms, complete with black dresses, lace collars, and John Lennon glasses perched on the tips of their noses. Their disciplinary action notwithstanding, the phrasing of the slogan remains unchanged, only prefaced by a perfunctory apology: "Pardon our grammar but/ Winston tastes good like a cigarette should." The grammatical correction— "as a cigarette should"—did not even need to be spelled out, for many in the audience were still well aware at the time of the prescribed form.

This miniature satire is revealing of speakers' uncertainty in the face of change, of concerted efforts to stop it, and of change's unstoppable march through time. How many of us fully understand the apology that prefaced the slogan nowadays, thirty years later, when political campaign promises are summarized by "like I said before" without the slightest hesitation? There may be some glaring eyes in the audience who would expect *like* to be replaced by *as*, but most of us would not notice any wrongdoing. It is true that, more recently, *like* has taken on a whole range of meanings in the lingo of the young generation, making it a linguistic jack-of-all-trades, the glue of conversational fluency. While this recent sweeping trend may outlive its usefulness, the sentence-linking *like* has firmly replaced the conjunction *as* used for the same purpose. Although the moment of initiation could be traced more than thirty years back, the change from *as* to *like* has taken place within one generation, in front of my generation's eyes.

A BACKWARD GLANCE

The history of the English language, its recorded fifteen centuries, offers a dramatic example of language change: Old English is so different from the modern variety that contemporary English speakers have to learn it as a foreign language. Its opacity is not caused by a different alphabet or by a foreign cultural reality encoded in a different vocabulary (although the latter is, naturally, a contributing factor), but to the largest extent by a different structure. We often say that the structure of Old English is more like that of Latin, in that its learners have to memorize scores of noun and verb endings in order to figure out the functions of the words in a sentence. The comparison with Latin would be fortunate, indeed, if it were accompanied by a clarification: that Latin did not die, but rather evolved into such modern-day languages as Spanish and Romanian and French. Old English also underwent massive changes on its way to becoming the language now spoken by 700 million people, "and only half of them native speakers of the language" (Quirk 1985, 1). Just as modern-day Latins continue to change, not least with infusions of English words, so does contemporary English.

Language change is a fact, hard to ignore from a historical perspective, but equally hard to accept at any one particular moment in history. In the sixteenth century, Sir John Cheke, appointed by Henry VIII as the first regius professor of Greek at Cambridge and knighted by Edward VI, took a firm stand against the onslaught of foreign words into English: "I am of the opinion that our own tung shold be written cleane and pure, unmixt and unmangled with borrowing of other tunges, wherin if we take no heed by tijm, ever borrowing and never payeng, she shall be fain to keep her house as bankrupt" (Hughes 1988, 103). Nowadays, whenever the French Academy launches a new war against English words "invading" the French language, I cannot help thinking that we are "payeng," and thus, over centuries, both languages become solvent. For languages change slowly, and as long as they have speakers, they will survive bankruptcy.

Cheke, the man who "taught Cambridge and King Edward Greek," was concerned with two areas of language change: the sounds of English and its vocabulary. He attempted to reform the spelling of English to bring it closer to the sounds that had undergone so much change over time. He tried to obliterate a significant consequence of the Great Vowel Shift—a series of pronunciation changes, started in the 1500s and still under way at his time—which is responsible to a large extent for the large discrepancy between sound and spelling in Modern English. At the same time, not unlike our contemporaries, who are changing the wording of religious texts to conform to current ideologies, Cheke, a supporter of the Reformation, sought to make do without borrowing words from Latin languages. For instance, he offered "gainraising" as a homemade alternative to the Latin-derived "resurrection" in his translation of St. Matthew's Gospel. His attempts to change both spelling and vocabulary from his Cambridge armchair were totally unsuccessful, just as similar attempts by others, at later times, turned out to be.

Pronunciation and vocabulary are the two areas of language where variation and change are more readily noticeable over long stretches of time and contemporaneously, and consequently are most easily targeted. In terms of sounds, English has changed over its history much more than, say, German, which did not undergo a vowel change of the magnitude of the Great Vowel Shift that shook English in its passage from Middle to Modern stages. But sound change continues in front of our eyes. Thus on Martha's Vineyard, a small island off the coast of Massachusetts, middle-aged fishermen subconsciously initiated a vowel change (e.g., /au/ in words such as *town* started being pronounced /əu/ as in *tone*) that started spreading to all the other permanent residents of the island (Labov 1972). This is an example of change in progress, observable at the level of a small community of speakers, radiating to the age groups closest to the one that started it, with fewer users among the oldest and the youngest of the residents. I am not suggesting here that this particular sound change will in time become standard, but it offers an exemplary nugget of the mechanism of sound change.

More noticeable than sound change is the continuous influx of new vocabulary into a language. Few contemporary English speakers are aware that *very* and the French *vrai* 'true' have the same source, and most speakers therefore have no qualms (not that they should) about saying "truly very sad." Few are aware that *coach* is basically the name of a town in Hungary (Kocs), where the closed carriage was first made, turned into a common noun from French into German and from German into English. But most are aware that *sushi* is a relatively recent borrowing from Japanese, just as speakers of Japanese may know that *seku-hara* is their rendition of the English "sexual harassment."

Not only does language change go on in all areas of language, from the sound system through the structure of the words to word order and the meaning of words, but quite often changes at one level of the language trigger change at other levels. An interesting small example among myriads is given by the vicissitudes of the Old English word *hād* 'quality', which became in Modern English the ending *-hood*, helping form words such as *neighborhood*. Nowadays it seems to be on its way to becoming another independent word, *hood* (different from the already existing noun *hood* 'head covering'), which means "space," "place" (as in the movie title *Boyz N the Hood*); for the time being it has the negative connotation of gangsterism, associated with *hoodlum*, of unknown origin. Over time, such contagious changes from word meaning to word structure and back to meaning are only to be expected in the language ecosystem.

My students, though, are confused by changes at yet another language level, that of word and sentence structure—changes that have marked English throughout its history and, like many other kinds of change, continue to occur in Modern English.

CHANGE HERE AND NOW

With a historical glance at language change as a foundation for understanding, we are now ready to tackle the last stage of the discovery process: to examine again some of the students' "language problems" and place them in the context of real speakers' language choices and attitudes. At this point we design together an informal empirical study of language change in progress. The project, outlined in some detail in the Appendix to this chapter, goes beyond identifying specific areas of word and sentence change into promoting reflection on the relationship between language change and writing, as well as on how different coexisting generations of speakers feel about change.

We first explore some "active" language areas, what Aitchison called "spaghetti junctions" (1989, 151), where language seems to be in a state of agitation, trying to choose from among several options for change. Here are a few such cases that are of concern to us: they are language forms in a state of flux, given here in sentence contexts. The evolving, or new, form, ever more frequent in speaking and informal writing, is represented first, and the older form, still the norm in formal writing, second.

Case 1: The Singular *Their*

(1) new: Everybody believes *their* own version of the story.

old: Everybody believes *his* own version of the story.

(2) new: Each person will pair off with the person sitting next to *them*.

old: Each person will pair off with the person sitting next to *him*.

The indefinite pronouns *everybody/anybody/nobody* or *each* now take the plural pronoun *they*, but continue to agree with the verb in the singular ("everybody *is*"). We might as well say that the pronoun *they* has acquired a new function, that of a singular indefinite pronoun (Allen 1997, 93). The older gender agreement with the masculine, the norm until not very long ago, was brought to the consciousness of English speakers, and editors have offered various solutions; the most common of them is the slashed pronoun *he/she*. They have all been rejected, however, just as quickly as the human body rejects incompatible organs. The message is clear: within the pronominal system there is no room for the creation of new forms. The new function of *their* is the solution reached tacitly and embraced organically by the speakers of English. We are reminded here of Sapir's words: "Language moves down time, in a current *of its own making*" (1921, 150; italics added).

Case 2: The Hypothetical *Was*

(3) new: If I *was* a millionaire, I would buy the Empire State Building.

old: If I *were* a millionaire, I would buy the Empire State Building.

In hypothetical, contrary-to-fact statements, the older invariant form *were* has been replaced by many speakers by the past-tense form *was* without any change in meaning: in both sentences in (3), the speaker continues not to be a millionaire, although the verb form has changed. We can look at this change from two perspectives: on the one hand, we can say that language opted for simplicity, in that now there is no formal difference between contrary-to-fact and simple past-tense statements; but at the same time, it chose to maintain two forms, *was* and *were*, instead of simply getting rid of one and simplifying the paradigm. The second perspective shows that in matters of language change, simplicity does not always win. The resilience of frequently used irregular plurals (e.g., *foot/feet*) offers additional proof against simplicity and regularity as the expected paths for change (McMahon 1994, 73).

Case 3: The Vanishing *Whom*

(4) new: They don't know *who* to blame.

old: They don't know *whom* to blame.

The object case of the relative pronoun *who*, one of the few remaining case inflections that connect Modern English to its ending-rich ancestor, Old English, is rarely seen and even more rarely heard these days. It is often replaced by *who*, its unmarked subject form. The change does not seem to be infectious: object case forms with the same ending, such as *him* and *them*, continue to thrive (e.g., I blame *him/them*).

Case 4: The Plural *Neither*

(5) new: *Neither* simplicity *or* regularity *or* resemblance can explain language change.

old: *Neither* simplicity *nor* regularity can explain language change.

The correlative dual negative coordinator *neither . . . nor* seems to be undergoing a double change. The number of coordinated items has grown from two, the older constraint, to several as speakers hone their ideas in the conversational flow and add information as they feel necessary. In addition, its second part, *nor*, has switched to the affirmative. Somehow, the scope of the initial negative *neither* has extended over the entire phrase, eliminating the need for a second negative. The elimination of the second negative is an organic development that seems ironically consonant with the grammarian-induced principle of one negation per sentence. While double negatives do seem to be resurfacing in some contexts (e.g., "You ain't seen nothing yet!"), in the case of our correlative, the second negative is dropped.

Case 5: The Quarrel between *I* and *Me*

(6) new: This is between you and *I*.

    old: This is between you and *me*.

(7) new: It may not be a problem to you and *I*, but it is to many others.

    old: It may not be a problem to you and *me*, but it is to many others.

If simplicity were the only direction of language change, one would expect all inflected pronominal forms to follow the path to oblivion taken by *whom*. But that is not the case. Another inflected pronominal form—*me*, the object case of the first-person-singular pronoun *I*—is gaining more ground in places where the prescribed form has been *I*, and it is creating unexpected confusion on its way. In some contexts (e.g., "it's *me*," "than *me*," "*me*, too") it seems by now almost unanimously accepted, although the occasional frowns are not absent. This produces hesitation in the use of the first person after a preposition, mainly when there are two coordinated pronouns, and the first person moves politely into second place. The new forms in (6) and (7) are cases of hypercorrection in which *me* is avoided and replaced by the subject case *I* in order to compensate for the occasional disapproval associated with the use of *me* in other contexts (e.g., "He's older than *me*").

Case 6: The Random Apostrophe

(8) new: The improvement of education is on *administrator's* and faculty *member's* minds. (the minds of administrators and faculty members)

    old: The improvement of education is on *administrators'* and faculty *members'* minds.

(9) new: Don't forget to clean the *chimney's*.

    old: Don't forget to clean the chimneys.

(10) new: At Little *Caesars* Pizza you can get free drinks. (the pizza sold at Little Caesar)

    old: At Little *Caesar's* Pizza you can get free drinks.

The vagaries of the apostrophe in contemporary English, although pertaining to orthography, a cosmetic rather than structural area of the language, provide an illustrative microcosm of language change: the confusion, hesitation, inconsistency, and hypercorrection that may accompany any language change before a balance is reached, and the new form finds a stable position and becomes the norm. When it comes to the apostrophe, many of today's writers are in a state of total disorientation, sprinkling the little orthographic marks over a sentence in the hope that they might fall in the right places.

The hesitation is between the genitive, or possessive, forms in (8) and (10), the place where, until not very long ago, it belonged, and the plural in (9), where it is appearing with increased frequency. The confusion is so pervasive that the plural marked by 's has acquired a name, "the green-grocer's apostrophe," for it is widely displayed on price cards for *banana's*, *raspberry's*, and *carrot's*; but it is by no means restricted to this noble trade.

The seeds of today's confusion between the written plural and possessive forms, and quite possibly the beginning of the apostrophe's demise in English, may be found in the overgeneralization by analogy of the -s ending from one of the many Old English classes of nouns (e.g., *stan* 'stone') to both plural and possessive singular of all nouns. But if that is the only reason, it is the longest germination period known to us. The causes of the apostrophe's status in contemporary English must be a lot more complex than that.

SPEAKERS, WRITERS, AND CHANGE: LESSONS LEARNED

With Sir John Cheke's words still resounding in our minds, we turn now to testing these and other junctions with three generations of speakers. Thus we create a more complete picture of historical change, with the added dimension of real speakers' attitudes toward language change. Students learn from their friends and relatives that the nagging problems they encounter in their writing are not slang, but simply symptoms of language change "in front of our eyes."

In their discovery process, they learn about people's attitudes toward language change: Younger speakers are more accepting and less judgmental of change than older speakers. Equally important, they realize that speakers across generations make a distinction between spoken and written modes of communication, and that writing is more resistant, but not impervious, to change: Writing is more conservative than speaking.

From their reflection on and testing of the changing forms, they learn that language change is very gradual, and that it happens not just toward simplicity and leveling, but in several directions at once: The direction of change is hard to predict. A final lesson about language change is that no matter how forceful the linguistic prescription is or how diligently speakers monitor their speech, change, once started, prevails: Language does not tolerate dictators.

Beyond these lessons about specific areas of language change in contemporary English and other speakers' attitudes to change, this step-by-step process of discovery is enlightening in larger ways. As April McMahon points out, "Understanding language change means understanding language better" (1994, 10). Part of that understanding is that language is alive, but also that the human-life metaphors we use in connection with language can easily take us down treacherous evolutionary waters, where thoughts of growth, maturity, decay, and death abound. Older speakers, as the students find out, are more prone than their younger contemporaries to think of change in progress as signs of "decay" and to blame the younger speakers for what is entirely beyond their and anyone else's power to control.

While carrying out their empirical studies of language change, some of my students notice (and others imagine) contradictions between what speakers say they do and what they actually do with language. For the study's questionnaire, one student constructed the sentence "Before you and I go to the movies, I need to stop to get money from an ATM." The sentence was given as an example of a hypercorrected use of the first-person pronoun after a preposition. The student was surprised that her English-teacher informant would use it always, in both spoken and written English. "I bet he's not teaching his students that kind of English!" was the young investigator's comment. She failed to notice, though, that in this sentence *before* is a conjunction and therefore outside the scope of "the quarrel between *I* and *me*." This is a splendid proof that the preposition/conjunction confusion is one of those weak links in contemporary English where change is bound to happen sooner or later. The Winston television ad of thirty years ago recorded for posterity the beginning of this change, whose exact direction cannot yet be determined.

APPENDIX: GUIDELINES FOR THE LANGUAGE CHANGE PROJECT

Questionnaire

Use the "questionable" language forms discussed and listed in class in sentence contexts (e.g., "Like I said before, double-space the entire paper, including the long quotations"). Create, in addition, a few "unquestionable" sentences (i.e., sentences most people would find acceptable in most circumstances) as distractors. Scramble the order of the sentences so that sentences with targeted forms are interspersed with distractors. Under each sentence give three frequency-of-order options each for spoken and written English. (For the "random apostrophe" you should offer only written options, of course.)

Example:

If I was you, I wouldn't tell anyone about the money yet.

Spoken	Written
always	always
sometimes	sometimes
never	never

Type the questionnaire and make copies for each of your six informants.

Informants

Find six English-speaking informants, two from each generation: your own, your parents', and your grandparents'. For some of you the Thanksgiving break may be a perfect opportunity to do the project. Ensure your informants' consent to participate in this study by explaining to them (*a*) that it is a school project, for a linguistics class; (*b*) that you are interested in finding out how language is used by different speakers; and (*c*) that their identity will be kept confidential at all times.

Procedure

Go through the questionnaire separately with each informant. Ask them to circle the option that applies to them. Some of them are bound to make comments about some of your sentences. Write those comments down. Summarize your results by awarding 3 points to "always," 2 points to "sometimes," and 1 point to "never." For each targeted form you will end up with six numbers: two (written and spoken) for each generation. Bring your answered questionnaires, the informants' comments, and your numerical summaries to class. We will compare the results and prepare to write a report of the study.

REFERENCES

Aitchison, Jean. 1989. Spaghetti junctions and recurrent routes: Some preferred pathways in language evolution. *Lingua* 77: 151–71.

Allen, Virginia. 1997. The organic approach to the apostrophe: An unwarranted consensus. *Composition Studies* 25: 83–99.

Hughes, Geoffrey. 1988. *Words in time: A social history of the English vocabulary.* Oxford: Blackwell.

Labov, William. 1972. *Sociolinguistic patterns.* Philadelphia: University of Pennsylvania Press.

McMahon, April M. S. 1994. *Understanding language change.* Cambridge: Cambridge University Press.

Partridge, Eric. 1970. *Slang*. 4th ed. New York: Barnes and Noble.

Quirk, Randolph. 1985. The English language in a global context. *English in the world: Teaching and learning the language and literatures*, ed. by Randolph Quirk and H. G. Widdowson, 1–6. Cambridge: Cambridge University Press.

Sapir, Edward. 1921. *Language*. New York: Harcourt, Brace and Co.; London: Oxford University Press.

9

GRAMMAR TEACHING IS DEAD—NOT!

Richard Hudson

Grammar is certainly not dead, to judge by the changes that are taking place under our noses. The "postsentential negator" in the title is almost certainly a recent innovation, and who knows whether it will still be around at the end of the next century?[1] This little bit of language is certainly an example of grammar (what else could it be?), and it is equally certainly "alive" in the sense that any other bit of our culture is alive. I live in England, where we not only drive on the left but also have a transitive auxiliary verb (e.g., "Have you any children?"), and I even use *jolly* as a degree adverb (*jolly good*), much to the amusement of my children, who find it quaint. All of these things are grammar, and all are full of life, change, variation, and interest to everyone.

HISTORICAL BACKGROUND

Yet most of our schools have stopped teaching children about grammar. Nobody could describe the state of grammar teaching in the schools of the United Kingdom as healthy: "The overwhelming majority of teachers in the UK . . . concede that attention to grammar and to the forms of language has been neglected" (Carter 1996, 8). The same is true in Australia: "[In Australia] the language system has completely disappeared from view in schooling" (Rothery 1996, 86). The United States and Canada seem to have taken the same route. In all these countries most school graduates do not know even the most elementary things about the grammar of their own language; for example, a recent survey of graduates who were training in a British university to become primary-school teachers found that half of them had no idea what a preposition or conjunction was (Williamson and Hardman 1995). Why?[2]

It is important to be clear that this is not a natural or inevitable state of affairs. It is not because grammar is inherently too difficult to teach, nor because it is obviously not worth teaching. For centuries it was one of the core subjects in English-speaking schools, to the extent that some UK schools are still called "grammar schools"; and there are many countries where it is still an important part of the school curriculum across the entire spectrum of academic abilities. For example, the grammatical analysis of sentences is taught in every primary school in France and Russia, and in every junior high school in China (Hudson 1998b).[3] I cannot say how good or how successful this teaching is, but grammar teachers cost as much as any others, so at least these societies must consider their services worth paying for.

As far as the Anglo-Saxon countries are concerned, however, grammar teaching was judged and found seriously wanting in the revolutionary days of the 1960s. A UK government report on English teaching, usually called the Bullock Report, concluded: "What has been shown is that the teaching of traditional analytic grammar does not appear to improve performance in writing" (HMSO 1975, 169). Similar worries were expressed in other countries. What was to be done? In the words of no less a commentator than Noam Chomsky (1969), should grammar teaching be "mended" or "ended"?

The Bullock Report sided with mending. It recommended explicit instruction in matters such as "punctuation, some aspects of usage, the way words are built and the company they keep, and . . . the modest collection of technical terms useful for discussion of language" (HMSO 1975, 172). What must be avoided was "explicit instruction out of context." However, it turned out to be all too easy for mending to turn into ending. At the time of the Bullock Report many English teachers had already stopped teaching grammar systematically in order to avoid "instruction out of context," with the result that the "right moment" hardly ever arose and grammar was simply not taught at all. (This point was made, interestingly, by a team of American observers in UK schools quoted in the Bullock Report, HMSO 1975, 172.) A generation later, the pupils of those days are the teachers of today, many of them with very little systematic knowledge of grammar and nothing to teach, whether out of context or in context.

The world has moved on since those heady days, and as far as the United Kingdom is concerned, I think that it would be fair to say that most English teachers now accept the need for grammar teaching. However, they are extremely resistant to the idea of decontextualized grammar exercises, so we are not simply experiencing a swing of the pendulum back to where it was in 1950. "The overwhelming majority of teachers in the UK . . . now willingly incorporate more formal knowledge about language into schemes of work which continue to stress the importance of audiences, purposes and social contexts of language use" (Carter 1996, 8). The U.S. scene seems somewhat different, with more resistance to grammar teaching of any kind. However, even there we find an influential movement called "whole language" that supports grammar teaching of the mended, contextualized, variety.[4]

THE PROBLEM: CAN GRAMMAR TEACHING BE BOTH CONTEXTUAL AND SYSTEMATIC?

The historical survey leaves us with an urgent question about grammar teaching. How can we reconcile the desire to teach grammar "contextually" with the apparent need to teach it systematically? To leave it till "the right moment" is to leave it to chance—the right moment may never come (Barton 1997). If the right moment does come, what then? Suppose that the student needs some instruction on the use of tenses; is that the moment for a private lesson on the English tense system, with or without exercises? What about the rest of the lesson (and the other students)? The problem would disappear if the student already knew about tenses from some earlier lesson on that topic; but without systematic teaching, how can we arrange this earlier lesson? In short, contextual teaching requires systematic teaching, but we are told that systematic teaching does not work because it is decontextualized.

The key to resolving this paradox is the idea that grammar teaching can have a variety of goals, of which only one is the improvement of writing. Other goals can provide "contexts" within which students can study grammar systematically, acquiring ideas, facts, and terminology that can then be used, as needed, in talking about their writing. There are plenty of other good educational reasons for looking explicitly at grammar: to increase self-awareness, to develop analytical thought patterns or scientific thinking, to prepare for parenthood, to prepare for learning other languages, and to prepare for learning Standard English. Any of these foci could provide a good context for a planned, systematic exploration of, say, tenses that could then be exploited, as needed, in discussions of students' writing.

The rest of this chapter is an attempt to make this suggestion more concrete. The next section reviews a number of recent initiatives in which grammar teaching has been both systematic and successful. The section after that summarizes some ideas for systematic grammar lessons, and the final section offers some general conclusions.

SOME RECENT INITIATIVES

One of the consequences of the interruption in the grammatical tradition has been that there has been scope for experimentation. Traditional grammar came with a package of aims and methods that tended to stifle new developments. Academic linguists have greatly improved the grammar itself, making its study into a highly sophisticated academic discipline; but at the same time, various groups of teachers and linguists have combined to try out new ideas about how grammar could be used in schools. All of these initiatives are small-scale projects that have produced important results at virtually no cost to the taxpayer, and those who are planning the future of grammar teaching will certainly pay attention to them. My collection of initiatives is certainly both incomplete and biased toward my local situation (in the United Kingdom), so the following survey should be read with this in mind. I have divided the survey into three broad areas: language awareness, literacy teaching, and grammar as science.

Language Awareness

Language awareness is the name given to a movement that originated in the work of Michael Halliday in the 1970s[5] and now has its own international association and journal (Hawkins 1987; James and Garrett 1991).[6] The main movers are schoolteachers and educationalists rather than linguists, but the driving force is the idea that schoolchildren should be taught things about their language partly for practical purposes, but partly because it is such an important part of their life and they have a right to understand it better. The scope of language awareness is very broad: dialects, accents and registers, history, the language of children, and grammar. Topics are chosen so as to be both accessible and interesting, but grammar qualifies as easily as any other topic, either in its own right or in connection with some other topic.

Different practitioners of language awareness are (of course) motivated in different ways, but one of the leading ideas is that explicit knowledge about the mother tongue helps in acquiring a foreign language. This seems rather obvious, but it flies against the practice in most schools. In a language-awareness school, the teaching about English and about, say, French would reinforce each other: for instance, the English teacher would introduce the terms *subject* and *verb* and show how inverting the subject and verb distinguishes statements from questions in English ("We are ready" versus "Are we ready?"), then the French teacher would tell students that French works basically in the same way as English, except that any verb allows this inversion ("Allons-nous?" versus the ungrammatical "Go we?"), which gives the English teacher the cue to talk about auxiliary verbs, and so on.

The same idea applies, perhaps surprisingly, to Standard English. Most people in the United Kingdom—perhaps 90 percent—are native speakers of a nonstandard dialect, and the proportion is likely to be similar in other English-speaking countries. One of the aims of public schooling is to ensure that everyone can write Standard English (and perhaps speak it, though this aim is more controversial). How should this be done? The philosophy of language awareness would suggest that the differences can be taught directly: "One of the most effective ways of learning Standard English is for pupils to compare and analyse differences between their own dialects and the dialect of Standard English, discussing explicitly how and when different forms are appropriate" (Carter 1996, 9).

Grammar-based Literacy Teaching

Grammar-based literacy teaching has the traditional aim of improving children's writing, but the examples discussed here avoid the problems mentioned earlier by concentrating on easily accessible areas of grammar, for example, very limited kinds of sentence analysis or grammatical patterns in vocabulary.

In Australia a number of teachers supported by Geoff Williams (a linguist at the University of Sydney) have found in controlled experiments that the simple quantity of what 10-year-old children write increases dramatically after they spend some time looking at one of the many ways in which sentences are structured (Williams 1995). In this project the children looked at the division of sentences into a topic ("theme") and the rest (e.g., "In England (topic) it often rains") but it may not matter much what they look at as long as their attention is on sentence structure. In the United Kingdom Geoff Barton, a secondary-school teacher with training in linguistics, reports (1997) that some of his weakest students benefit "dramatically" from an exploration of simple, compound, and complex sentence types. He supplies models and the students produce further examples (long, short, sensible, or silly) without (apparently) worrying at all about the lack of "context" for the examples.

Most interesting of all, Mary Mason, another linguistically qualified teacher, designed a complete three-year course on "academic language" for 12–14-year-olds that has now been taught over a number of years in several schools (Mason, Mason, and Quayle 1992). The course covered a general introduction to language, the formation of Latinate vocabulary, and the organization of sentences into coherent discourse. The effects reported include a general overall improvement in examination results across all subjects as well as improvements specific to language performance: aptitude for learning a foreign language, comprehension, and writing (Heap 1991).

In the light of these admittedly limited experiments, it is hard to maintain that grammar teaching never has any effect on pupils' own writing (or other uses of language). On the other hand, it is still unclear what precisely it is that produces these beneficial effects. No doubt the content of what is taught matters in some cases, but it is possible that almost anything is better than nothing: all that matters is that the child's attention should be directed to the fine detail of word or sentence structure. If this is true, it is good news for teachers since it means that they can achieve something even by studying one small area of grammar (e.g., how words divide into stems and affixes).

Grammar as Science

The idea here is to use grammar itself as an area of scientific investigation where children can learn to formulate hypotheses and test them, just as in academic linguistics. This is an idea that has been pursued actively by a group of linguists in the United States based on the linguistics department at MIT (and largely motivated by the Chomskyan revolution in academic research on grammar). For linguists, grammar is a science in the sense that it tries to explain facts about usage by building and testing alternative theories. What makes linguistics different from other sciences, and more amenable to this treatment in schools, is that the data to be explained consist of our everyday behavior. One advantage of theorizing about our own behavior is that we are interested in it, and another is that it is freely available to inspection; but the method of working on these data is just ordinary scientific method, as applied in chemistry or physics.

The aim, then, is to teach children how to think scientifically by getting them to think about the grammatical patterns in their own language. For example, the teacher writes up the sentences "I bought the book" and "I bought a book" and asks whether they have the same meaning; if not, what is the difference? The children try out any hypotheses that they can think of—maybe you only buy *the book* if you intend to buy that particular book? The teacher helps them to test their hypotheses (e.g., in this case by changing the verb to "lost"—you can lose *the book* even though you do not intend to do so) and guides them gradually to the (or at least a) right answer (Fabb 1985; Goodluck 1991; Honda and O'Neil 1993).

The most sophisticated evaluation of the program to date is a doctoral thesis by Maya Honda (1994), who reported trials with mixed-ability seventh- and eleventh-graders that showed statistically significant improvements in two measures of the children's ability to reason scientifically. Perhaps the most impressive fact about this work is that the improvements followed just two weeks of work with each group. What emerges from all these initiatives is that grammar teaching is not only good for children, but that when it is taught well, children enjoy it and use words like *fun* and *helpful* in describing the experience.

SOME IDEAS FOR DISCOVERY LEARNING IN GRAMMAR

For the sake of concreteness I shall finish with a collection of specific ideas for grammar-based lessons graded roughly according to age, starting with 6-year-olds and leading up to 16-year olds.[7] The list is intended to illustrate the enormous range of things that can be done in the name of grammar, so the only unifying theme is the use of "discovery learning," in which children work out the rules for themselves (as in several of the other initiatives described in the previous section). As we all know, active learning is always more successful than passive, but the main point of this list is to show how grammar teaching can be systematic without being pointless. Each of these activities provides technical concepts and terminology that can later be used, as needed, in discussions of the children's own writing.

• Inflections and dictionary words: Get the children to work out the rules for plural nouns—how to segment *dogs* into *dog + s*, how the ending varies from word to word in spelling (e.g., *church + es*) and in pronunciation (*cat + s*). Consider the implications for the notion *word*: are *dog* and *dogs* different words, or the same? How would a dictionary treat them? All these things can be done by discovery learning.

• Ambiguity in jokes: Ask the children to explain a few jokes that turn on ambiguities, aiming at two broad classes of ambiguity: alternative meanings for one word (e.g., question: How can you keep cool at a football match?" "Stand next to a fan.") and alternative relationships among words (She: "The police are looking for a man with one eye called Murphy" He: "What's his other eye called?"). It does not matter how these relationships are described; for example, one completely satisfactory answer would be that *called Murphy* describes the eye or the man. The main thing is to lay the foundations for the study of sentence structure. A more general discussion of ambiguity could arise: Is ambiguity restricted to jokes? Is it a problem for readers or listeners? How can it be avoided?

• Tense: Explore the meaning differences between pairs like *I am little* and *I was little*, leading to the terms *present* and *past*. You can have a look at the inflections involved, but the main point is to discuss the choice of tenses in a narrative extract in which the teacher has doctored the second paragraph by "detensing" all the verbs (e.g., *am* or *was* changed to *be*), leaving the students to choose the tenses. The aim is for them to see how choice of tense affects the reader.

• Phrases and the apostrophe: This is about the difference between the plural ending *-s* and the possessive marker *'s*. Start with an example such as "We know every boy's name" and get the students to insert words between *boy* and *'s* (e.g., "We know every boy + in this room + 's name." Then do the same with "We know all the boys," but not "We know all the boy + in this room + s." In the process they are learning not only how to use the apostrophe, but also why correct use helps the reader. (The grammar behind this is that *'s* is added to noun phrases, but plural *-s* is added to nouns.)

• Vocabulary and style: Look carefully at the wording of a short paragraph from a well-written narrative to see how it achieves its effect, for example, how you know in each sentence or clause whose view it expresses. Pick out the particular words (or grammatical patterns) that act as clues, and explain their effect. For example, by changing *went* to *came* in "She went to him" we shift to seeing the scene from his point of view.

• Subjects, verbs, and dialects: Carry out a careful, open-minded exploration of the details of subject-verb agreement in both Standard English and the local nonstandard English, covering examples like "His family are all away," "We was talking" and (maybe) "She live here." This can lead into discussions of correctness, status, and so on as well as grammatical details, while (incidentally) allowing some teaching of the details of Standard English.

• Purposes and indirectness: Why do teenage magazines wrap information up in so many words? (Why: "X is itching to spill the beans on Y?" Why not: "X wants to talk about Y?") Take an extract and translate it into the prosaic minimum of words; then consider what has been lost in terms of excitement, challenge, mystery, and so on.

• Presuppositions: What is the meaning of *yet* in "Have you got a car yet?"? Why is it so hard to argue against the presupposition that *yet* carries? This can be extended into an exploration of advertisements and other persuasive texts.

• Passives: Collect some examples of passive verbs in a scientific text and a newspaper article and compare the reasons (good and bad) for using passives rather than actives. The immediate point is to deepen the students' understanding of grammatical conventions, but such activities also relate to general topics such as genre differences and probably help children's own use. The "active/passive" terminology is just a useful byproduct.

• End-weight and readability: Present a sentence with a long subject and ask for alternative (and preferably better) ways of organizing the same words without loss of meaning. For example, start with this pair:

(1) a. That we missed the bus upset me.

   b. It upset me that we missed the bus.

Ask the students which they prefer, and why. Is their preferred one shorter or longer than the other? Then ask them to complete this pair:

(2) a. That the rabbit escaped when I left the hutch open is a nuisance.

   b. ??

To do this, they must be able to recognize a subordinate clause (*that the rabbit escaped when I left the hutch open*) that is the subject of a higher clause and that itself contains a smaller subordinate clause (*when I left the hutch open*). Finally, work out with them the rule for converting between the two patterns, using whatever terminology is helpful—"subject," "subordinate clause," or even "extraposition" (the name for pattern b). Extraposition is an important item in any writer's tool kit, so why not give it a name for future use in context? Moreover, it would be hard to discuss the pros and cons of extraposition without considering the needs of readers, which is perhaps the most important general topic in the training of any writer.

CONCLUSION

Grammar teaching seems to be on the way back after a period of absence, but we must make sure that it is free of the fatal weaknesses that almost killed it. I should like to highlight just three morals of the recent history:

• Grammar teaching must not be tied to the teaching of Standard English. However much politicians and others may wish to make this connection, it should be resisted. In this chapter I have hardly mentioned Standard English, and I have assumed throughout that grammar applies just as well, and just as usefully, to nonstandard words and constructions as to those of Standard English. Identifying "grammar" with Standard English alienates those students whose native language is rejected as simply wrong. This was one of the main weaknesses of the 1950s.

• Grammar teaching must focus on the facts and on the children. In old-fashioned grammar teaching, grammar was defined by the tradition, so there was no point in looking at actual usage, least of all the usage of the children; the teacher was the expert, and the children's role was to learn this expertise. In modern grammar, the facts are paramount, and the children are coexperts in studying the facts. The teacher's expertise lies in analysis and in knowledge of certain kinds of language (academic and Standard), but the children are experts on the language of their home and the local community. The teacher's role is to guide the pupils through the grammar they know already, providing established ideas and terminology as required. This is much harder for both teacher and pupil, but much more fun.

• Grammar teaching must have a clear purpose. Old-fashioned grammar teaching was often decontextualized and pointless. The exercises led nowhere, and the terminology was never used except in the exercises. The approach taken here is that grammar teaching has many purposes, all of which are educationally respectable. Teaching children to write better is one important use of grammar, but only one.

Grammar teaching really needs justifying—NOT!

NOTES

In writing this chapter I have been helped by Ewa Jaworska, Nigel Fabb, Geoff Barton, and Catherine Wallace, but most of all by Rebecca Wheeler, whose enthusiasm, energy, efficiency, and sensitivity have been exemplary.

1. Apparently a "NOT-spotter" has found one in a novel published as early as 1910. There was a discussion of this construction on the *Linguist* list in early 1992, archived at *http://linguistlist.org*; the citation (by Larry Horn) is in message 3.320. Here is a more recent example of the postsentential NOT, produced by no less a person than Stephen Pinker (1994, 356): "Aha! The theory is circular! . . . Natural selection is 'the survival of the fittest' and the definition of 'the fittest' is 'those who survive.' Not!!"

2. The arguments against grammar teaching are reviewed conveniently in Weaver (1996, chap. 2). There is a very useful survey by the same author at *http://www.heinemann.com/hbbc*. Some of this research is weak or inconclusive; for criticisms, see, e.g., Tomlinson (1994), Honey (1997, 185–90), and especially Qualification and Curriculum Authority (1998). Some research even shows that decontextualized grammar teaching can improve students' writings, e.g., Bateman and Zidonis (1966).

3. I collected the information reported here via the *Linguist* list in September 1997. My summary can be found in the archive, *http://linguistlist.org*, in message 8.1330.

4. See Weaver (1990). The web site for whole language is at *http://ericir.syr.edu/Eric*.

5. Apart from a large number of books and articles, Halliday was responsible for a very important set of materials for teaching language at the secondary level, published as Doughty, Pearce, and Thornton (1971). These materials are still regarded as among the best ever produced, but their uptake in schools was disappointing. The most likely explanation is that they required too sophisticated an understanding of language by the teachers; they were not "teacher-proof." This is a recurrent theme in attempts to develop language teaching in schools: the best plans and materials can be thwarted by the lack of teachers who can put them into practice. If anything, the demand for "decontextualized" grammar teaching makes the teacher's task even harder because it precludes preparation.

6. The journal is called *Language Awareness* and is published by Multilingual Matters (*multi@multi.demon.co.uk*). The association is the Association for Language Awareness, whose membership details can be found in the journal or from the publisher.

7. These ideas are spelled out in more detail in Hudson (1992). As for the details of sentence analysis, I suggest a new system in Hudson (1998a). This approach is a blend of modern linguistics with old-fashioned approaches that some students find easier to learn than other modern systems.

REFERENCES

Barton, Geoff. 1997. Grammar without shame. *Use of English* 48.2: 107–18.
Bateman, D., and F. Zidonis. 1966. *The effect of a transformational study of gram-*

mar on the writing of ninth and tenth graders. Champaign, IL: National Council of Teachers of English.

Carter, Ronald. 1996. Politics and knowledge about language: The LINC project. *Literacy in society*, ed. by R. Hasan and G. Williams, 1–28. London: Longman.

Chomsky, Noam. 1969. Should traditional grammar be ended or mended? *Educational Review* 22.1 (November): 5–17.

Doughty, Peter, John Pearce, and Geoffrey Thornton. 1971. *Language in use*. London: Arnold.

Fabb, Nigel. 1985. Linguistics for ten-year-olds. *MIT Working Papers in Linguistics* 6: 45–61.

Goodluck, Helen. 1991. More linguistics for ten-year-olds. *Innovations in Linguistics Education* 5: 35–41.

Hawkins, Eric. 1984. *Awareness of language: An introduction*. Cambridge: Cambridge University Press.

Heap, Brian. 1991. Evaluating the effects of an LA course. *Language awareness in the classroom*, ed. by Carl James and Peter Garrett, (247–53). London: Longman.

Her Majesty's Stationary Office (HMSO). 1975. *A language for life*. London: Her Majesty's Stationery Office.

Honda, Maya. 1994. Linguistic inquiry in the science classroom. Harvard dissertation, MIT Occasional Papers in Linguistics 6.

Honda, Maya, and Wayne O'Neil. 1993. Triggering science-forming capacity through linguistic inquiry. *The view from building 20: Essays in Linguistics in honor of Sylvain Bromberger*, ed. K. Hale and S. J. Keyser, 229–55. Cambridge, MA: MIT Press.

Honey, John. 1997. *Language is power: The story of Standard English and its enemies*. London: Faber and Faber.

Hudson, Richard. 1992. *Teaching grammar: A guide for the national curriculum*. Oxford: Blackwell.

———. 1998a. *English grammar*. London: Routledge.

———. 1998b. Is grammar teachable? *English 4–11*. 2: 11–14.

James, Carl, and Peter Garrett, eds. 1991. *Language awareness in the classroom*. London: Longman.

Mason, Mary, Bob Mason, and Tony Quayle. 1992. Illuminating English: How explicit language teaching improved public examination results in a comprehensive school. *Educational Studies* 18: 341–53.

Pinker, Steven. 1994. *The language instinct*. London: Penguin.

Qualification and Curriculum Authority. 1998. Recent research on grammar teaching. *The grammar papers: Perspectives on the teaching of grammar in the national curriculum*, 45–56. Hayes: Qualification and Curriculum Authority. The QCA is the governmental authority responsible for the curriculum in the schools of England and Wales. Its publications are available from QCA Publications, PO Box 235, Hayes, Middlesex UB3 1HF (phone: 0181 867 3333; fax: 0181 867 3233).

Rothery, Joan. 1996. Making changes: Developing an educational linguistics. *Literacy in society*, ed. by R. Hasan and G. Williams, 86–123, London: Longman.

Tomlinson, David. 1994. Errors in the research into the effectiveness of grammar teaching. *English Education* 28: 20–26.

Weaver, Constance. 1990. *Understanding whole language.* Portsmouth, NH: Heinemann.

———. 1996. *Teaching grammar in context.* Portsmouth, NH: Heinemann.

Williams, Geoff. 1995. Learning systemic functional grammar in primary schools. Macquarie: Macquarie University Style Council.

Williamson, John, and Frank Hardman. 1995. Time for refilling the bath? A study of primary student-teachers' grammatical knowledge. *Language and Education* 9: 117–34.

III

LANGUAGE AND WRITING

10

Writing Standard English IS Acquiring a Second Language

Susan K. Heck

As I sat down to grade my students' first essays of the semester, I was a bit overwhelmed by the massive stack of papers in front of me and somewhat bewildered by the task. I could not help but wonder what challenges these students faced; after five weeks of class, I was reading their first efforts at formal essays. Resigning myself to the fact that I would be working for a while, and knowing that the only way to finish was to go one paper at a time, I pulled the first essay off the stack, propped my feet up in my recliner, and began to read about a student's hiking trip the previous summer.

"My rendezvous with the earth's enigmas revealed such salubrious divinities that an ineffable allurement encompassed me. Nature miraculously engulfed me with her exquisite loveliness." I was flabbergasted. This student's in-class writing and homework sounded nothing like what I was reading. How should I respond? Surely matters of purpose, audience, and concise language were relevant, but I wanted to be careful not to insult or discourage her. She was very confident in her writing ability. My initial reaction, however, was simply to ask her how many times she consulted her thesaurus. I hesitatingly put her essay aside, deciding to respond to it later. I desperately hoped that I would have a moment of inspiration before I finished reading the other essays.

Although the example from my student may seem extreme, the situation is not uncommon. Beginning writers have tremendous difficulty learning the conventions of academic discourse, even though they are writing in the "same language" that they have been speaking since they were children. The results are often awkward, and they become frustrated and discouraged. I began to realize that while my student had reached the point of understanding that spoken and written language are different, she had not yet come to command the relevant differences. That is, in seeking to communicate in a new dialect, she had overshot her mark. Of course, as Williams (1994) points out, such overshooting is a necessary step in writing acquisition. I needed to acknowledge that she understood the distinction between spoken and written language and that she had an extensive vocabulary. Only then could I begin to teach her about considering audience and purpose.

Indeed, the numerous differences between spoken and written language (Ong 1981; Brown and Yule 1983; Chafe 1986; Rubin and Dodd 1987) complicate the process of writing acquisition for beginning students. "Acceptable" speech patterns suddenly become "unacceptable" academic writing, and this understandably frustrates them. Although the language seems the same at first, when students begin to encounter and acknowledge the differences between spoken English and written English, they are, essentially, learning a new "language" (Falk 1979).

I began to think that there might be a parallel between learning written English and learning second languages as I was reading a text by Larsen-Freeman and Long (1991) on second-language acquisition (SLA). The text discusses the second-language phenomenon of *blending* and *blurring* words and phrases. For example, a student learning English as a second language might create a sentence such as "She looked at the problem from both *standpoints of view*," blending "standpoints" with "points of view." This helped me understand something my student had done in her essay. She created the word *encountenance*, mixing the words *encounter* and *countenance*. She was not the only one, either; I quickly found another example from a student who wrote, "Independence, as he knew it, *deceased* to exist," blending *deceased* and *ceased to exist*. Even though both students speak English as a first language, I began to think that there might indeed be a parallel between their acquisition of writing skills in English and the acquisition of a second language. If so, then perhaps I could understand and explain their errors just as a language teacher would explain the differences between Spanish and English to a Spanish-speaking student learning English as a second language.

Confirming my suspicions, I began to find examples of other second-language phenomena in my students' writing. Along with blending and blurring, examples of *overgeneralization* were especially prominent. Overgeneralization is the application of a newly learned rule to situations where it does not apply. For example, a common overgeneralization that students learning English as a second language make is the extension of the rule for past-tense formation to all verbs, adding -*ed* even to irregular verbs. Thus one ESL student wrote, "I *goed* to school yesterday" instead of "I went to school yesterday." Based on the student's knowledge of English at that time, it made good sense to write *goed*. She was following her own linguistic standard that was based on her prior knowledge of English and the rules she knew, and she was learning. Now she simply needed to learn the exceptions to the rule.

Overgeneralization also seemed to explain a native-English-speaking student's difficulty with mastering the rules of comma usage. As I graded her first essay, I noticed that she completely avoided using internal punctuation in her writing, producing a series of simple subject-verb-object sentences with no variation:

> My mother and I got in the car.
> We went to the mall.
> We went shopping and had lunch.

I concluded that she might be unsure of the rules of punctuation, so we talked extensively about the use of commas before the next essay, especially the use of commas with coordinating conjunctions. Her second essay contained revisions such as "My mother, and I got in the car, and then went to the mall." At first, I considered my attempt at teaching comma usage to be a failure. However, when I looked at her writing as an indication of the development of a "second language," I recognized that learning was taking place. She was not avoiding the use of commas anymore, and she had learned (and overgeneralized) that commas often are placed in front of words like *and, but* and *however*. Although she had not yet mastered the rules of comma usage, the idea of using commas before coordinating conjunctions had entered her written English. Again, she was following her own linguistic standard, based on her competency in spoken English and what she had learned about Standard Written English, and she was learning, just like the ESL student who overgeneralized the rule for past-tense formation.

Students also overgeneralize the structure of academic discourse in their essays. One student, when faced with the task of writing a narrative essay about a significant event, promptly began to write an outline in standard five-paragraph theme format, complete with a three-point thesis, paragraphs to develop each point, and a conclusion that summarized the three points. During a conference, I asked him why he chose to apply this strict format to a narrative essay, and he responded, "Well, I thought that five-paragraph themes were good writing in college." I showed him examples of other narrative essays, and we began to talk about different options that authors use for organization and how different genres often require different approaches.

Another common second-language learning challenge that I saw in my students' writing was *transfer*. Transfer occurs when students use elements of their first language to help in the acquisition of other languages. For example, beginning English-speaking students learning Spanish often reverse adjective-noun word order in Spanish to match the word order in English. They create phrases like *el blanco perro* 'the white dog', which matches English word order, instead of using the Spanish word order for nouns and adjectives, *el perro blanco* 'the dog white.' Without exposure to other languages that order adjectives and nouns differently, the English speaker assumes that the word order of other languages will be the same as in English.

Beginning writers also often transfer the similarity of the sounds they hear in spoken English to spelling in written English. Students write sentences such as "The bag was *to* small for *it's* contents," confusing the spelling and meaning of *too/to* and *it's/its*. Other common confusions are *your/you're* ("I hope that *your* doing fine") and *their/they're/there* ("We know that *their* taking English 101 this semester"). Another student wrote, "I *now* that my father is coming to visit this weekend," again demonstrating transfer of the sounds of spoken English to written English. It is easy to forget the *k* at the beginning of the word when it does not "sound" like it belongs there. Eventually, students become more aware of these errors as they differentiate between spellings when there is little difference in sound.

Beginning writers also transfer the speaking patterns of English into their writing. While describing his senior high-school football season, one of my students wrote: "We just crushed every opponent. No one got in our way. We ran it inside, outside, and right down their throats. But the sixth game had loss written all over it. It was a Saturday game and our school is 'O' for the century on Saturday." When we spoke about his essay, he had difficulty recognizing the informal, oral language conventions he was using in his writing. Naturally, they "sounded" normal to him, especially when he read the essay out loud, and he could not think of any other way to express the same ideas without using the same words. His transfer of the speech patterns of his oral dialect into his written English is similar to an ESL student's transfer of sounds, words, and grammatical constructions from his or her native language into English.

These challenges, combined with the examples of blending, blurring, and overgeneralization, suggest that beginning writing students are truly struggling to learn the conventions of a new language. As I began researching the acquisition of writing in beginning composition students, I found many scholars who agreed with my premise that learning to write Standard English is parallel to learning a second language. Several scholars agree that beginning writers develop writing skills and achieve proficiency similarly to the way other adults develop second-language skills (Horning 1987; Falk 1979; Esau and Keene 1981). They encounter difficulties, produce developmental errors, and progress through learning stages similar to those of students learning a second language, even though they are writing in their native language. The key to understanding writing students' developmental processes and helping them progress is acknowledging that they are en-countering a new language system, Standard Written English (SWE), that is distinct from the oral dialects they have been speaking since they were children. In fact, as they develop their writing skills, the language they produce is a combination of their oral language and what they know about the conventions of Standard Written English. Their errors, instead of being problems, often become guideposts to their progress, showing increasing mastery of new conventions.

Understanding the parallel between writing acquisition and second-language acquisition helps teachers better understand the sources of student writing errors so they can help students to progress toward mastery of written English. Shaughnessy (1977) claims that beginning writers' errors are "intelligent," and that their errors can be used to help them learn. Teachers must realize that beginning writing students already have consid-erable linguistic skill in their oral language, and they use this skill when they are learning to write (Farr and Daniels 1986). Unfortunately, the in-telligence of student writing errors is not always acknowledged, and in-stead, teachers reprimand students for their errors. Explaining to students why they make certain errors will be more helpful to them than simply forcing them to memorize the rules of written English. They will be more likely to remember the difference between the modes of discourse if they understand their mistakes.

By understanding the parallel between writing acquisition and second-language acquisition, teachers will also improve their perceptions of basic writers' challenges and their attitudes toward errors in writing (Horning 1987). In addition, recognizing a writing student's oral language ability not only changes the teacher's perception, but encourages the student. Realizing that students have already learned to use oral language effectively on their own terms will increase their confidence as they face the challenges of learn-ing to write Standard English as well as providing the composition instruc-tor with a foundation on which to begin building the student's writing skills. A teacher who acknowledges and draws upon prior knowledge can use it to measure student progress and encourage the student toward mas-tery of a new language.

REFERENCES

Brown, Gillian, and George Yule. 1983. *Discourse analysis*. Cambridge: Cambridge University Press.

Chafe, Wallace. 1986. Writing in the perspective of speaking. *Studying writing: Linguistic approaches*, ed. by Charles R. Cooper and Sidney Greenbaum, 12–39. Beverly Hills: Sage.

Esau, Helmut, and Michael Keene. 1981. A TESOL method for native-language writing instruction: In search of a model for the teaching of writing. *College English* 43: 694–710.

Falk, Julia. 1979. Language acquisition and the teaching and learning of writing. *College English* 41: 436–47.

Farr, Marcia, and Harvey Daniels. 1986. *Language diversity and writing instruction*. New York: ERIC.

Horning, Alice. 1987. *Teaching writing as a second language*. Carbondale: Southern Illinois University Press.

Larsen-Freeman, Diane, and Michael Long. 1991. *An introduction to second language acquisition research*. London: Longman.

Ong, Walter. 1981. Literacy and orality in our times. *The writing teacher's sourcebook*, ed. by Gary Tate and Edward P. J. Corbett, 36–49. New York: Oxford University Press.

Rubin, Donald, and William Dodd. 1987. *Talking into writing*. Urbana, IL: ERIC.

Shaughnessy, Mina. 1977. *Errors and expectations: A guide for the teacher of basic writing*. New York: Oxford University Press.

Williams, Ann. 1994. Talk written down? The sociolinguistics of school writing. *Writing vs. speaking*, ed. by Svetla Cmejrkova, Frantisek Danes, and Eva Havlová, et al., 283–90. Tübingen, Germany: Günter Narr.

Reading, Writing, and Linguistics: Principles from the Little Red Schoolhouse

Gail Brendel Viechnicki

In my college-level composition courses, I frequently encounter paragraphs like the following in my students' papers:

> (1a) Oral history has played an important role over the millennia because it helps to represent groups and people who are illiterate. Accounts can be transferred from person to person anywhere in the world, and it can be done without pencils and paper. Later, when the culture becomes more advanced or when outsiders happen upon the illiterate groups, the accounts can be written down. This is one reason why we know the little that we do about ancient cultures.[1]

The stylistic problems of this paragraph are typical of advanced academic prose: something strikes us as awkward about it, but it is difficult to see exactly how it could be improved. Our first reaction might be to mark this paragraph "unclear" or "awkward"; a more ambitious teacher might even comment that its sentences "do not flow." These sorts of comments are not incorrect: we do stumble a bit when we read this paragraph, and we may be tempted to reread it. However, by making general comments like "confused," we are simply giving our reactions to, or feelings about, the text. Because we feel confused by the text, we label it "confused."

This confusion can be the beginning of the instructional moment between the writer and her or his teacher, but it should not be the end. For real learning to occur, the writer needs to understand not just that her or his text confused me, but what about the text confused me. If the writer can predict my reactions to her or his future writing, if she or he can predict what will make me write "clear" instead of "confused," she or he will be a more successful writer. In fact, readers' reactions to texts are largely predictable, as shown by substantial linguistic, psycholinguistic, and reader-comprehension research. Linguistic research can form the bridge between readers' intuitive reactions to texts, on the one hand, and, on the other hand, principled revision strategies that help writers get the reactions that they want from their readers. Thus I claim that the teaching of academic writing can benefit from linguistic insights. Such linguistic insights about the structure of language and about how readers understand texts are captured by the University of Chicago's Little Red Schoolhouse (LRS) writing program. LRS uses readers' reactions to certain combinations of linguistic structures in order to articulate specific strategies for revision; because of this, it is sometimes called a "reader-based" approach to teaching writing (Williams and Colomb 1993, 258–59).[2] In what follows, I argue that this approach to teaching writing has proven so successful precisely because of its linguistic foundation. I will illustrate this claim with a brief discussion of the revisions that I suggested to three student writers.

One of the stylistic problems that LRS handles particularly well is that of information flow. The basic premise is this: readers need old information in order to understand new information, and readers need these two kinds of information to be in specific locations within each sentence. Substantial linguistic and psycholinguistic research shows that readers prefer old information to be at the beginning of sentences, while they prefer new information to be at the ends of sentences (Firbas 1964, 1992; Clark and Haviland 1977; Clark and Clark 1977). New information in one sentence becomes old information in the next; the current ideas chain together sentences into a coherent whole. This type of information structure facilitates comprehension: we use the (new) information at the end of a sentence to help us understand the following sentence, and hence the rest of the text.[3] When a text violates this information structure, it is often hard to follow. For example, one of the reasons that (1a) is difficult to understand is that new information precedes old information; as we said before, "it does not flow."

In particular, the first sentence of (1a) ends with the phrase "people who are illiterate." Because it is at the end of the sentence, readers expect the next sentence to build on the concept of illiteracy. However, the writer starts her next sentence by mentioning "[a]ccounts," a "new" concept, and then ends her sentence with a reference ("without pencils and paper") to the "old" concept of illiteracy. Again, in the third sentence, she puts the by-now-"old" idea "accounts" at the end of the sentence. In effect, she has reversed the expected flow of information. Suppose that we revise her paragraph according to LRS's principles of information structure:

(1b) Oral history has played an important role over the millennia because it
helps to represent groups and [people who are illiterate]$_{new info}$. [Without

pencils or papers]$_{old info}$, people anywhere in the world can transfer [accounts of history]$_{new info}$. Later, [those oral accounts of history]$_{old info}$ can be [written down when the culture becomes more advanced or when outsiders happen upon the illiterate groups]$_{new info}$.

Suddenly, her paragraph becomes more "readable" and "clear" than it had been, simply because we restructured its flow of information. The information-flow strategy proved useful not only for this paper: in subsequent papers, this student used this revision technique to write papers that her readers found much clearer.[4]

Reversed information flow is not the only stylistic problem that I confront in advanced undergraduate papers. Consider paragraph (2a):

(2a) The application of the "law of diminishing marginal demand" to the market is easy to understand. Over-saturation of the market with one consumer good can quickly and easily cause the decrease of the value of the good. [. . .] To explain the "law of diminishing value of return" we will use another example. On a large task the cooperation of many workers working together to get the job done may cause mass confusion. This confusion will decrease the productivity of the group.[5]

This is also problematic, but it evokes a different set of reactions than (1a) did; we call (2a) "wordy," "too abstract," "hard to understand." These words communicate how we as readers feel about the text: we have a hard time understanding this paragraph, and we feel that there are "too many (abstract) words." Comments that form a basis for the upcoming revision process might be something like "write more specifically" or "make the relationship between your ideas clear." But unless we give concrete suggestions for revision, we may only frustrate our students. How does one "write more specifically"?

To provide a solution to this writer's difficulties, we turn to another linguistically grounded principle. Research has shown that readers prefer that the crucial "actions" of a sentence be located in verbs, and that the "characters" performing these actions be located in subject positions (Williams 1996a, 5). Instead of following this preferred pattern, however, writers of academic prose often displace actions away from verbs by turning them into derived abstract nouns ("nominalizations") and displace characters from subjects by moving them elsewhere (to be objects of prepositions, or possessors of nouns, for example), or by deleting them altogether.[6] In a typical article in a scholarly journal, the action of most sentences is hidden in abstract nominalizations, and as a result, most sentences have twice as many prepositional phrases (preposition plus abstract nominalization) as they have verbs (Williams 1996b, 18). In fact, it is this feature that distinguishes academic writing from other genres. Even though this writing style is widespread, readers consistently judge it to be "difficult to understand," "too abstract," and even "pompous." Readers want actions in verbs and characters in subjects.

My students, however, typically object at this point. They think that if they replace abstract nominalizations and prepositional phrases with finite verbs and subjects, they will produce simple, nonacademic "Dick and Jane"–type prose. The students who object have correctly recognized that part of their educational task is to learn the language of the academic community. Indeed, one of the hard parts of teaching composition is balancing the need for clarity with the need to "speak the lingo." Furthermore, some students argue that the ideas in most academic papers are just too complicated to be written about simply. It is true that the action of an academic sentence is seldom a simple prototypical action like movement, for example; and its characters are often abstract, complex ideas. But the complex sentences sometimes required in academic writing do not have to be hard to read or understand. We can write very complex sentences that readers can move through quite easily. The point of this principle is to remove gratuitous difficulty by avoiding not all nominalizations, but only the ones that hide crucial action (Williams 1996a; Williams 1996b, 19; see also note 6). This will improve clarity without making prose sound too simple.

Moreover, when students overuse and misuse abstract nominalizations, the logical relationships between ideas are often obscured. For example, in (2a), what character does the "oversaturating" and "applying" is not made clear. I have found that students imitate a style with many abstract nominalizations especially when they are unfamiliar with a topic. For example, the writer of (2a) was just learning about economics when she wrote this paper, and she was unable to talk or write about the subject without using the heavily nominalized language that her textbooks had used to describe it. For her, abstract nominalizations were "psychological sanctuaries" that enabled her to discuss economics without clearly stating how various ideas related to one another. Thus to revise this paragraph our writer will have to address these ambiguities.

The clarity of (2a) can be improved by removing its abstract nominalizations. As it stands now, the "action" resides in verbs-turned-nouns: "application," "oversaturation," "lowering," "value," "cooperation," "confusion," "productivity." The characters who perform the action are not in subject positions, but are either the objects of prepositional phrases ("of many workers," "of the group"), or they are deleted altogether (there is no character expressed who does the "oversaturating" or "applying," as already noted). Our LRS principle correctly predicts that these sentences will be awkward because the characters and actions are not in the syntactic positions where readers expect to find them. Consider the following revision:

(2b) When [we]$_{character}$ [apply]$_{action}$ the "law of diminishing marginal demand" to the market, [we]$_{character}$ [find]$_{action}$ that the concept is easier to understand. When [manufacturers]$_{character}$ [oversaturate]$_{action}$ the market with one consumer good, [they]$_{character}$ [can quickly and easily decrease]$_{action}$ how much the good is worth. [. . .] To explain the "law of diminishing value of return" we will use another example. When [workers]$_{character}$ [cooperate]$_{action}$ to complete a large task [they]$_{character}$ [become confused]$_{action}$ and when [they]$_{character}$ [do]$_{action}$ [they]$_{character}$ [work]$_{action}$ less productively.

The revision of this paragraph seems to us "clearer" and "less confused," and our reaction is entirely predictable: we like this version better than (2a) because here the action is in verbs, and the characters performing that action are in subject positions. Not only does this revision sound better to us, but by suggesting that this student limit her use of abstract nominalizations, we compelled her to make clear the relationships between her ideas. In fact, it is largely due to this one principle that this student's thinking and writing about economics improved tremendously over the ten-week quarter.

Finally, consider a third kind of problematic sentence I find in academic writing:

(3a) One interesting example of oral history, written down in the early twentieth century by historians who interviewed ex-slaves after the Emancipation, is slave narratives.[7]

This is another example where our comments to the student, perhaps "hard to follow," reflect our reaction to the text: we have a hard time following this sentence. How do we arrive at a concrete revision strategy from a personal reaction? To answer this, we again turn to a linguistically based principle. This time the generalization is that readers want the subject and the verb close together and early in the sentence (Williams 1996c, 4). Psycholinguistic research has found that readers store the subject of a sentence in short-term memory until they read the verb (Clark and Clark 1977, among others). After they locate a subject-verb "core" (SV core), they store it in long-term memory and are then able to process the rest of the sentence. In our example 3a, notice where the subject is located ("One interesting example of oral history"). Then mark where the verb is ("is slave narratives"). The two are separated by quite a long stretch of text (fifteen words and three modifying clauses, to be specific). The distance between subject and verb does not bother the writer of the sentence because she already knows what verb she intends. Readers, however, do not know what verb is coming, so a sentence like this one can pose a processing problem for them. Revising according to the SV-core principle, that is, simply moving the verb closer to the subject, renders the sentence dramatically better.

(3b) [One interesting example of oral history]$_{subject}$ [is slave narratives]$_{verb}$, written down in the early twentieth century by historians who interviewed ex-slaves after the Emancipation.

In this version, we readers again get what we expect: the SV core is intact and comes early in the sentence. Because she learned a psycholinguistic generalization about memory limitations, this student paid attention to the location of subject and verb and, in so doing, secured the reaction that she wanted from her readers.

The student writers of all three of these examples benefited from a linguistic perspective. Not only are the specific principles discussed here supported by linguistic and psycholinguistic research, but also this approach to teaching writing is linguistic in general. When students are taught with this approach, they learn to look at their writing as a collection of linguistic structures on the page. That is, they learn that not only are the words they write important, but so too is the syntactic position where they locate those words. For example, students may unconsciously know that they have subjects and verbs in the sentences they write, but when we make them actually look at what words on the page are in the "subject" position and which are in the "verb" position, they ask themselves, "What is this monstrosity that is functioning as my subject?" or "Why the heck is my verb all the way over there?" That students are asking these questions at all shows that such principles have the advantage of decontextualizing text. In other words, linguistics offers writers tools they can use to distance themselves from a text; these tools help to ignite the revising process, or reopen the text, so that writers can reengage with their words (Robert Marrs, personal communication). Most writers achieve distance from a text simply by putting it down for a while and picking it up again later. But students do not have this luxury: they typically receive a paper assignment and are expected to complete it all within ten days; so for them, these linguistic tools are invaluable. In addition, these linguistic tools are transferable: students can use these revision strategies in other papers and in other classes.

Another aspect of the linguistic approach to teaching writing is that it prompts students to consider their audience. Talking about "how readers read" makes students aware that what they are writing will be read, and that the specific words and combinations of words that they write have predictable effects on their readers. For example, if they consistently put new information before old information, readers will call their writing "confused." In this way, the notion of "audience" becomes much more real for them.

Furthermore, as students become aware of their audience, they are reminded that they are readers too, and peer-review seminars become more productive in a number of ways. First of all, student reviewers discuss what they as readers understood to be old information and new information in some sentence, for instance, rather than assaulting the writer with more typical comments like "this is confused" or "you didn't make sense here." As a result, the experience is far less face-threatening for the writer, and hence the writer is more open to revision suggestions. Students absorb linguistically based suggestions for revision more easily because they realize that a large part of being judged a "good writer" simply involves giving readers what they want. Finally, students consistently report that they like linguistically oriented peer-review seminars better than they like traditional peer-review seminars: in my view, quite an accomplishment.

So, in our quest for constructive comments on these example paragraphs, we began at the level of personal reaction, but found it to be the beginning, and not the end, of the instructional moment; we needed to provide the student with principled suggestions for revision. LRS offered such principles based on broader studies of how readers read and the structure of language, and we saw three examples of how these linguistic principles could benefit students' work. Thus from personal reaction we come full circle to cognitive theories of comprehension. None of this will much interest your composition students, but it will improve their academic writing skills.

NOTES

I owe many thanks to Robert Marrs and Joseph Williams for their reactions to various drafts of this chapter. All mistakes, of course, are my own.

1. From a student paper in English 225, Academic and Professional Writing, Winter 1996, the University of Chicago.

2. A "reader-based" program like LRS is most useful for advanced undergraduate and graduate students who have little difficulty finding something to write about, but who still need help revising what they have written.

3. This concept of information flow holds at various levels of a text. At the level of the sentence, old *words* and *phrases* must precede new *words* and *phrases*. In a string of sentences, however, what comes at the beginning of each sentence should be the *topic* of that sequence of sentences (that is, old information with respect to those sentences). At the larger level of discourse, old information and new information are defined even more broadly (Williams 1996d).

4. Note, of course, that what LRS offers are strategies for *revision*. It would be unreasonable to expect students or anyone else to think about these principles while actually writing.

5. From a different student paper in English 225, Academic and Professional Writing, Winter 1996, the University of Chicago.

6. Note, of course, that not all nominalizations are "bad" for writing. *Farmer* from *farm* is fine. So is *suggestion* from *suggest* (where the nominalization names the object of the original verb "I suggest *X*"). Some nominalizations are standard

and are used all the time: election, photosynthesis, literary criticism. Also, some nominalizations can act like characters (e.g., "Research indicates . . ."), and some are useful when they refer back to something in the text (e.g., "These claims are based on . . .") (Williams 1996b, 7–10).

7. From the student paper cited in note 1.

REFERENCES

Chomsky, N. 1972. Deep structure, surface structure, and semantic interpretation. *Studies on semantics in generative grammar*, ed. by Noam Chomsky, 62–119. The Hague: Mouton.

Clark, H., and E. Clark. 1977. *Psychology and language: An introduction to psycholinguistics*. New York: Harcourt Brace Jovanovich.

Clark, H., and S. Haviland. 1977. Comprehension and the given-new contract. *Discourse production and comprehension*, ed. by Roy O. Freedle, 1–40. Hillsdale, NJ: Lawrence Erlbaum Associates.

Firbas, J. 1964. On defining the theme in functional sentence analysis. *Travaux Linguistiques de Prague* 1: 267–80.

———. 1992. *Functional sentence perspective in written and spoken communication*. Cambridge: Cambridge University Press.

Jackendoff, R. 1972. *Semantic interpretation in generative grammar*. Cambridge, MA: MIT Press.

Williams, J. 1996a. The little red schoolhouse. Session one: The principles of clarity, I: Characters/actions = subjects/verbs. Unpublished manuscript.

———. 1996b. The little red schoolhouse. Session two: The principles of clarity, II: Subjects and characters. Unpublished manuscript.

———. 1996c. The little red schoolhouse. Session three: The grammar of clarity, III: SV-Core. Unpublished manuscript.

———. 1996d. The little red schoolhouse. Session four: The architecture of clarity, IV: Information-Flow. Unpublished manuscript.

———. 1996e. *Style: Ten lessons in clarity and grace*. 5th ed. New York: Longman.

Williams, J., and G. Colomb. 1990. The University of Chicago. *Programs that work: Models and methods for writing across the curriculum*, ed. by Toby Fulwiler and Art Young, 83–113. Portsmouth, NH: Boynton/Cook Publishers.

———. 1993. The case for explicit teaching: Why what you don't know won't help you. *Research in the Teaching of English* 27.3: 252–64.

Copious Reasoning: The Student Writer as an Astute Observer of Language

Todd Oakley

The teaching of writing has become big business on college and university campuses. Not only do we have the universal requirement of freshman composition, but we have supplemental courses in advanced composition, technical writing, and business writing. With this expansion, we have also seen a concomitant proliferation of composition specialists, writing-program directors, writing centers, graduate programs, scholarly conferences, journals, and book presses. Despite these institutionalized efforts, the general sentiment among those within and without the university is that the quality of prose is not improving.

Some argue that the current "degraded" state of students' prose is due to their unfamiliarity with the grammatical rules of formal written English. Others argue that students lack adequate knowledge of the topics as well as critical-thinking skills necessary to sustain a coherent academic argument. The solution is often either to acquaint each student with the rules by rote practice or to eschew such formal concerns in the hope that they will take care of themselves once the student has developed an elaborate knowledge base.

I think that there is a more fundamental problem. Students lack fluency and refinement in the skill of *presentation*: "the act," write Francis Noël Thomas and Mark Turner, "of placing before the reader something the writer has already recognized" (1996). Interestingly, college students are virtuoso presenters in conversational situations, displaying great aptitude for orchestrating the rich compositions of sound, gesture, facial expression, body movement, and immediate response inherent in these social environments into one cohesive activity. Next to the full orchestration of speech, writing appears utterly impoverished. Not only is the detailed score of sound, gesture, facial expression, and body movement reduced to marks on paper, but no immediate response is forthcoming. Consequently, breaks in the coherence of the score occur and often go unrepaired.

Neither the "rules" nor "topics" approaches by themselves help students orchestrate written presentation. Drills in traditional grammar do not work well (Lester 1990, 333–66), because learning a set of discrete conventions— subject-verb agreement and sentence boundaries, for example—does not constitute a coherent orchestration. The topics approach assumes that continued research and reading will build a knowledge base sufficient to produce good writing without systematic understanding of the forms of discourse.[1] After all, good writing is good thinking, and good grammar is a byproduct of good thinking.

Though I agree in principle that good writing issues from good thinking, good writing is not a bundle of skills nor an accumulation of knowledge on a subject; it is a coherent intellectual activity that issues from the systematic development of a perspective on language use that the topics and rules approaches will only develop randomly and episodically. To present something to a reader, writers need not only to be virtuoso performers of language, they also need to become astute observers of language, dispassionately and disinterestedly analyzing the rhetorical effects of their own and others' writing. Is there an approach to the teaching of writing that shows promise in developing students' ability to examine patterns of the language systematically? Can we get a student to understand, for instance, why a certain word order produces one effect (perhaps one that she or he did not intend to produce) while another order produces a different effect (perhaps one that she or he did intend)? I believe that there is. I call this approach *copious reasoning*.

Copious reasoning presumes that what is important to teach is not the "correctness" of an expression or set of expressions but its "effectiveness" when considered against the possible motives of the writer and demands of the reading situation. From this perspective, correctness of forms is a byproduct of understanding the rhetorical effectiveness of those forms. For instance, what is the difference between the two grammatically correct sentences "Floyd broke the glass" and "The glass was broken by Floyd"? Both express the same objective event. If one is asked to picture the event, the first sentence instructs one to create a story that begins with Floyd's action and ends with the broken glass, while the second sentence instructs one to create a story that begins with the broken glass and proceeds backward in time to end with Floyd's action. Once one can make this conceptual distinction, one can then ask the pertinent question, what is the selective advantage of moving from cause to effect or effect to cause when telling this story? Prompting students to write, rewrite, and rearrange phrases and sentences that express ostensibly the same event or idea is copiousness, a method of language instruction developed most elaborately by the Renaissance humanist and theologian Desiderius Erasmus (1466–1536).

In *De ratione studii*, his summary program for a liberal education, Erasmus maintains (as I and other critics of the rules and topics approaches do today) that interminable drilling of rules will not teach students to present their ideas eloquently. Instead, discriminating reading and continuous practice, particularly in presenting the same subject in many different styles, will develop knowledge. Knowledge of things proceeds through knowledge of words; hence Erasmus concludes that "a person who is not skilled in the force of language is, of necessity, short sighted, deluded, and unbalanced in his judgement of things as well" (1978, 666).

Like many of the grammar mavens writing today, Erasmus noticed that young students lacked the ability to present their ideas effectively, and this observation prompted him to compose *De copia* (1512), a treatise designed to help those striving for "divine eloquence" from falling "into a kind of futile and amorphous loquacity" (1963, 11). Accumulation of linguistic material—like the Floyd sentences—forms the basis for good thinking and writing, for it is only from a wealth of material, argues Erasmus, that students can begin to balance the competing virtues of concision and amplification: the ability at once to focus attention and weed out irrelevancies and to magnify complexities and expose subtleties of a given subject (Laib 1990, 457). Through his own demonstrations, Erasmus offers students extensive instruction on how to develop a "knowledge of things" by refining their "knowledge of words." Most memorable among these exercises is chapter 33 of *De copia* (Erasmus 1978, 348–65). In it, Erasmus varies the sentence "Tuae litterae me magnopere delectarunt" ("Your letter pleased me greatly") 200 times and the sentence "Semper dum vivam tui meminero" ("Always, as long as I live, I will remember you") 195 times.

Erasmus understood writing and rewriting the same idea to be tantamount to thinking and rethinking it; thus what is to emerge from such exercises is a greater understanding of the linguistic means available to a speaker for expressing a given idea for specific persuasive purposes. What is important above all is variety, because it matches the ideal human condition. As Erasmus explains, "Nature above all delights in variety," and

just as the eyes fasten themselves on some new spectacle, so the mind is always looking round for some fresh object of interest. If it is offered a monotonous succession of similarities, it very soon wearies and turns attention elsewhere, and so everything gained by a speech is lost all at once. This disaster can easily be avoided by someone who has it at his fingertips to turn one idea into more shapes than Proteus himself is supposed to have turned into. (1978, 302)

A human being's need for variety is reflected in my own writing exercise, an up-to-date version of Erasmus's famous chapter 33. Consistent with his exercise, I ask each student to first describe a situation and then create at least five different sentences epitomizing that situation (see the Appendix to this chapter).

Rejoicing in variety does draw out the virtuoso in the student writer, but Erasmus's version does not draw out the sharp observer who can consciously channel these capacities. In isolation, the creation of these sentences is analogous to the practicing of musical scales. It makes the mind nimble, but little more. The major drawback of Erasmus's approach is its failure to provide a heuristic for thinking about how to use this material, leaving his student much like the musician who knows only scales. In my version, students not only produce abundant linguistic material, they also produce abundant commentary on the different rhetorical uses of each one. What concepts, emotions, or expectations might each sentence produce? For an explanation, I turn to the linguistic sciences.

One linguistic theory in concert with Erasmian copiousness and hence with the aim of my writing courses is Ronald Langacker's *cognitive grammar*. Like Erasmus, Langacker is not interested in "correctness" so much as he is interested in explaining "the ability of speakers to shape and construe a conceived situation in alternate ways" (1990, 213). To account for a human being's naturally endowed virtuosity with language requires building a theory and instituting a vocabulary for observing the subtle differences between such sentences as "Your letter pleased me greatly" and "I was greatly pleased by your letter." Langacker's theory does this.

Langacker starts from the premise that language structure follows the movement and order of our experiences rather than the strict order of logic. For instance, the sentence "The hammer broke the glass" can be said to refer to the same event in which Floyd is the culprit, but in this case the speaker chooses not to present Floyd's actions, but the event itself. Logically, events are causally linked to actions, but human beings often experience the events separately from the actions and, at times, are concerned only with the event itself.

Langacker offers two complementary conceptual models of thought to mirror our experiences. One way to observe the workings of the English language is to imagine words as physical entities interacting in an environment. Langacker calls this the *billiard-ball* model. This model is nested in a more general model for understanding the observance of verbal behavior, in which individuals can imagine a stage whereby characters in a setting act out variations of these billiard-ball-like happenings. We also can imagine that the events unfold before our eyes, as if viewing them from an external vantage point. Langacker calls this the *stage* model. Together these two models provide an intuitive way for analyzing linguistic material. Let us test Langacker's hypothesis that language structure follows the movement and order of "staged" experiences by considering the following examples, reminiscent of Erasmus's famous exercise:

1. Your letter pleased me greatly.
2. I was greatly pleased by your letter.
3. The letter you sent me pleased me no end.
4. She saw how pleased I was with your letter.

Observation of the inner workings of these different sentences begins by understanding these words as metaphoric entities interacting in a particular setting. Sentence 1 highlights a situation in which an unnamed person, "me," is affected by an action. Let us cast this person in the role of *patient*. The pronoun "your" corresponds to an unnamed person who is the creator of the "letter." When these two elements combine, we can now complete the cast by adding the instigator of the action, or *agent*, as well as the conveyor of the action, or *instrument*. The writer of this sentence has, in effect, assigned these particular roles to particular real-world references, thus framing a small story type in which an agent, "your," creates an object, "letter," that is used as an instrument for affecting a patient, "me." Notice that the word ordering mirrors precisely this conceptual ordering: agent, instrument, patient, and their relationships. It is a stock example of an action chain, the minimal conception constituting Langacker's billiard-ball model of events. The mental effect of receiving the letter is metaphorically patterned after a physical event of receiving an object.

Sentence 2, while maintaining the same cast of characters, orders them differently. This sentence does not mirror the canonical action chain. Instead, the movement of experience proceeds from the affected patient, "I," to the causal agent, "your," to the facilitating instrument, "letter." Though the words themselves stay the same, the story has been fundamentally altered so as to begin at the canonical ending (with the recipient's response to the letter) and end at the canonical beginning (with the creation of the letter). Understanding the conceptual difference between sentences 1 and 2 prepares the way for student writers to reflect on the contrasting rhetorical effects of each.

Sentence 1 leads the reader to expect an elaboration on the qualities of the letter itself, since it is a common assumption that grammatical subjects specify topics of discussion. Hence one might expect something like the following:

> Your letter pleased me greatly. The eloquence of your wording and the tact with which you describe your situation make it a model for all good epistolary writing.

By contrast, sentence 2 leads the reader to expect an elaboration on the recipient's mental state, such as the following:

> I was greatly pleased by your letter. When I read your greeting, I knew I had found a lifelong friend.

Let us push on a little further and consider sentence 3, "The letter you sent pleased me no end." While sentences 1 and 2 present stories of creating and reading a letter, leaving in the background the physical story of sending and receiving it, sentence 3 blends the story of the recipient's pleasure in reading the letter with a story of the physical act of delivery itself. More specifically, the grammatical subject, "you," is now ambiguously the agent or writer of the letter (the letter could have been written by someone else), but is unambiguously its messenger, now cast in the role of the *source* (a starting point of motion). But the direct object, "letter," is unambiguously cast simultaneously in the roles of instrument and of *mover* (an entity undergoing a change of location), and the pronoun, "me," is unambiguously cast simultaneously in the roles of patient and of *goal* (an endpoint of motion). In short, sentence 3 constitutes the weaving together of two story types: the static, mental story of pleasure as represented in the agent, patient, and instrument role assignment; and the dynamic, physical story of movement along a path as represented in the source, goal, and mover role assignments. The blending of these two stories is completed by the introduction of the adverbial phrase, "no end," which cues readers to conceive the recipient's mental state of pleasure in terms of continuous rectilinear motion. Our experience with motion along a path becomes the conceptual basis for presenting an abstract mental state. Blended stories, it can be pointed out, are efficient ways of presenting two different but related events in one tight package.

Sentence 4, "She saw how pleased I was with your letter," adds the role of an outside observer. Let us cast her in the role of *experiencer* (being[s] engaged in mental activity, be it intellectual, perceptual, or emotional). The simple addition of new elements changes greatly the whole purpose of the expression. No longer is the purpose simply to assert the existence of a mental state, but to verify it. The writer sets up the expectation that further sentences will elaborate on just how "she" can observe a mental state.

The models and constituent terms offered in Langacker's linguistic theory permit teacher and student to talk precisely about the inner workings of phrases and sentences. But it also has the added advantage of providing a model and vocabulary that make the activity of expository writing itself coherent. Sometimes a student will have trouble presenting a complex process in writing, say, a laboratory procedure. The possible elements one could choose are staggeringly diverse. A student may sharpen her or his focus if she or he thinks globally of the writing situation as a stage where the reader is cast as the observer. The teacher then prompts the student to ask, who are the principal actors, and in which ones is the observer most interested? Is she or he interested in the agent performing the experiment or in the order of operations? Once the student can answer these questions, she or he can then make informed decisions about what particulars to present.

If we combine instruction in the global knowledge of a situation with the local knowledge of words, we just might develop the discriminating writer and reader that Erasmus and we want to produce. But producing discriminating writers and readers requires a systematic way of helping them become astute observers of the written word. The copious-reasoning exercises attempt to cultivate the astute observer in our students by (1) establishing grammar as a legitimate and intellectually stimulating topic of study in its own right, (2) reaffirming students' belief in their own linguistic virtuosity and powers of observation, and (3) providing a means for students to look at their own writing as crafted artifacts whose effectiveness varies with audience and purpose.

APPENDIX: ACCUMULATION EXERCISE

This exercise is designed to be repeated periodically throughout the term. You should record approximately 10 versions of this study in your journal during the semester.

You begin by describing a situation or scenario and then you "express" that same situation in different ways, *emphasizing* certain information and *suppressing* other information. For example:

Situation: Floyd's little sister, Andrea, has been teasing him incessantly all morning. Angry and desirous of revenge, Floyd picks up his toy hammer, swings it, and shatters Andrea's favorite drinking glass. The shards fly in all directions; one of them hits Andrea on the arm and cuts it.

Expressions:
Floyd broke the glass with the hammer.
Floyd cut me with the glass.
The shards of glass cut Andrea's arm.
The hammer broke the glass.
The force of the hammer hitting the glass caused shards to fly in all directions.
The glass shattered, cutting Andrea's arm.
Floyd banged the hammer against the glass.
Andrea was teasing me!

As you can see, a wide variety of possibilities exist for expressing this situation. As you can also see, this process is highly selective. For each sentence, many aspects of the overall situation are left out, not being evoked or alluded to in any way: Andrea's teasing, Floyd's desire for revenge, where the hammer was lying before Floyd picked it up, and so on. *What elements get profiled depend largely on what aspects of the situation the speaker wishes to evoke for specific expressive purposes.*

After describing a simple situation like the one just given, and after expressing it in at least five different ways, you should provide a brief commentary on the rhetorical effects of each. Here are some basic tools for analyzing the inner workings of phrase and sentences.

Semantic Roles

The following roles should be thought of as highly abstract conceptual patterns that relate to specific words in a sentence. They are not the same as grammatical categories.

agent = instigator of the action or event

patient = something/someone affected by the agent

instrument = object used to affect the patient via direct contact

experiencer = beings engaging in mental activity, be it emotive, perceptual, or intellectual

mover = an entity undergoing a change of location

source = starting point of an event or motion

goal = endpoint of an event or motion

location = place of object or event

Grammatical Categories

The English language is said to follow predominantly this pattern: subject—verb—object. The sentence "I like him" follows this pattern, where "I" functions semantically as the agent and "him" as the patient or theme. Although this pattern is predominant, speakers of English use a variety of other patterns, such as direct object—subject—verb, as in "Him I like." (The semantic roles remain the same.) Some patterns, however, do not work so well, for instance, verb—subject—direct object for "Like I him" or verb—direct object—subject for "Like him I." I encourage you to play with these "weird" structures as well. If you create an "ungrammatical" sentence, describe why you consider it so. Subjects, verbs, and direct objects are the three main grammatical categories, but they are not the only ones. Other categories include *indirect objects* and *prepositions*. For example, "I baked Cindy a cake for her birthday" follows this pattern: subject—verb—

indirect object—direct object—prepositional phrase, where the subject (I) acts as the agent-source, the indirect object (Cindy) as the goal, the direct object (cake) as the patient, and the prepositional phrase (for her birthday) as the goal because of its association with the indirect object.

Sample Analysis

The sentence "Floyd cut me with the glass" profiles the subject "Floyd" as the agent of the act and the preposition "with the glass" as the instrument for bringing it about. The direct object "me" functions as the patient. Andrea would most likely be the speaker because she wishes to assign blame. By contrast, the sentence "The glass shattered, cutting Andrea's arm" suppresses the agent and instrument of the act altogether, focusing instead on the resulting effects. This is an example of a patient-subject sentence. Floyd or a third party (Floyd's friend) might be the speaker because the use of this construction suppresses agency, thereby mitigating blame. The sentence "The force of the hammer hitting the glass caused shards to fly in all directions" suppresses both the agent and patient roles in favor of the instrument role, "force of the hammer," as the grammatical subject. The direct object, "shards," functions in the mover role. The speaker may be a physicist whose only interest is physical contact between hammer and glass. The status of what lies "upstream" (the agent, "Floyd") or ultimately "downstream" (the patient, "Andrea") is not important.

You should begin with a simple situation like the one described here, but as the semester progresses you will (with my help) choose more abstract situations, perhaps some directly relevant to your paper topics.

NOTE

1. The rules and topics approaches correspond to Linda Flower's distinction between *schema-driven planning* and *knowledge-driven planning* (1994, 132–35).

REFERENCES

Erasmus, Desiderius. 1963. *On copia of words and ideas.* Trans. and intro. by Donald B. King and H. David Rix. Milwaukee, WI: Marquette University Press.
———. 1978. *Collected works of Erasmus.* Vol. 24, *Copia: Foundations of the abundant style.* Trans. by Betty Knott. Toronto: University of Toronto Press.
Flower, Linda. 1994. *The construction of negotiated meaning: A social cognitive theory of writing.* Carbondale: Southern Illinois University Press.
Laib, Nevin. 1990. Conciseness and amplification. *College Composition and Communication* 41:443–59.
Langacker, Ronald. 1990. Settings, participants, and grammatical relations. *Mean-*

ings and prototypes: Studies in linguistic categorization, ed. by S. L. Tso-hatzidis, 213–38. London: Routledge.

Lester, Mark. 1990. *Grammar in the classroom.* New York: Macmillan.

Thomas, Francis Noël, and Mark Turner. What's wrong with college English. Clear and simple as the truth Web site, 1996, *http://www.wam.umd.edu/~mturn/WWW/thinking.html* (January 1, 1998).

Writing Well in an Unknown Language: Linguistics and Composition in an English Department

Victor Raskin

Linguistics and rhetoric and composition often reside in the same departments, which are most commonly departments of English, but occasionally these two disciplines may be housed also in a speech and language or even a communication department. My own experience is about eighteen years of active and happy interaction between an English linguistics program and a rhetoric and composition program in a fairly large English department, and I will focus on this kind of arrangement (following a somewhat unusual and boring path for an academic, namely, talking about things one knows well).

Having started originally as language units, departments of English in this country, much more than in other English-speaking countries, became predominantly, if not exclusively, literature departments. A typical composition of a medium-size English department is a couple of dozen literary scholar-teachers, divided among the various periods of British and American literature, poetry, and drama, perhaps an Old/Middle English scholar, and possibly a writing-lab director. In some universities, there may be a separate linguistics program or even a small department and/or a smattering of linguists in a foreign-languages department, a communication department, or some other adjacent unit.

Within the last two decades or so, however, pretty sizable programs in writing and in linguistics have emerged within the larger English departments. At the same time, smaller units have started advertising for linguists and/or writing specialists as well. A typical story behind these developments is the hiring of one successful rhetorician or a linguist who is well read and appreciative of belles lettres. If that newly hired linguist's or rhetorician's courses become successful and overfilled, the department will hire another specialist, and another, and so on and so forth. I am actually plagiarizing this story from the history of the emergence, early last century, of the Jewish community in Lafayette, Indiana, one of the oldest and most successful Jewish communities in the Midwest, which has enjoyed almost idyllic relations with the Gentiles over almost two centuries. Unexpected and frivolous as this comparison may seem, this history is not a bad path for the rhetoricians and linguists to try to emulate. It is also very close to the history of my own department.

The reality in an English department has not always been that rosy. A predominantly literary department will tend to continue on its path for a while, often ignoring the needs of the nonliterature faculty and students. In many cases, it is a benign neglect. Nevertheless, the rhetoricians and linguists will have to work toward different requirements and other allowances for their students. It is a long and at times tortuous task, but it results in a very positive development: the forging of political and, eventually, academic ties between these two minorities.

These days, that late in the game, it is no longer uncommon for an English department to be past this transition phase and to have become reasonably diverse and pluralistic, especially at large institutions, and the faculty of various coexisting programs have largely learned to be tolerant and understanding of each other's needs and peculiarities. This is good, but we can do better than that. For some pairs or even groups of programs, this situation has created a unique opportunity for interdisciplinary cooperation without crossing departmental barriers. English linguistics and rhetoric and composition provide a truly fertile ground for a most interesting interface, with far-reaching and enlightening ramifications for both disciplines. This chapter explores the following issues:

- Differences and similarities between the two disciplines
- Nature of the overlap(s) between them
- The best manner of interdisciplinary cooperation between them
- The related theoretical issue of metaphorical extensions in applications

DIFFERENCES AND SIMILARITIES BETWEEN LINGUISTICS AND RHETORIC AND COMPOSITION

The most striking similarity between the two disciplines is that both deal with language. But so what? Linguistics, often defined as the scientific study of language, cannot claim any monopoly of this subject of research: in fact, there are many different disciplines that center on language, such as literary criticism, communication, and much of philosophy. We must do better than that to establish affinity between linguistics and writing.

Linguistics has been predominantly theoretical in this century, and it tends to study language as a rule-governed abstract entity, internalized in the mind of the native speaker and serving as the basis of a natural communicative faculty. Some linguists would say that there is linguistics and then there is sociolinguistics, which studies, basically, how socioeconomic differences in society are reflected in language. Often experimental and statistical, sociolinguistics is probably relevant for our topic here only in the sense that some stylistic distinctions may be sociolinguistic in nature, but we will not discuss this issue in this chapter.

Theoretical linguistics assumes that the rules of language are encoded in a manner of which the native speaker is not aware even as he or she follows these rules in using the language. Linguistics observes and analyzes speech in order to identify the main elements of language and establishes the rules holding between and among these elements. The ultimate goal of linguistics is, then, the discovery of the mental mechanisms underlying language. As such, linguistics has emerged in the last two decades or so as one of the main components of the study of the mind and perhaps a most promising venue for penetrating this perhaps final frontier in human cognition.

Rhetoric and composition (two branches of the same discipline, theoretical and pedagogical, respectively, which is why the conjunction is treated as a noun in the singular in this chapter and similar writings), on the other hand, concerns itself with the use of language for writing. It takes language nature for granted, as a whole, and does not research it, assuming that linguistics has already done that. It is not important for success in the field to be really well informed about linguistics (conversely, the linguists' ignorance of rhetoric and composition cannot be exaggerated). Language is largely a tool for rhetoric and composition, and the rhetorician assumes full intuitive familiarity with the rules of language on the part of the writer.

Rhetoric and composition focuses on the ways of using this "unknown"—actually unexamined—language effectively to express the writer's thoughts, to communicate, to convince. Lately, it has been interested in analyzing the authorial voice, the power play behind the voice, and thus the true intentions of the text (I will have more to say about intention later). One can easily say that rhetoric and composition also explores certain rules of language. The differences in the way linguistics, on the one hand, and rhetoric and composition, on the other, view language are summarized in table 13.1. Let us now consider these four very significant differences in more detail.

Rules of Language

Unlike linguistics, rhetoric and composition deals with consciously acquired rules. Linguistics is also interested in language acquisition, of course, but it is not in the business of teaching native speakers their language: on the contrary, linguistics studies the native speakers' competence to under-

Table 13.1
Language as Viewed by Linguistics and by Rhetoric and Composition

The phenomenon as seen by	Linguistics	Rhetoric and Composition
Rules of language	Excavates the unconsciously internalized rules from the minds of the native speakers	Formulates and teaches consciously acquired rules of good writing
Method of inquiry	Formal, logical, explicitly rule oriented	Informal, diverse, not always focusing on rules
Prescriptiveness and usage of language	Aggressively not prescriptive by choice; accepts usage as is and describes it	Naturally and deliberately prescriptive; sets out to change the usage to adapt to a predefined norm
Type of language studied	Casual, ordinary, everyday	Noncasual written language

stand how language works. Unlike linguistics, rhetoric and composition has a large teaching branch, composition, which actually preceded and motivated rhetoric. This branch distributes the received wisdom of how to write well. This wisdom often comes in the form of prescriptive rules: dos and don'ts, shoulds and shouldn'ts, you'd-betters, and or-elses. Such rules cannot be assumed to be naturally available to native speakers: they are native speakers, not native writers. Even literacy has to be taught, but the ability to write well requires a considerable pedagogical effort (even though successful autodidaction, through trial and error, is not excluded). The rules that composition doles out are "man-made," consciously formulated or invented and consciously learned. They may change from epoch to epoch and from style to style, even if the language does not change that much in the same time frame.

The rules that linguistics studies are rules that the native speaker subconsciously applies to produce well-formed or at least acceptable utterances in his or her native language. The rules formulated by rhetoric and pedagogically propagated by composition are the rules of creating well-written text. Obviously, well-written text should also be well formed linguistically, but the reverse is not true: a written text consisting only of well-formed utterances is not necessarily well written. In other words, the rhetorical rules subsume linguistic rules and add a whole new layer of additional rules that linguistics is not necessarily concerned with—and certainly has not been, to a very large extent.

Let us look at a few examples. In (1), language rules, the stuff of linguistics studies, are violated at increasingly high levels: (1a) violates English syntactic rules, (1b) semantic rules, (1c) pragmatic rules, and (1d) discourse rules.

(1) a. *I read book.

 b. *I am reading a doughnut.

 c. *John and Mary are husband and wife, but they have never been legally married and their marriage is not an ordinary-law one.

 d. *And then John said to Mary that he quits. It is much colder in the North. Two plus two makes four. And Bob really should not have eaten the orange.

In (1a), the absence of an article before the noun *book* makes the sentence violate a simple unconscious rule of English that makes any reasonably competent native speaker, regardless of his or her intelligence or education, use an article before a noun or a noun phrase, except in some well-known exceptional cases. In (1b), no syntactic rule is violated, but the verb *to read* and its direct object are not compatible semantically: a good lexicon will indicate that the verb typically requires texts as direct objects, at least in nonmetaphorical cases, and, symmetrically, the class of verbs that *doughnut* typically requires does not include *to read*.

As we go up the level of language structure, the examples become lengthier and more complex. In (1c), if John and Mary are married, this does imply that they have either undergone a legal procedure making them husband and wife or, alternatively, in some societies, are seen as married by virtue of having lived as husband and wife for a long period of time. But the sentence says that neither is the case. It does not violate any syntactic or semantic rule, but it negates its own implication or inference. An unconscious rule of pragmatics prevents a competent native speaker from uttering such sentences.

In (1d), we have a sequence of four sentences. Each is perfectly all right syntactically, semantically, and pragmatically. In fact, each is all right by itself. It is only when they are put together in a single text that they emerge as deviant. We expect a text to be cohesive, to share a topic, to make sense as a whole. It is the unconscious knowledge of rules of discourse (or, more specifically, of cohesiveness) that prevents a competent native speaker from uttering texts like (1d).

All of these rules and many others account for a well-formed text—if none of them is violated, of course. Linguistics does not go beyond well-formed texts, and certainly there is a great deal to learn and study here.

But rhetoric and composition goes a lot further. Let us compare the two examples in (2). (2a) is a well-formed English text because no language rule is violated there. But English rhetoric does not see (2a) as a well-written paragraph because it does not begin with a topic sentence, so in an English composition class, students agree to be taught to rewrite (2a) as (2b), which conforms to an extra, nonlinguistic, consciously formulated and acquired rule.

(2) a. Lafayette streets are kept clean, even though some of them are rather curvy and narrow. The Police Department is quite successful in keeping crime down. There are good shopping opportunities. People are largely civil and pleasant and, unlike in, say, New York City, they smile at each other on the streets. Polite driving is the norm. A few years ago, Lafayette was voted an All-America city.

   b. Lafayette was voted an All-America city a few years ago for several reasons. Its streets are kept clean, even though some of them are rather curvy and narrow. The Police Department is quite successful in keeping crime down. There are good shopping opportunities. People are largely civil and pleasant and, unlike in, say, New York City, they smile at each other on the streets. Polite driving is the norm.

People can easily say something like (2a), but they are taught to write (2b). The rules underlying (2a) are natural—they do not have to be taught. The rules underlying (2b) have to be taught—they are optional, constraining, and for some creative writers, arbitrary, so they violate them on purpose, which is a different story.

Talking of creative writers, literary rules are added on top of rhetorical rules: not all rhetorically correct paragraphs constitute literature. Most are seen as not good, and only very few are characterized by special literary qualities such as the beauty of the language, the special style adapted for the author's purposes, originality, and so on. So linguistics stops far short of where rhetoric and composition goes, but, in turn, the latter stops far short of literary goals.

Method of Inquiry (Modus Operandi)

Linguistics is very concerned with its *modus*. We immediately recognize a mathematical text as such. Linguistics aspires for the same distinction. It proceeds in a similarly well-defined fashion, which seems to imply that our pretty plain-English exposition here is not really linguistics. The discipline sees itself these days as heavily theoretical. In fact, it is perhaps the most theoretically developed discipline this side of science. Linguistic theory, fashioned mainly in terms of mathematical logic, is seen as an axiomatic theory with undefined primitive terms, rules of combining these terms into propositions, axioms, or true statements, and truth-preserving rules that generate all true statements in the theory from the axioms. Linguistic theory underlies, formats, and drives each specific language description. It also determines a methodology, a toolbox, for obtaining these descriptions. Ideally, a linguist's work is, then, to provide a description of a set of phenomena in a language or group of languages in a way that is compatible with linguistic theory, using the tools provided by the theory. In practice, because linguistic theory is still "under development," even if its format is not, linguists produce descriptions to argue certain theoretical and methodological points and to claim that linguistic theory should or should not include certain terms, rules, and statements because their absence or presence will affect the descriptions of important phenomena adversely.

And how, pray, does rhetoric and composition operate? Very differently and much more diversely. Rhetoric and composition includes a wider and less well-defined range of interests and concerns, and its methodologies reflect this diversity. One will not find the logical precision linguistics requires, but one will discover a whole slew of approaches. At its humanities-like extreme, one finds critiques of classical rhetoric as well as histories of rhetorical schools of thought, largely unaffected by specific theoretical and methodological concerns. At the social-science-like extreme, there are well-designed experiments with randomization, quantification, control groups, advanced statistics, factor clustering, and other psychology-type paraphernalia (this is where rhetoric and composition may border on sociolinguistics, though it happens surprisingly rarely in real-life research). On the humanities side, rhetoric and composition may border on, and even cross into, literary criticism and theory, history, and philosophy. On the social-science side, there are obvious parallels with communication, psychology, sociology, and—to a lesser extent—anthropology.

One obvious practical conclusion from this difference in the methodology is that the linguists cannot speak their language to the rhetoricians. Fortunately, good linguistic research easily relieves itself of formalism and renders itself into plain English. So, to contradict what was said earlier, this chapter may still be good linguistics. To accommodate linguistics, rhetoric and composition must stick to its premises and definitions as set out in advance and not shift them without an explicit notice because the linguists, just like the tough rebel leader in a broken-taco commercial, just "hate it when that happens."

Prescriptiveness and Usage

The issue of prescriptiveness is a sticky point. Linguistics studies ordinary language as it manifests itself in speech. Sociolinguistics studies the varieties of language as used by various groups. Does not this make linguistics precisely the field that should be in charge of correct usage? In fact, most lay people think that a linguist is either a person who knows how to speak and to write correctly or a person who knows a lot of languages, but both of these suppositions may be false. Forget the foreign languages, a painful point for many Americans. We know by now that writing correctly is the rhetoric and composition territory. But surely, linguistics must know how to speak correctly. It actually does, but it will not admit it. Why? The story is long and complex, but here is the extra-short version.

Linguistics likes to delimit itself. Its boundaries vary from one theory to another, but they are always there. Starting with de Saussure and, definitely, through Chomsky, linguistics has declared its lack of interest in the correct use of language—an amazing statement, if a linguist manages to shed the shackles of his or her brainwashing in this respect. The linguist, the slogan went and still goes, describes, not prescribes. Everything the native speaker says is correct and warrants the linguist's attention. This is not at all dumb. A century or so ago, only standard prestigious dialects were considered worthy of attention. Local and social dialects were disparaged and treated as distortions of the norm if they deviated from the standard. We still have recurrences of this syndrome these days, for instance, in the matter of Ebonics, which the media really mishandled (yes, Virginia, it is a perfectly legitimate dialect of English, and no, Jesse, don't worry: it is not a good idea to use it similarly to Spanish in bilingual education).

So linguistics came to respect dialects and rejected prescriptiveness. This may have been justified historically but not conceptually, and, as an unintended result, linguistics has ceded its perspective on concurrent language development to pop grammarians, who, in their magazine language columns or on talk shows, attempt to stop any such development, to freeze language at the stage they like, and to impose their preferences on the speaking masses (the one famous exception is William Safire, who has a degree in linguistics and always consults fellow linguists on tricky questions—he also refrains from issuing prescriptive edicts).

The only redeeming feature of this situation is that this lucrative—and often ludicrous—pontification keeps these pundits from academia, where they would probably do more damage—and, of course, nobody listens to them anyway, just as native speakers render such state-sponsored language-regulatory agencies as the French Academy in France or the Hebrew Academy in Israel increasingly redundant. Can we even imagine that a bunch of unruly kids would ever watch somebody telling them not to use *hopefully* in the sense of "hoping that," to restore the form *whom*, or never to end a sentence with an emphatic *NOT*? Even if they did watch such programs, would they follow the advice? Ex-CU-U-Use me!

Contrary to linguistics, rhetoric and composition is all about correct usage, not the verbal, oral version of it (which is, basically, orphaned, except that communication may sometimes claim oratory), but, rather, correct written usage. As I already briefly mentioned earlier, the field is openly and unabashedly prescriptive about writing, especially as far as its teaching pedagogies in composition are concerned. Moreover, students of writing are willing to learn these rules and to apply them because they know that their writing will be considered unacceptable if they do not. In other words, in writing instruction, there is none of that well-recorded unconscious or conscious resistance that native speakers invariably show to prescriptions as to how they should speak. A beginning student of composition may—and sometimes does—argue with his or her instructor that (2a) is just as good as or better than (2b), but later, students realize that certain conventions are in place, and they have to be abided by if one's writing is to be seen as acceptable—always, of course, for a certain intended audience and purpose under the appropriate circumstances.

Casual, Ordinary, Oral Language versus Noncasual, Stylized, Written Language

In view of the previous discussion, it is not at all surprising that linguistics focuses on casual language, that is, language as expressed in ordinary, everyday speech. In this century, this focus has been exclusive: if linguistics even looks at written texts, it does so only when the real thing, transcriptions of spoken language, is not available. There is a good reason for this emphasis: linguistics wants to understand only the linguistic rules that the native speaker has acquired naturally, not the write-well layer added by a composition instructor. Linguistics wants all of language that was not taught to the native speaker in class.

This classroom-taught layer of language is precisely what rhetoric and composition is interested in, namely, noncasual, special, effective usage of language in writing. There has been some serious research done recently in linguistics, still mostly in blissful ignorance of rhetoric and composition, on the differences between written and oral varieties of the same language (see, for instance, Tannen 1982). The differences are very significant: nobody speaks the way he or she writes—nor should anyone. If fact, if somebody does, the audience will be bored. The differences are so ingrained and expected that it is not unusual for a culture to have a foreign language used for writing (e.g., Latin for Gentiles and Hebrew for Jews in medieval Europe).

INTERACTIONS BETWEEN LINGUISTICS AND RHETORIC AND COMPOSITION

As we have already stated, linguistics concerns itself a great deal with well-formed sentences. Rhetoric and composition's good writing subsumes well-formedness and goes far beyond it—alone—to well-written text. Somewhere beyond the scope of this chapter, literary scholarship kicks in at an even higher degree of noncasualness, where a simply well written text becomes a beautifully written text—or, at least, the author intends it to be so. A seemingly simple progression, but, again and again, reality, that mortal enemy of academic research, makes it all much more complex.

Nature of the Overlap

While linguistics is supposed to be concerned with all levels of linguistic structure, from the phoneme and up, in the last three and a half decades, it has definitely privileged the sentence as its primary focus. Rhetoric and composition pays relatively little attention to the sentence and clearly privileges the paragraph as its main focus, with the whole discourse, that is, whole chapters or even whole books, very long texts, being not such a remote second. In principle, linguistics is responsible for the rules governing these larger language units as well; in practice, however, it knows much less about them than it does about the sentence and the smaller units (word, morpheme, and phoneme).

Text linguistics, or discourse analysis, was supposed to be the linguistic study of paragraphs and texts. It started very ambitiously in the early 1970s (see, for instance, van Dijk 1977; Beaugrande and Dressler 1981) but has not produced a body of knowledge comparable to that accumulated by linguistics at the sentence level and below. To add insult to injury, an earlier attempt to reduce composition to sentence level, known in the field as sentence combining, fizzled out, mercifully, very fast.

The subject-matter overlap, then, between linguistics, on the one hand, and rhetoric and composition, on the other, is in the area of the larger language units, which is on the periphery of the current linguistic interests. As a result, linguistics has less to offer to rhetoric and composition of what is ready-made, what is already available in the course of normal linguistic work. It would be nice for a linguist to look in the warehouse of the field when a rhetoric and composition customer stops by for an off-the-shelf product, but, in many cases, the product is not there—the work needs to be done, often from scratch, and it does need to be done in linguistics anyway, whether rhetoric and composition calls or not.

By its very nature, the still-growing area of linguistic pragmatics is probably of most value to rhetoric and composition, sometimes almost in the off-the-shelf form. After all, pragmatics often has to go beyond the individual sentence. It ventures into the areas of cohesiveness and coherence (see, for instance, Levinson 1983; Brown and Yule 1983); it may even deal with the rules of politeness (Brown and Levinson 1987). So if rhetoric and composition is concerned with a formal, polite style, and it generally is, it can pick up the linguistic-pragmatic rules of politeness and take them to its classroom.

A very promising area of pragmatics that was clearly on the immediate interface between linguistics and rhetoric and composition opened up in the early 1980s. It was a study of the so-called new-given opposition in the sentence (see, for instance, Prince 1981), previously known, for most of this century, as the functional perspective of the sentence, or the theme-rheme opposition, or presupposition-focus (also, topic-focus) opposition. The given information in the sentence was either introduced earlier or is assumed to be present in the speaker's and hearer's minds for some other reasons: for instance, if you and I are standing in front of an enormous and weirdly shaped barn, you can tell me, "It is enormous and weirdly shaped" and I will immediately understand, even on a day when I had to get up before noon, that by *it* you mean the barn.

Similarly, in (3), the given is underlined and the new italicized. Note that the seemingly tiny difference between the indefinite and definite article reverses how the information is presented and organized in the sentence.

(3) a. *A man* came into the room.

b. The man *came into* the room.

It is pretty clear that rhetoric and composition should be interested in the arrangement of given and new in each sentence and across sentences. In fact, the topic-sentence-first requirement for the paragraph can be reformulated in these terms:

- Introduce your given up front in the topic sentence.
- Introduce the synopsis of your new there as well.
- Do not change the given throughout the paragraph.
- Detail the new throughout the paragraph.

Linguistic pragmatics does also generally, if not directly, delve into style, and the ancient discipline of stylistics, very rarely taught these days (it has not been offered in my department for years), may be seen as "co-owned" by linguistics and rhetoric and composition. So linguistics will be able to "approve" a paragraph syntactically, semantically, and even pragmatically and stylistically, and yet, again and again, such a paragraph may fall short of being a sample of good writing because it may have not conformed also to the additional set of rhetoric and composition rules dictated by the culture-dependent and changing rhetorical norms, sometimes also referred to (I like the term, and you will too, after you have encountered it a million times) as "recursive practices."

This issue of cultural dependence of recursive practices deserves a brief discussion. Not everybody realizes that an "ideal" translation of a very well written, say, German newspaper article will not be a well-written American newspaper article because German (along with just about every language of continental Europe, certainly including my native Russian) follows the historical-narration model, while American English, as we have already seen, puts the most important information up front, especially in a newspaper. Accordingly, a German journalistic account of a fire will begin with the time when the house was built and will follow the development chronologically, not arriving at the fire itself until the very end of the article. By this time, an American reader of the ideal English translation of that article will have stopped reading the article beyond the opening paragraph because of a total lack of interest in the completion of an unknown house in Bremen in 1694.

Conversely, the German readers of the ideal translation of an American fire report will be astonished to read about the fire itself in a telegraphic first paragraph, followed by a seemingly chaotic and lengthy list of details about the event that is continued on page C23, all the time trying hard to reconstruct the historical perspective that they expect from this genre. Let us note, sadly, that linguistics still knows very little about the informational structure of a text, even after that promising given-new venture, a deficiency that comes to haunt it in natural-language processing, where the computer has to build up its knowledge resource in order to provide proper extralinguistic context to sentences that cannot be correctly interpreted otherwise.

While the study of the paragraph and whole discourse is the major overlap between the two disciplines, a new front of cooperation is provided by the rich concept of intention (see, for instance, Searle 1983), which underlies both the linguistic meaning and rhetorical goals. My intention to express a certain content is what precedes every utterance I make, and if only I could figure out the nature of that intention, its components, and how they are represented, I would have a much clearer notion of what sentence meaning was—because, clearly, what I intend to say is that meaning.

In linguistics, intention is a recent import from the philosophy of language and goal in cognitive science, but linguistic achievements in the study of these concepts, driven largely by computational linguistics, are very likely to be useful for rhetoric and composition. Again, the linguistic intention, in the native speaker's subconscious, is to utter a well-formed proposition. It is debatable even if the scope of this intention may range over a whole sequence of propositions. The rhetorical intention subsumes the linguistic intention and adds to it an extra intention, perfectly conscious or at least easily made so, of producing a well-written and well-composed text. Even with this new opening via intention, the same systematic difference between linguistic text and rhetorical text keeps popping up.

Manner of Cooperation

The manner of cooperation between the two disciplines has been explored perhaps in more detail than any other interdisciplinary interface, and this has been a result of fruitful coexistence of the disciplines within the same department. The cooperation takes primarily the form of applying linguistics to rhetoric and composition (see, for instance, Raskin 1986; Raskin and Weiser 1987, especially chap. 15). Many rhetoric and composition scholars expect linguistics to deliver a great deal of help to them and complain at its failure to do so.

In fact, any attempt to convince such scholars that linguistics can be helpful to their field only to a certain clearly limited extent may cause a considerable amount of disappointment and aggravation. Thus, Weiser and I were amused, even if not surprised, when our 1987 book on the subject (Raskin and Weiser 1987), generally very well received and honored with a *Choice* magazine best-book-of-the-year award, came under severe criticism for the part that I had contributed and that asserted, with proof and argumentation, partially if briefly repeated here, that linguistics can be useful for rhetoric and composition only to a limited extent.

In fact, this is always the case. In a rigorous application (see Raskin 1985, chap. 2), the concepts, ideas, and methods of the source field (in this case, linguistics) are used to study the material and problems of the target field (rhetoric and composition) in order to obtain insights into the latter that cannot be obtained without such an application. An application is always limited in scope, and it cannot cover the target field completely—in fact, if it does, the disciplinary distinction of the target field from the source field should be called into question, which it is most certainly not in this particular case.

The cooperation between linguistics and rhetoric and composition may not be symmetrical, but it is certainly not unilateral. While the benefits for rhetoric and composition may appear more obvious, linguistics reaps benefits from the interaction as well. Rhetoric and composition provides new challenges to handle (e.g., the informational structure of text), material to describe (language entities larger than the sentence), and foci to consider (e.g., cohesiveness in discourse). The truly functional aspect of semantics and pragmatics, that is, what practical effect using this or that particular meaning or this or that arrangement of meanings, or, in other words, what particular expressions or their specific arrangement actually do for the speaker and/or hearers, all of which is largely marginalized in linguistics per se, gains in significance as a result of the cooperation.

Sometimes, a third player may also affect the cooperation between these two fields. Thus, as mentioned earlier, linguistics would have remained unaware (and some of it still is) of the need to address the way information is handled in a text if it were not for the pressures from computational linguistics, also known as natural-language processing. But the moment this pressure is registered, linguistics may attempt to borrow some wisdom from rhetoric and composition, which has addressed this issue, even though not necessarily in the way that linguistics wants it addressed.

Metaphorical Extensions

A rigorous application of linguistics to rhetoric and composition is limited in scope by definition: it basically does not go beyond the notion of a well-formed text. As mentioned earlier, rhetoric and composition uses a much richer notion of a well-written text ([2b]) as opposed to ([2a]). Linguistics can take a rhetorician only so (not very) far toward the latter notion.

In a certain contradiction to this—and somewhat hopefully for those who tend to expect more from linguistics—it has been noted over the last decade of the dialogue between linguistics and rhetoric and composition that the latter can also benefit from extending linguistic ideas and methods beyond linguistics' own parochial concerns. If this is done emulatively, according to the rules of the linguistics game, the result is a "metaphorical extension" of one discipline into another. Chomsky (1959) made this term very pejorative when he used it to destroy Skinner's empiricism, and a metaphorical extension can, in fact, be badly abused if a discipline is extended beyond its legitimate scope surreptitiously or ignorantly. It is a different matter, though, when a scholar is aware of abandoning the proper scope of a discipline and provides the necessary intellectual and methodological basis for the extension.

Quite a few years ago, a doctoral advisee from rhetoric and composition announced to me happily that she was going to write her dissertation on life scripts, using my script-based semantic theory. My first reaction was panic because, of course, that plan would take my rather technical, well-defined approach to sentential meaning far beyond its legitimate domain of application. It became clearer to me later that there was not much to be nervous about. The brilliant student, while inspired by the notion of linguistic script, proceeded to define it for her purposes every step of the way, describing the components of life scripts, formulating the rules of putting them together, and figuring out what belongs in the script and what does not. She may have not defined the meaning of life, but she did a very good piece of research. This was a textbook example of a good metaphorical application. One can argue, of course, that linguistics qua linguistics did not really help her much, but the counterargument will be that it actually did—by lending to her field a concept that could be extended, along with the careful methods of its definition and justification.

Metaphorical extensions of linguistics into rhetoric and composition may thus be quite fruitful, and, besides yielding interesting results (for instance, in a growing array of jointly produced doctoral theses in my department, theses that are increasingly making their way into print, as well as getting good academic jobs for their authors), they also provide more general justification for this method of interaction between any other two disciplines. In other words, the interaction between linguistics and rhetoric and composition, if it is carefully and knowingly taken beyond the limitations of a rigorous application, may still yield significant results for interdisciplinary cooperation in general.

CONCLUSION

Open minds, intellectual curiosity, and mutual education would be beneficial for any two academic disciplines sharing some points of interest. Linguistics and rhetoric and composition are prime candidates for such cooperation. We have briefly discussed the academic and intellectual whys and hows (and how-nots) of such cooperation. It is not redundant, however, especially for a linguist, to be reminded of the practical political and administrative benefits of such cooperation.

Besides the necessity to fight together for their places in a department dominated by other fields and often to form a strong alliance in the process, linguistics profits immensely from cooperating with rhetoric and composition and actively contributing to the preparation of specialists in rhetoric and composition. In my department, the Rhetoric and Composition Program is three to four times larger than the English Linguistics Program, and some of our linguistics courses are recommended or even required for these specialists. Alternatively, it is not unusual for a graduate student in English linguistics to take rhetoric and composition as the secondary field or graduate minor. Our new doctoral graduates in English linguistics typically find employment more easily if they can show preparation in rhetoric and teaching experience in rhetoric and composition (and the reverse is true also). Needless to add, the students in both fields are the primary clear winners in this cooperation.

Chomsky once dismissed an arbitrary juxtaposition of two disciplines as a futile attempt to obtain fire from friction. In the cooperation between his discipline and rhetoric and composition, no thanks to that purist and isolationist in linguistics, a great deal of fire has been produced without much friction. Just don't read a report on this fire in a German newspaper!

REFERENCES

Beaugrande, Robert de, and Wolfgang Dressler. 1981. *Introduction to text linguistics*. London and New York: Longman.

Brown, Gillian, and George Yule. 1983. *Discourse analysis*. Cambridge: Cambridge University Press.

Brown, Penelope, and Stephen C. Levinson. 1987. *Politeness: Some universals in language usage*. Cambridge: Cambridge University Press.

Chomsky, Noam. 1959. Review of *Verbal behavior*. *Language* 35: 1.

Levinson, Stephen C. 1983. *Pragmatics*. Cambridge: Cambridge University Press.

Prince, Ellen F. 1981. Toward a taxonomy of given-new information. *Radical prag-matics*, ed. by Peter Cole, 223–55. New York: Academic Press.

Raskin, Victor. 1985. *Semantic mechanisms of humor*. Dordrecht: D. Reidel.

———. 1986. On possible applications of script-based semantics. *The real-world linguist: Linguistic applications in the 1980's*, ed. by Victor Raskin and Peter C. Bjarkman, 19–45. Norwood, NJ: Ablex.

Raskin, Victor, and Irwin Weiser. 1987. *Linguistics and writing: Applications of linguistics to rhetoric and composition*. Norwood, NJ: Ablex.

Searle, John R. 1983. *Intentionality*. Cambridge: Cambridge University Press.

Tannen, Deborah, ed. 1982. *Spoken and written language: Exploring orality and literacy*. Norwood, NJ: Ablex.

van Dijk, Teun A. 1977. *Text and context: Explorations in the semantics and pragmatics of discourse*. London and New York: Longman.

IV

LANGUAGE AND LITERATURE

WATERSHIPS ALL THE WAY DOWN: USING SCIENCE FICTION TO TEACH LINGUISTICS

Suzette Haden Elgin

The usefulness of science fiction for teaching is obvious. It appeals to young people who are uninterested in reading, it takes advantage of strong loyalties to popular-culture complexes such as *Star Trek* and *Star Wars*, and it gives teachers tools for countering typical student resistance both to "literature" and to scientific methods and principles. Its role in the curriculum for many disciplines, from literature courses through physics and on to law, is already well established.

There are three additional excellent reasons for extending this practice specifically to the field of linguistics. First, because you are free to invent your own science fiction languages, you can be totally in control of your data without sacrificing any of your scholarly principles. Second, even if you restrict yourself to languages already constructed by others, no native speakers of these languages exist to challenge your judgments. Third (and in my opinion most importantly), science fiction languages get you past many of the knee-jerk negative reactions that students have to linguistics information, because you are using languages that carry no political freight. This gives you the same distance-from-the-trees viewpoint that so-called "exotic" human languages offer, without any of the accompanying problems of maintaining political correctness. No existing human language— including the students' native languages, which may be passionately despised by them as a classroom topic—can give you that advantage.

In this chapter I'm going to describe some of the possible ways in which science fiction can make it less difficult to teach linguistics or teach about linguistics. Because this field is one in which the theory seems to be replaced by The Very Latest Thing about twice a week, I will do my best to be as generic and as jargon-free as possible.

EXPLORING BASIC CONCEPTS AND PRINCIPLES OF
LINGUISTICS THROUGH SCIENCE FICTION

Use science fiction to pose large general questions that are linked to basic concepts and principles of linguistics. For example:

Question: Suppose you are an extraterrestrial linguist writing an article titled "How to Recognize a Terran Language." What are at least ten items that you would have to include?

For this exercise, you will want students to list the characteristics that identify the languages of Earth as human languages. A list that would be acceptable might include the following:

- All Terran languages are composed either of sounds or of gestures.
- All contain some nounlike elements.
- All contain some verblike elements.
- All have ways to indicate singular and plural.
- All have ways to make statements and ask questions.
- All have ways to make statements negative.
- All have ways to give commands.
- All have ways to combine two or more propositions into one larger proposition.
- All have ways to specify time and location.
- All have ways to add new items to the vocabulary when they are needed.
- All have ways to communicate about things that are contrary to fact, or hypothetical.

Students will learn a lot about language and linguistics from answering this question and discussing their answers in class. It will give you a chance to take up a multitude of other questions and to make a dent in the common conviction that no language could possibly get along without some feature (the copula, for example, or the adjective) that is part of English. It will let you introduce the important distinction between a language and a code; it will give you a chance to discuss the controversies about sign languages. And it's one of the best possible diagnostic probes for bringing to light the myths and misunderstandings about human language that students typically bring with them.

Question: Based on current knowledge in linguistics, is *Star Trek*'s "Universal Translator" device scientifically probable? Why or why not?

The Universal Translator (UT), which looks much like a flashlight, is a crucial device for keeping *Star Trek*'s stories moving. Hypothetical crew member Brekk, native speaker of English, meets an extraterrestrial (ET) whose native language is one of the Jovian tongues; Brekk points the UT at the ET and turns it on; whatever Brekk says is heard by the ET as the Jovian tongue in question, while whatever the ET says is heard by Brekk as English.

Given the enormous amount of work required to program today's powerful computers to translate accurately between two related Terran languages such as French and Spanish (let alone unrelated ones such as Navajo and English), the UT is not much more probable than a magic wand. Like a magic wand, it's a literary convention—part of the fiction in science fiction rather than part of the science. Students tend to forget that before a device like the UT could work, it would still have to be programmed by a human being, presumably a linguist, or an ET. You can teach a lot of linguistics in the course of a discussion about how a human or extraterrestrial linguist would do that programming, what tasks it would consist of, and the like.

Question: What are the major linguistics errors typically found in science fiction?

The Universal Translator is one, of course. The other four most common ones are:

1. The idea that an entire planet would have only one language, such as Martian
2. The idea that people who can travel backward and forward in time over many centuries would still always be able to speak the language wherever and whenever they find themselves, except for being a tad quaint with their slang
3. The idea that it is possible to prevent language change by passing laws against it
4. The idea that if we do encounter ETs with whom we can communicate, their languages will be just like human languages in all the ways that really matter to us

That last item is a matter of intense controversy within the science fiction community. You will find people passionately arguing on convention panels that any language that doesn't have a way to ask questions or doesn't have any nounlike elements (and so on through the list) simply is not a language, by definition. That is precisely the point. Human beings have defined "a language" in a way that appears to be specified by the human brain, and they are therefore incapable of imagining any language that doesn't meet that definition. I have often told students that if they run into someone who can suggest a language of any other kind, they should assume that the person is in fact an ET. So far, the only "violation" of the definition anyone has been able to come up with is extending "languages are composed of sounds and/or gestures" to "languages are composed of sounds and/or gestures and/or colors and/or smells." But that is not really a change, since the true generalization is that languages are composed of meaningful units, and the definers are merely substituting units of color or smell for units of sound or movement.

If we human/Terrans are going to insist that we will only recognize a system of communication as a language if it meets the specifications for human languages, we are probably in for trouble. We have no justification for assuming that sentient beings without humanoid brains—sentient gas clouds, say, or sentient quartz crystals—will require their languages to have nouns and verbs, or to have a way to indicate singular and plural, and so on. This question gives you an opportunity to bring up the controversy over whether language is hard-wired in the human brain or not (and if it is, to what extent) and discuss it in a context that students will actually find interesting.

> **Question:** How could we tell if extraterrestrials were trying to communicate with us?

This question follows naturally from the previous one, or can be used in its place. We need to realize that it might well be that ETs have been patiently trying to talk to us for centuries, but that—because we refuse to accept anything as a language that does not have nouns and verbs (or some other specification from that list)—we haven't noticed and aren't likely to notice. This discussion inevitably leads to some student's proposing that telepathy is the obvious solution to communication between humanoids and nonhumanoids, which will give you a chance to introduce some important concepts in semantics.

LOOKING INTO SCIENCE FICTION LANGUAGES

Have the students look at specific science fiction languages just as you would have them look at French or Cherokee, for analysis and discussion. Have them write papers on the phonology, morphology, and syntax (and so on) of one or more of the languages you choose. This gives you a chance to introduce as much of the core terminology and concepts and techniques of linguistics as you wish, depending on the level and purpose of your class.

Languages for which it is easy to put together an adequate glossary and set of example sentences include Ursula Le Guin's Kesh (in *Always Coming Home*); the Elvish languages in J.R.R. Tolkien's books; *Star Trek*'s Klingon, as codified by Marc Okrand; and the language called Láadan that appears in my *Native Tongue*, for which (as for Klingon) a dictionary and grammar and tape are available. You will also find (or can easily assemble) brief glossaries from many other novels, including Frank Herbert's *Dune*, Marion Zimmer Bradley's *Darkover* books, and numerous novels by C. J. Cherryh.

SCIENCE FICTION READINGS TO TALK ABOUT IN CLASS

Assign specific science fiction readings to establish an interesting and nonthreatening context for discussing major issues in linguistics. The following examples are of course just suggestions, but they will give you an idea of the possibilities.

- For a discussion of the Sapir-Whorf hypothesis (also called the linguistic relativity hypothesis), assign *The Languages of Pao*, by Jack Vance. In this book, the government of Pao tailors its population for their roles in adult life by controlling the choice of which language they learn in infancy. Those who will grow up to be soldiers acquire one native tongue, those who will grow up to take positions in trade and business learn another, and so on. The government is overthrown when a group secretly learns more than one of these designer languages natively, thus giving it much broader perceptions than the rest of the population.
- For a discussion of language acquisition and language learning, assign *The Embedding*, by Ian Watson, and/or my *Native Tongue*.
- For a discussion of problems in translating from one language to another, assign *A Door into Ocean*, by Joan Slonczewski.
- For a discussion of language policy and language engineering, assign George Orwell's *Nineteen Eighty-four* (and/or *The Languages of Pao*).
- For a discussion of communication barriers between speakers with very different languages and cultures, assign *Foreigner*, by C. J. Cherryh.

Finding science fiction novels that will set the stage for serious linguistic discussions is easy; they are abundant. What's hard is finding books that are still in print, a problem for which I know no solution. (Works by Le Guin, Cherryh, and Orwell are more likely to remain in print than the others I have suggested.) If your class is small, you can usually manage by putting three or four copies of the selected book on reserve in your library. Often writers will give you permission to make photocopies of an out-of-print book as long as you specify that they are for classroom use only and will not be resold. (Be sure you write or e-mail the writer directly, because letters sent to them in care of publishers can sit on a desk for six months or more before being forwarded; you can find almost any living science fiction author by just typing in his or her name in the blank space for an

Internet search.) Sometimes you can structure your classes so that photo-copied excerpts will be enough; sometimes a used-book store, alerted to what you'll need well in advance, will be able to find an adequate number of copies for you. (None of these strategies will help get the books back in print, of course; to do that, people would have to write the publishers and raise cain.)

SOLVING PROBLEMS IN SCIENCE FICTION LANGUAGES

Give your students linguistics problems and exercises using data from science fiction languages. Here is a very simple example, with brief explanatory comments, to show you what I mean; the language in question is probably "Lapine," but its creator never said so specifically, and I have therefore stuck to "rabbit language" and "Rabbitspeak."

Look at the data that follow, taken from the rabbit language in Richard Adams' *Watership Down*. Write the rule (or rules) for making nouns plural in this language and use them to fill in the missing items. We will discuss your solutions in class.

	Singular	*Plural*
homeless rabbit	hlessi	hlessil
fox	homba	hombil
motor vehicle	hrududu	hrududil
hedgehog	yona	yonil
badger	lendri	—
doe (or mother)	marli	—
rowan tree	threar	—
enemy of rabbits	—	elil

Students will suggest at least two ways of writing the rules. (I cannot know which of the many possible formalisms—sets of symbols and squiggles—you might prefer to teach them for this purpose; I will therefore stick to plain English prose. However, the opportunity to teach your favorite squiggles with these problems will be obvious.) The two solutions students will bring you follow; the first one is far more likely than the second.

1. If the noun ends in *i*, add *l*; otherwise, drop any final vowel and add *il*. Or . . .
2. Drop the final vowel (if any) and add *il*.

Both of these proposed solutions fit the data and will make it possible for the students to fill in the first three blanks. *Lendri*'s plural will be *lendril*, *marli*'s will be *marlil*, and *threar*'s will be *threaril*. So far, so good. But the students will have had trouble with the task of finding the singular for *elil*, because they have no way to know whether it is *el* alone (just add *-il*) or *el* followed by some vowel. (They may not have noticed that this was a problem, of course, in which case they will profit from having it pointed out).

This gives you a chance to make some remarks about the kinds of problems that linguists run into when trying to do historical reconstruction of a language. It gives you a chance to introduce some symbols such as *elV* and/or **elV* and to explain why that's a useful thing to do. It also offers an opportunity to send the students to the novel to make a glossary for themselves and to look at all the rest of the items of Rabbitspeak to see if they can find any clue that would solve this dilemma. (I couldn't find one, by the way.)

Next you will want to discuss the question of whether it's possible to decide which of the two ways of writing this plural rule is better, and why. This gives you the opportunity to introduce the scientific principle of *economy* (or *parsimony*, or Occam's razor, as you like), which comes down on the side of "Drop the final vowel, if any, and add *il*." This choice will seem overwhelmingly obvious to you, but it is not the intuitive one. Students will object to the idea of dropping an *i* and then putting it right back again as part of *il*. They need to learn that strange as that may seem, it is the most efficient and most scientific way to go. (Those who then recognize this as good programming will be pleased.)

The final step I recommend is to have the students compare pluralization in Rabbitspeak with pluralization in English. Show them this (or similar) data:

book	book + s	books (*s* pronounced as *s*)
bird	bird + s	birds (*s* pronounced as *z*)
beach	beach + es	beaches (*s* pronounced as *z*)

Depending on the level of your class, either have them work out the rules for this data or present the rules yourself. There are a number of respectable ways to do this; these two are representative:

1. a. Add an *s* to the noun.

    b. If the result gives you two fricatives (buzzing/hissing sounds) in a row, insert an *e* between them.

    c. Make the final *s* agree in voicing with the sound it follows.

2. Add the plural marker, -s, which must agree in voicing with the sound that it follows.

Explain that the second, more economical, solution is possible because *every* English word is constrained by the fact that English never allows a sequence of two consecutive fricatives and routinely breaks up such forbidden sequences by inserting an *e*.

Have them notice that in both languages it is possible to reduce the entire process to a single relatively simple rule. Point out that because we don't have any information about the way the rabbit language sounds (as is also true for much historical reconstruction), we cannot know whether a constraint of some kind from the sound system is involved in Rabbitspeak pluralization. When this is over, you will have introduced a respectable number of basic terms and concepts from linguistics, including the revolutionary idea that *English* has rules that make sense.

WRITING GLOSSARY STORIES

Have your students, either individually or as a group effort, write a *glossary story*. This is a narrative form seen occasionally in science fiction, in which the entire story is told using nothing but dictionary entries. The students can make up definitions of either coined English terms or terms of their own devising from a hypothetical ET language. (It's a good idea to limit them to no more than thirty items, and they will need to be told to write the story first, before trying to come up with their terms and definitions). The example that follows is one that I did for my newsletter in 1995 and is therefore short enough to fit in this brief chapter; it uses lexical items from a hypothetical future English.

Tale in Twelve Terms

1. *jellhorry*	a christening ceremony for an infant who has been posted
2. *caddrag*	someone who refuses to spend the money necessary to put on a *proper* jellhorry and is stingy about it; especially pejorative when the caddrag is a man whose posted child has been released to him for surrogate decanting
3. *fizstats*	health statistics (blood counts, blood sugar, pregnancy status, enzyme counts, electrolytes, and the like), derived from urine

4. *to post*

(*a*) from "to postpone," used only of human children; to abort a baby and store the embryo at an authorized fedkresh in accordance with federal law; (*b*) obsolete—to write data in a file, or display an item

5. *fedkresh*

government facility at which abortions are performed and where women store the one to three aborted children allowed by law

6. *to decant*

to reimplant a posted child in the uterus so that its mother may bring it to term and bear it in the usual fashion

7. *brindesse*

a crime of women; the attempted concealment of a pregnancy, miscarriage, abortion, or birth; now rare

8. *lugbone*

mild reproof, as in "You lazy little lugbone!"; used to young girls who are careless about the daily checking of their fizstats; less common since the forwarding of all fizstats to the National Institutes of Health (NIH) has become computer automated, but still used in rural areas of the United States

9. *"Kraggaine's choice"*

a woman's dilemma when, faced with a fourth unwanted pregnancy, she must decide which child to post and which to decant; from the infamous case in 3097 of Gwendolyn Kraggaine, who committed suicide to avoid bearing any of her four children

10. *kellameer*

therapy for parents of a decanted child who is stillborn or dies within seventy-two hours of birth

11. *mortmother*

surrogate in whose uterus a baby is implanted after its biological mother's death

12. *baskyhood*

the difficult (and fortunately very rare) situation of men who—upon the death of the mother of their posted children—must deal with their legal and religious obligation to decant all such children to mortmothers and assume full responsibility for all of these persons; support groups for men struggling with baskyhood are called "Nasker groups" after Charles Trenton Nasker, the longtime companion and lover of Gwendolyn Kraggaine (see *"Kraggaine's choice"*)

This exercise will teach your students large amounts of basic information about the way that words are created, the way sounds are combined, the importance of clear definitions, and many other useful things. (It will also give them an understanding of economy that is not linked to computer programming, and it is an excellent introduction to the difficult genre of documentation and instructions.)

I hope I have made my case. I know from long experience that introducing people to linguistics can be a traumatic experience for both students and teachers, especially if, as is often the case, the students arrive with all the usual phobias about anything that strikes them as remotely resembling math. Science fiction offers many resources that will go a long way toward turning that unfortunate situation around.

REFERENCES AND SUGGESTED READING

Adams, Richard. 1975. *Watership down*. New York: Avon Books.

Allan, James D., ed. and comp. 1978. *An introduction to Elvish*. Hayes, UK: Bran's Head. (Distributed in the United States by Jitco, 1776 East Jefferson Street, Rockville, MD 20852.)

Burgess, Anthony. 1962. *A clockwork orange*. New York: Norton.

Cherryh, C. J. *Foreigner*. 1994. New York: DAW Books.

Delaney, Samuel R. 1976. *Babel-17*. Boston: Gregg. (Warning: Contains a spectacular error in dealing with the phonemic/phonetic distinction.)

Elgin, Suzette H. 1984. *Native tongue*. New York: DAW Books.

———. 1988. *A first dictionary and grammar of Láadan*. 2nd ed. Madison, WI: Society for the Furtherance and Study of Fantasy and Science Fiction (SF3).

———. 1994. *Linguistics and science fiction sampler* (booklet). Huntsville, AR: OCLS Press.

Herbert, Frank. 1965. *Dune*. Philadelphia: Chilton Book Company.

Le Guin, Ursula K. 1985. *Always coming home*. New York: Harper and Row.

Meyers, Walter E. 1980. *Aliens and linguists: Language study and science fiction*. Athens: University of Georgia Press.

Okrand, Marc. 1985. *The Klingon dictionary*. New York: Pocket Books.

Orwell, George. 1963. *Nineteen eighty-four*. New York: Harcourt, Brace and World.

Slonczewski, Joan. 1986. *A door into ocean*. New York: Avon Books.

Tolkien, J. R. R. 1974. *The lord of the rings*. 3 vols. London: Allen and Unwin.

———. 1977. *The Silmarillion*. Boston: Houghton Mifflin.

Vance, Jack. 1958. *The languages of Pao*. New York: Ace Books.

Watson, Ian. 1973. *The embedding*. London: Gollancz.

IN FICTION, WHOSE SPEECH, WHOSE VISION?

Elizabeth Closs Traugott

> Dave struck out across the fields, looking homeward through paling
> light. Whut's the use talkin wid em niggers in the field? Anyhow, his
> mother was putting supper on the table. Them niggers can't understan
> nothing. One of these days he was going to get a gun and practice
> shooting, then they couldn't talk to him as though he were a little boy.
> He slowed, looking at the ground. Shucks, Ah ain scareda them even
> ef they are biggern me! Aw, Ah know whut Ahma do . . . Ahm sev-
> enteen. Almost a man. He strode, feeling his long loose-jointed limbs.
> Shucks, a man oughta hava little gun aftah he done worked hard all
> day. (Richard Wright, "The Man Who Was Almost a Man," 1396)

Who speaks here? Whose vision are we privy to? Why, in the first paragraph of this short story, do we have so many switches from standard to
nonstandard language use? These are questions about "point of view" or
"perspective." Traditionally, point of view has been thought of rather sim-
plistically: is the narrative first or third person, is the narrator all-knowing
("omniscient"), limited, unreliable, or objective (unable to access the
characters' minds), is the first-person narrator a major or a minor participant in the story? However, such issues hardly do justice to the questions
writers constantly pose about how identity, awareness, and consciousness
in general can be represented. Not only is language inadequate to express
everything that can be felt, but there is always tension between what one
can know about oneself and what one can know about others.

   While certain writers of fiction exploit and draw attention to ways in
which points of view can be represented, a key point for students should
always be that the features of language under discussion are all part of

everyday language use. Any story we tell our friends is likely to have some of the characteristics highlighted in this chapter, even if it is about our personal experiences, since we shape and represent them through language.

WHOSE VOICE IS THIS?

To understand who speaks and who sees in fiction, a student must in the first place cross two crucial hurdles. The first is coming to grips with the fact that fiction is not autobiographical. The narrator is always a projection of the author, even in the first person. Richard Wright may or may not have witnessed Dave's story; Angela Carter is not the young girl in the fairy tale "The Erl-King," though she may have had analogous experiences. The second hurdle is to separate "story" or "plot" (what happens—"just one thing after another, a what and a what and a what" [Margaret Atwood, "Happy Endings," 77]) from "discourse" or "narration" (how what happens is represented—the "How and Why" [ibid.]).

Once these hurdles have been passed, an exploration can begin into "authority to tell," specifically into what the first person (I) or a third person can know about someone other than him- or herself. Why is it that I can say, "I am sad," and I am unlikely to be questioned about the truth of what I have said, but I am likely to be challenged if I say, "You are sad" or "She is sad"? Without access into the minds of others, I have no real authority to comment on their experiences unless they have revealed those experiences to me either by what they have said or by their behavior.

There are obvious constraints on plot in first- versus third-person narrative. Some are trivial, such as the constraint that, except in ghost stories, first-person narrators cannot recount their own death, but narrators can always recount the death of third persons. On a deeper level, first-person narrators can express their own feelings, thoughts, perceptions, and subjective perspectives without qualification. However, unless they adopt an omniscient, internal perspective, narrators must position themselves to be authorities about the feelings, thoughts, and perceptions of third persons. One way to do this is to start with an external perspective and gradually, sometimes seamlessly, shift to an internal one. Verbs like "seem" and "appear" and adverbs like "doubtless" and "probably" abound as the external narrator introduces a scene in third-person narrative: "It did not *appear* to be the duty of these two men to know what was occurring at the centre of the bridge; they merely blockaded the two ends of the foot plank which traversed it. . . . *Doubtless* there was an outpost further along" (Ambrose Bierce, "An Occurrence at Owl Creek Bridge," 162, italics added). This narrator, who at the beginning can only describe what he sees and speculate about it, three paragraphs later can comment on the inner thoughts of the man he had observed being prepared for hanging: "He wondered what it was, and whether immeasurably distant or near by" (163).

Authors may draw attention to the difficulties of conventions concerning the narrator's authority to tell by various means, for example, developing a plot around the nature of authorship and narrative stance, a device that goes all the way back to Laurence Sterne's *Tristram Shandy*. Alternatively, they may be very subtle. At the end of Michael Ondaatje's book *The English Patient*, a novel in which multiple narrators weave their stories with little overt attention being paid to the craft of narrative, we are startled at the end by the highlighting of this tension in narrative authority. The third-person narrator of this final chapter shows us Kirpal, the former bomb-disposer, now a doctor, thinking about Hana, with whom he has shared several months in the Italian villa where Hana nursed the "English patient." Now, several years later, Kirpal has a "limited gift" of being able to "see" her but does not "know what her profession is or what her circumstances are" (300). There is a brief shift in the next-to-last paragraph to first person, who presumably is the narrator ("if writers have wings") not Kirpal, who is no writer:

> And Hana moves *possibly* in the company that is not her choice. She, at even this age, thirty-four, has not found her own company, the ones she wanted. . . . Ideal and idealistic in that shiny dark hair! . . . She still remembers the lines of poems the Englishman read out loud to her from his commonplace book. She is a woman *I don't know well enough to hold in my wing*, if writers have wings, to harbour for the rest of my life. (Michael Ondaatje, *The English Patient*, 301, italics added)

The reason for this deliberate distancing from Hana, who has been one of the focal points of the first three hundred pages, may be a move to strengthen the ideological value placed at the end on family and reaching fulfillment, embodied by Kirpal. Hana, by contrast, "has not found her own company, the ones she wanted" (301). As in many examples of shift in perspective, local shifts, whether with regard to person or spatiotemporal or psychological relationships, may also serve to draw attention to larger-scale ideological points of view.

Why does one typically speak of first- and third-, but not of second-person narrative? In daily life, access to the feelings and thoughts of second and third persons is essentially equally difficult. There is an added problem with second persons in narrative: the difficulty of distinguishing the addressee/reader from the character, the generic, plural "you" meaning "everyone" from the singular individual "you." The following is from a novel in which chapters alternate from first- to second- to third-person narrative, exploring the role of person in fiction:

> *You* were looking at the other faces for clues when Misra's image came right before *you*, placing itself between *you* and the men *you* were staring at. *You*

would remember the same image when, years later, at school and in Mogadiscio, *you* were shown the pictures of Egyptian mummies by one of Salaado's
relations. (Nuruddin Farah, *Maps*, 123, italics added)

This "you" refers to the protagonist, Askar, as if addressing himself in a
mirror, allowing for a self-analytic perspective. In *Maps* specific events involving unique individuals and places (Misra, Mogadiscio) are narrated in
the past tense to ensure that there is no potential for confusion with a
generalized "you" who might include the reader, as in "The woods enclose.
You step between the first trees and then *you* are no longer in the open
air; the wood swallows *you* up" (Angela Carter, *The Erl-King*, 217, italics
added). Here the plurals (*woods, trees*) as well as the present tense (*enclose,
step*) serve to appeal to the reader to identify with the protagonist in the
events.

WHOSE VISION IS THIS?

Who speaks and who sees often coincide in first-person narrative, in
third-person narrative they often do not, but students should never assume
a correlation. The question "Who sees?" involves the question "From
whose perspective are the events brought into focus (or "focalized")?" The
distinction between who speaks and who sees allows us to account for
shifts at the micro level, either the sentence or within the sentence, in ways
that attention to first- and third-person narrators cannot. It also allows us
to recognize double perspectives.

The shifting spatial relations represented by *come* and *go*, or *this* and
that can make the distinction especially clear. *Come* and *this* involve a
positive or close ("proximal") orientation toward the speaker or center of
attention ("They/you come toward me"). By contrast, *go* and *that* can express either the opposite, that is, a negative or distal orientation away from
the speaker ("They/you go away from me"), or a neutral perspective ("This
class is going well"). Choice of *come* over *go* or *this* over *that* focalizes
and orients toward the subject of the sentence when that subject is a person.
The *come* at the beginning of Leslie Marmon Silko's "Storyteller" focalizes
the *she*, not the narrator, as the experiencer of the sunrise and as the center
of attention to whom things are positively oriented. "Every day the sun
came up a little lower on the horizon, moving more slowly until one day
she got excited and started calling the jailer" (1145, italics added)—we
know that unless there is a shift, we as readers are invited to share her
perspective, to be empathetic with *she*. By contrast, Silko's first-person narrative "Yellow Woman" starts, "My thigh clung to his with dampness, and
I watched the sun *rising* up through the tamaracks and willows" (1214,
italics added). Since the narrator is a first person, there is no distinction
between the narrating voice and the seeing eye. What students need to be

aware of, however, is that although we are invited to empathize with this first-person narrator, we are to understand that she is keeping her distance, observing (watching, not just "seeing") what she interprets as a magical event. This we understand in part because of the use of *rising* rather than *coming*. Students should also note that when the subject of the sentence is not a person, the orientation tends to be understood as toward the narrator and reader, as in "The hills across the valley of the Ebro were long and white. On *this* side there was no shade and no trees and the station was between two lines of rails in the sun" (Ernest Hemingway, "Hills like White Elephants," 653, italics added). Contrast the effect of "On *that* side," which would evoke a scene oriented away from the narrator's and reader's position.

Another well-known example of the distinction between who speaks and who sees is provided by the kind of representation known as "free indirect style" or "narrated monologue." Often associated with Virginia Woolf, this style is widely used to give a filtered perspective on inner thoughts and feelings, aligning narrator and character, yet also keeping them apart. In the following excerpt we listen in on Martha's thoughts:

> I shall not tell Mark that I'm leaving. Today. I don't want to be involved in all this. . . . She meant, this atmosphere of threat, insecurity, and illness. Who would have thought that coming to this house meant—having her nose rubbed in it! Yes, but that wasn't what she had meant, when she demanded from life that she must have her nose rubbed in it. (Doris Lessing, *The Four-gated City*, 106)

In the first sentence the narrator represents Martha's own thoughts directly (something that only an internal narrator can do in third-person narrative). In the fourth sentence there is a shift to third person. Who speaks or thinks "She meant"? If it is Martha, we should be able to reconstruct "I (Martha) mean, this atmosphere of threat, insecurity, and illness." This is possible, and *this* suggests that it is likely. But it is also possible that the narrator is interpreting and elucidating her vague thoughts to us (along the lines of "I [narrator] conclude that what she was thinking about was . . ."). This ambiguity provides an imperceptible transition between Martha's unfiltered thoughts at the beginning and the next sentence, which is clearly anchored in Martha (*this, come,* and the colloquial *having her nose rubbed in it*). But the third person evokes a double perspective: Martha's and that of the narrator who is no longer artificially "in her head," as in the direct-thought sentence "I shall not tell Mark that I am leaving," but truly narrating—representing a consciousness rather than displaying it.

Students can practice sensitizing themselves to this kind of representation by converting direct thought or speech into indirect and comparing the differences. Indirect thought would typically give them something like "She asked herself whether anyone would have thought that her going to that house would have resulted in her being reminded of her failure," a version that is relatively neutral in perspective. They can also notice that nonstandard and dialect characteristics are wiped out by indirect style (and indeed by free indirect): Both "I won't do anything" and "I won't do nothing" become, in indirect form, "She said she would not do anything."

If students take this kind of approach to the passage from Richard Wright quoted at the beginning of this chapter, they will see that in the first sentence the narrator is speaking and presenting a scene without any particular orientation. The second, being in nonstandard English, is direct speech. (It is important for the student to understand that this story was written in the 1930s, when the "N word" was not a subject of the same kind of political force as now, and furthermore that, as an African American writer writing about an African American youth, Wright would even now have the authority to use this word. The political force itself has point of view built into it—groups that are subject to prejudice often appropriate negatively oriented terms to themselves, as has recently occurred with the term *queer* or, in the nineteenth century, with *Yankee*.) The third sentence, "Anyhow, his mother was putting supper on the table," with the casual *anyhow*, must, by contrast, be in the form of free indirect thought.

Once free indirect style has been recognized, its function deserves attention, particularly if it is used only at certain points in a narrative. Wright uses it at the beginning of "The Man Who Was Almost a Man" to focalize attention on and sympathy with the young man while at the same time perhaps easing the reader into the use of nonstandard English. The style is used again later at certain structural points of plot development. When Dave gets his gun, he plans to take his boss's mule Jenny down to the fields and practice shooting. In a passage that picks up the spatial imagery of the beginning, we read: "He hitched Jenny to a plow and started across the fields. Hot dog! This was just what he wanted" (Richard Wright, "The Man Who Was Almost a Man," 1355). Likewise, in "Cat in the Rain" by Ernest Hemingway, an author not often associated with internal perspective, free indirect style is used at a turning point in the emotional experience of the American wife as she yearningly goes out in the rain to seek a cat she has seen from her hotel window: "The cat would be around to the right. Perhaps she could go along under the eaves" (66). Immediately afterward the realities of the situation impinge on her as the maid opens an umbrella behind her.

The complexities of who speaks and who sees increase as we move to satiric and ironic perspectives. Here the perspective is ideological: the narrator's "stance" or "mind-set" toward the events is being represented. The speech of others, society at large, or individuals is often echoed and made fun of by the narrator speaking in the narrative voice as the focalizer. One very brief example must suffice here, from Charles Dickens's *Our Mutual*

Friend. The Veneerings are an upstart nouveau riche couple who value only what is "bran-new" and socially important. They value people exclusively in terms of the social roles or descriptors associated with them. The Veneerings go to a dinner, meet an Engineer, a Payer-off of the National Debt, a Poem on Shakespeare, a Grievance, a Public Office (49), and then themselves invite these same people to dinner, not as people but as social roles. The narrator speaks, echoing the Veneerings, but in a distanced, satiric way, implying that he would never use these terms himself. We know this because the dinner invitation is embedded in a passage that preposterously introduces as a piece of furniture a character who we later learn is called Twemlow: "There was an innocent piece of dinner-furniture that went upon easy castors and was kept over a livery stable-yard in Duke Street, St. James's, when not in use, to whom the Veneerings were a source of blind confusion" (48). The Veneerings could presumably not have known that they were a source of confusion to this person (Twemlow); they may or may not have thought of him as a piece of furniture. It is the narrator's perspective that assigns this designation, caricaturing what they might have thought.

SOME KEY FEATURES FOR STUDENTS TO LOOK FOR

The language of point of view is highly complex. However, some general tendencies hold and can be used by students as guides to thinking about questions of who speaks and who sees.

Spatiotemporal Perspectives

The key features of spatial and temporal perspective are choices of verbs with shifting meanings (these and other words with meanings that shift depending on the viewpoint of some center of attention can be called "shifters" or "deictics"). As we have seen, "proximal" orientation is interpreted as being directed toward the perspective of the viewer, for example, *come*, *bring*; distal as distancing, moving away from the viewer, for example, *go*, *take*. Parallel with the choice of verb is the choice of demonstrative (*this* versus *that*), and of the temporal adverb *now* versus *then*. Avoidance of orientation requires a verb like *pass* or *move* or the article *the*. The force of spatiotemporal perspective becomes particularly clear if such a perspective is absent, as at the beginning of Charles Dickens's *Little Dorrit*.

Much narrative is in past tense, as in "John and Mary fell in love and got married." But it can be in the present: "John and Mary fall in love and get married" (Margaret Atwood, "Happy Endings," 75). When the present tense is used in connection with verbs expressing events such as coming to a place, arriving, winning, or killing, that is, events that are understood to occur in sequence one after another, we usually understand that an event that occurred at some point in the past has been projected onto the present to make it more immediately visible to us. For the question of "Who sees?" a shift from present to past or from past to present is particularly interesting. The end of Bierce's "Occurrence" is a case in point. Farquhar imagines that he escapes. The reader is invited, on first reading, to experience his breaking free with him and to believe that it is occurring, partly because the past tense is continued from the earlier narrative of the hanging: "As Peyton Farquhar fell straight downward through the bridge, he lost consciousness. . . . The cord fell away; his arms parted and floated upward" (65). Several paragraphs later there is a shift to the present tense at the moment that he imagines he reaches home and sees his wife, and a false moment of epiphany is experienced. The reader is then jolted by a shift back to past tense, accompanied by a shift from an internal mental experience to an external view of his body, highlighted by a shift from the pronoun *he* to his name:

> Ah, how beautiful she *is!* He *springs* forward with extended arms. As he *is* about to clasp her, he *feels* a stunning blow upon the back of the neck; a blinding white light *blazes* all about him, with a sound like a shock of a cannon—then all is darkness and silence!
>
>   Peyton Farquhar *was* dead; his body, with a broken neck, *swung* gently from side to side beneath the timbers of the Owl Creek bridge. (168, italics added)

Speech and Thought Representation

The key features of free indirect style are third-person pronoun, past tense, modal verbs with past-tense form (*would*, not *will*), present temporal adverbs (*now*, not *then*), proximal verbs (*come*, not *go*), proximal demonstratives (*this*, not *that*), colloquial language (but not dialect), and questions with verb inversion, for example, "What would she be doing now?" In free indirect style modal verbs (e.g., *must, could*) and adverbs (e.g., *possibly, doubtless*) are understood as the evaluations made by the focalized character. For example, Farquhar's false epiphany starts out with his own contemplation of his experience and warrants the shift to present tense: "*Doubtless*, despite his suffering, he fell asleep while walking, for *now* he *sees* another scene" (168, italics added). By contrast, in narrative that is not represented in free indirect style, modals usually express a narrator's evaluative point of view, as we have seen in connection with the example from *The English Patient*.

Manner

Manner adverbs like *sulkily*, or *happily* are usually based in the narrator's perspective. So are verbs that express an action done in a certain kind of manner, such as *sulked*, or adjectives that describe such qualities, such as *sulky*. At the beginning of D. H. Lawrence's "Odour of Chrysanthemums" a locomotive engine is characterized as a living being moving toward a focal point of attention (the mining village), but people are characterized as shadows, passive entities in an active world of machines. The narrator juxtaposes machines and humans in part by evaluative commentary: "The trucks thumped *heavily* past, one by one, *with slow inevitable movement*, as she stood *insignificantly* trapped between the jolting black wagons and the hedge" (859, italics added). As Elizabeth in this story moves from bitter resentment and insensitivity to self-knowledge, so the narrative stance shifts. Initially the stance is that of external observation and largely negative evaluation highlighted with manner adverbs that Elizabeth herself probably would not have had the insight to use, for example, "Elizabeth Bates said this *bitterly*, and *with recklessness*" (865, italics added), "she said *pitiably* to herself" (866, italics added). Then there is a shift to the narrator's external speculation about a possible positive act, "Then she *must* have bent down and kissed the children" (866, italics added), and finally to internal evaluation devoid of most negative assessment, other than Elizabeth's own. Although free indirect style is used early on to signal beginning changes in her perception, for example, "What a fool she had been to imagine that anything had happened to him!" (865), it is not used to any great extent until the end. Whatever manner adverbs there are toward the end are evaluations that she and the narrator can both share. The last line is "But from death, her ultimate master, she winced *with fear and shame*" (873, italics added).

The example of "Odour of Chrysanthemums" highlights once again the importance of recognizing not just one but several clues together in understanding point of view. This brings us back to the passage by Richard Wright at the beginning. As we have seen, the narrator shifts almost imperceptibly from external observation, as in the first sentence, to the boy's inner thoughts, to free indirect style. Then the view is more external again: "He slowed, looking at the ground." Although it is possible that the boy, Dave, was aware of his slowing and looking at the ground, it is more likely that this is the narrator's observation, as is "He strode, feeling his long loose-jointed limbs." The shifts, following so fast one upon another, establish the empathy between narrator and character, despite their differences, evoked by, for example, the use of Standard English narrative and of thought and speech represented in nonstandard English.

Nonstandard Forms

Although the use of nonstandard varieties of English, and of languages other than English, is not usually considered a feature of point of view and has perhaps not been discussed much in the theoretical literature because it does not occur in free indirect style, nevertheless, it plays an important role. Used until the writings of Mark Twain almost exclusively for purposes of comic effect, nonstandard Englishes and other languages over the years have become increasingly important in fiction, especially in developing awareness of and empathy with multicultural voices: "Acting like a *bolilla*, a white girl. *Malinche*. Don't think it didn't hurt being called a traitor. Trying to explain to my ma, to my *abuela*, why I didn't want to be like them" (Sandra Cisneros, "Little Miracles, Kept Promises," 330; italics original). For Wright, one issue was on the one hand to highlight the plight of the oppressed by representing their voices, and on the other to emphasize the similarities in the human condition among the oppressed. He therefore chose not to represent distinctly African American features of language. At the same time he strove to represent voices as speaking authentic varieties, not "degenerate" or "bastardized" forms of English. The absence of apostrophes, for example, in "Ahm going by ol Joe's sto n git that Sears Roebuck catlog n look at them guns" (1396) instead of "Ahm going by ol' Joe's sto' 'n' git that Sears Roebuck cat'log 'n' look at them guns" can be seen as signaling the narrator's ideological perspective on the world he evokes.

CONCLUSION

Stories can teach us about the world. Not just the story, but the points of view on it, can help us see things from several perspectives. Motives and secret lives become visible. It is the language of fiction that makes us see, but only if we can follow all its subtleties.

REFERENCES

Atwood, Margaret. 1983. Happy endings. *Murder in the dark: Short fictions and prose poems.* Toronto: McClelland and Stewart. Reprinted in Charters 1999, 74–77.

Bierce, Ambrose. 1891. An occurrence at Owl Creek bridge. *Tales of soldiers and civilians.* San Francisco: E. L. G. Steele. Reprinted in Charters 1999, 162–68.

Carter, Angela. 1979. The Erl-King. *The bloody chamber and other adult tales.* New York: HarperCollins. Reprinted in Charters 1995, 216–22.

Charters, Ann, ed. 1995. *The story and its writer: An introduction to short fiction.* 4th ed. Boston: Bedford Books of St. Martin's Press.

———, ed. 1999. The story and its writer: An introduction to short fiction. 5th ed. Boston: Bedford Books of St. Martin's Press.

Cisneros, Sandra. 1991. Little miracles, kept promises. *Woman Hollering Creek*, New York: Vintage Books. Reprinted in Charters 1999, 323–331.

Dickens, Charles. 1971 [1864–5]. *Our mutual friend*. London: Penguin Books.

Farah, Nuruddin. 1986. *Maps*. New York: Pantheon. Cited in Monika Fludernik, Introduction: Second-person narrative and related issues. *Style* 28 (1994): 281–311.

Hemingway, Ernest. 1927. Hills like white elephants. *Men without women*. New York: Scribner's. Reprinted in Charters 1999, 653–56.

———. 1944. Cat in the rain. *The first forty-nine stories*. London: Jonathan Cape. Reprinted and discussed in Ronald Carter, Style and interpretation in Hemingway's "Cat in the Rain," *Language and literature: An introductory reader in stylistics*, ed. by Ronald Carter, 65–80. London: Allen and Unwin, 1982.

Lawrence, D. H. 1933. Odour of chrysanthemums. *Complete short stories of D. H. Lawrence*. New York: Viking Penguin (1961). Reprinted in Charters 1999, 859–73.

Lessing, Doris. 1969. *The four-gated city*. New York: Alfred A. Knopf.

Ondaatje, Michael. 1992. *The English patient*. New York: Vintage Books.

Silko, Leslie Marmon. 1981a. Storyteller. *Storyteller*. New York: Seaver Books. Reprinted in Charters 1995 1144–56.

———. 1981b. Yellow woman. *Storyteller*. New York: Seaver Books. Reprinted in Charters 1999, 1214–22.

Wright, Richard. 1987. The man who was almost a man. *Eight men*. New York: Thunder's Mouth Press. Reprinted in Charters 1999, 1396–1405.

FURTHER READING

Carter, Ronald, ed. 1982. *Language and literature: An introductory reader in stylistics*. London: Allen and Unwin.

Culler, Jonathan. 1997. *Literary theory: A very short introduction*. Chap. 6, "Narrative." New York: Oxford University Press.

Fowler, Roger. 1986. *Linguistic criticism*. Chap. 9, "Point of view." New York: Oxford University Press.

Leech, Geoffrey N., and Michael H. Short. 1981. *Style in fiction: A linguistic introduction to English fictional prose*. Chap. 8, "Discourse and the discourse situation"; Chap. 10, "Speech and thought presentation." New York: Longman.

Linde, Charlotte. 1993. *Life stories: The creation of coherence*. Chap. 4, "Narrative and the iconicity of the self." New York: Oxford University Press.

The Poetics of Everyday Conversation

Deborah Tannen

Poets, playwrights, and listeners to everyday conversation are in love with the speaking human voice. In poems, in plays, and in telling friends about something that happened, writers and speakers strive to capture the lilt, the verbal twist, the particular nuance of what someone said.

Many fiction writers locate the roots of their art in conversational stories. The Black South African writer Mark Mathabane, for example, grew up in the ghastly shacks of apartheid-era Alexandra, Johannesburg, in a world where no books were in view and neither of his parents could read or write. Years later, when an American talk-show host asked how he developed his love of literature, Mathabane answered:

> The seeds of this love for knowledge and for reading were planted . . . when my mother would gather us around the fire— usually we were wracked with pangs of hunger, because there was nothing to eat—and she would tell such mesmerizing stories, vivid images, deeply entertaining and instructive. And then we'd forget that we were hungry. And I think that her knowledge of these stories became our library, and if I am asked, "Where do you trace your creativity to," I think to those days.[1]

Most of us tend to think of literature as the artful use of language, and of everyday conversation as a messy, graceless use of it. But the magnetism of stories told in conversation, and the fascination that everyday language holds for so many verbal artists, belies that belief. In my research, I have tried to figure out how the voice talking in conversation casts its magical spell. The answer, I have concluded, is through literary-like features that are pervasive in everyday talk. I have found that forms of language that we think of as "literary" are basic to everyday conversation. That is what I have in mind when I speak of a poetics of conversation.

These poetic linguistic elements drive both conversational and literary language by means of patterns of sound and sense. Sound patterns make up the musical level of language, including rhythm and intonation. Just as the rhythm and sound of music involve dancers with each other and with the dance, so the rhythm and music of language involve the audience with the speaker or writer and the discourse by sweeping them along, luring them to move in its rhythm.

At the same time, involvement is created on the level of sense, as listeners do some of the work of creating meaning from the words they hear. Conversation is not a game of serial passivity, in which one person actively speaks while the other passively listens. Engaging in conversation is always active for both speaker and listener, thanks to these two types of involvement: a listener is caught up in the music of the speaker's language, often nodding in rhythm, and also does active work helping to make meaning from the words spoken.

Three poetic elements of language that are fundamental to conversation as well as to literary language are repetition, dialogue, and details. Repetition establishes rhythm and also meaning by patterns of constants and contrasts. Dialogue—the representation of voices (what some people call "reported speech")—creates rhythm and musical cadence as well as setting up a dramatic scene in which people interact with each other and engage in activities that listeners recognize. Details provide seeds from which listeners sprout characters, meanings, and emotions.

It is easy to identify all these poetic features in any everyday conversation. Take a tape recorder with you for a day as you talk to people, and ask their permission to tape the conversations. If anyone is uncomfortable, don't turn the tape recorder on. But when you talk to one or more people who don't mind being taped, then record the conversation. Afterwards, listen to the tape and choose a segment to transcribe. It could be just a few minutes long, or up to five minutes at most. When you transcribe the conversation, write down every word you hear and check it carefully against the tape several times, until you are sure you have captured all the words that were spoken, including hesitations like "uh" or "um." Then you can examine the transcript for poetic features, just as you would a novel, short story, or poem. It does not have to be a conversation that seems important. The more trivial the conversation, the more exciting it is to find patterns in the transcript.

SAY IT AGAIN: REPETITION

One of the easiest patterns to find in transcripts of conversation is repetition. Just as poems often repeat lines to emphasize meaning and to create nuances of meaning, so do speakers in everyday conversation. Here is a short excerpt from a dinner-table conversation that I taped some years ago. The speakers were all friends: Steve was the host, Peter was his older brother, Steve and I had been close friends since our teen years, and Chad was a new acquaintance—a friend of a friend.

In this part of the discussion, we were talking about how Peter's wife had recently told him that she wanted a divorce. He was explaining that his relationship with his wife had always been difficult, but he would have stayed with her nonetheless. As a participant in the conversation, I supported what Peter said, and he accepted my support. His brother, Steve, however, made a comment (and a joke) by turning Peter's words around to disagree:[2]

Peter: It was <u>very very</u> difficult.
            Both of us were-
                   Deborah: mhm
            both of us were struggling,
            and even when I think of s-
            yknow I would've <u>stayed</u> in the relationship
            but it wasn't .. from .. that it was so <u>great</u>,
                   Deborah: mhm
            it's just that I felt .. like .. in terms
            of bringing up your children, and

Deborah: That's what you do, yeah.

Peter: ... That's what you do.
                   Deborah: mhm
                   ...

Steve: I hate to tell you, Peter,
            but that's not what you do anymore.
            [all laugh]

Deborah: <u>This</u> is what you do.

Chad: This is what you do?

Peter: It's pretty crazy though, it's really /?/

Deborah: Either way it's crazy.

Steve: I think it's crazy to stay together.
            You're miserable.

When Peter said that he would have stayed with his wife for the sake of their children, I paraphrased his line of argument by saying, "That's what you do." This paraphrase is a meaning repetition that says, "I understand your point so well that I can rephrase it for you." Peter ratified my contribution by repeating it: "That's what you do." This repetition implies, "Yes, that's what I meant: I approve of your contribution, so I will incorporate it into my own discourse, to show you that you got it right and I appreciate your empathy."

Steve then used the words of our now-joint phrase to turn it around: "That's not what you do anymore." This repetition implied, "People no longer stay together for the sake of the kids. What people do now is get divorced, just as you're doing." If Steve had made this statement in new words, no one would have laughed, because it could be a serious point, but because he took our words and turned the meaning around, it came across as humorous, and everyone laughed. I then used the same strategy to support Steve's reversal: "*This* is what you do." At this point Chad joined the conversation by repeating my words as a question: "This is what you do?" Repetition made it easy for Chad to take part, even though he did not know the other people present very well.

Peter, maintaining his serious key and his position that one might as well stay in a difficult relationship, disagreed with his brother by saying, "It's pretty crazy though," because he did not want the divorce; his wife did. My response, "Either way it's crazy," borrowed—and thereby ratified— Peter's words to agree with him, but also to agree with Steve's counter-claim that couples no longer stay together despite marital difficulties. Steve rounded out this "verse" by also picking up the phrase "it's crazy" and re-shaping Peter's (and now my) words to strengthen his own position: "I think it's crazy to stay together."

Line by line, you can see the repetitions performing a variety of functions in the conversation, adding new meanings in creative ways. On the relationship level, by repeating each other's words, we picked up threads of each other's discourse to weave a coherent conversation in which we all felt connected to each other.

SO HE SAID/SO I SAID: DIALOGUE

The term *reported speech* is often used to refer to quotations that actually represent what someone said rather than paraphrasing it. When people tell each other about their own experiences or about other people and events, representing the voices of those in the stories creates a more vivid scene than simply paraphrasing what was said. More often than not, the words represented in the story are not literally the words that were spoken. Rather, creating dialogue makes the point of the story in a more dramatic way. For that reason, I have coined the term *constructed dialogue* to replace the term *reported speech*.

It is sometimes obvious that dialogue created in conversation was not actually spoken by anyone. For example, a student in my class recorded a conversation in which a guest addressed a question to a cat, and the host answered by creating speech for the cat. The cat was sitting on the win-dowsill looking out:

Guest: What do you see out there, kitty?

Host: She says, "I see a beautiful world out there just waiting for me."

The host used a high-pitched, childlike voice to show that he was speaking as the cat, not as himself.

Another situation in which it is obvious that the dialogue is created, not reported, is when listeners provide lines of dialogue for stories that recount events they did not witness. Another student recorded a conversation in which someone told about the time her brother cast a fishing rod and accidentally sunk a lure in their father's face. The speaker, Lois, described her father arriving at the hospital holding the lure in his face. Joe, a listener, offered a line of dialogue spoken by a hypothetical nurse that satirizes the absurdity of the situation:

Lois: So he's walkin' around-

Joe: "Excuse, me, Sir, you've got a lure on your face."

Since Joe was not there, we know that he is not "reporting" what he heard but rather constructing a line of dialogue to contribute to the story. This serves a function very much like my paraphrasing the point of Peter's story in the earlier example: it shows that Joe was listening and following the story, and that he was eager to be involved in telling it as well. By allowing Joe's dialogue to become part of her story, Lois ratified his contribution and created connection between them.

Even when speakers recount their own experiences, there is no reason to believe that the words of dialogue they represent in their stories are the exact words that were spoken—though even if they were, choosing just those words to repeat in the story is still a creative act, constructing an effective story. One last example of dialogue comes from another story recorded by a student in my class. A medical resident returned home from a stint in a hospital emergency room and told about how three young men had come into the emergency room and caused a commotion. One of them was covered with blood, but his wound was relatively superficial:

They come bustin' through the door,
blood is everywhere.
It's on the walls, on the floor, everywhere.
[sobbing] "It's okay Billy! We're gonna make it!"
[normal voice] "What the hell's wrong with you."
W-we-we look at him.
He's covered with blood yknow?
All they had to do was take a washcloth at home
and go like this . . .
and there'd be no blood.
There'd be no blood.[3]

The young doctor could have stated that the wounded boy's friends were reassuring him that everything would be all right. Instead, he took on the voice of the friends, giving the words a sobbing quality and thereby communicating that the young men were out of control, highly emotional, and causing a stir. The emotional way that he created the dialogue—[sobbing] "It's okay, Billy! We're gonna make it!"—contrasts with the calm voice of the doctors who asked: [normal voice] "What the hell's wrong with you." I have written this sentence with a period at the end rather than a question mark because the intonation did not go up at the end; instead it remained steady, part of the contrast between the hysterical young men and the calm, cool, and collected doctors.

In all these examples, by creating dialogue, speakers tell about experiences in a more dramatic way, just as writers of stories and plays create drama through dialogue.

DETAILS

It is not unusual to hear someone say, "Skip the details. Get to the point." But when you are having a casual conversation with a friend, it would be just as likely—maybe more—to hear someone say, "Give me the whole story, with all the juicy details." Indeed, the juice of a story is often in the details. When you hear details, you recognize an experience or a scene and can fill in the rest with your own memory or imagination.

An interest in details can also be a way that listeners show interest in other people because by giving details, speakers are giving a sense of their experience. A woman told me that her family referred to her grandmother, pejoratively, as "I had a little ham, I had a little cheese." This captured what they regarded as Grandma's boring habit of telling details they did not need to know, such as what she ate for lunch. I recalled this woman's grandmother when my own great-aunt, many years a widow, had a love affair when she was in her late 70s. Obese, balding, her hands and legs misshapen by arthritis, she did not fit the stereotype of a woman romantically loved. But she was—by a man, also in his 70s, who lived in a nursing home but occasionally spent weekends with her in her apartment.

In telling me what this relationship meant to her, my great-aunt recounted a conversation. One evening she had had dinner at the home of friends. When she returned to her own home that evening, her man friend called. In the course of their conversation, he asked her, "What did you wear?" When she told me this, she began to cry. "Do you know how many years it has been," she asked, "since anyone asked me what I wore?" Asking for a detail like what she wore showed personal interest in her—the kind of interest usually reserved for intimate relationships.

How often, when people tell what happened to them, do they begin by trying to recall the exact time ("It was what? '92? '93?") or the exact place (as a man recalled about an experience that occurred on a street corner in Washington, D.C., "It was 18th and M, or 18th and L"). It usually makes little difference to the point of the story whether it occurred in 1992 or 1993, or on which specific corner. But we all know the experience of trying to recall exactly where and when something occurred, so watching others try to retrieve such details from their memory gives us an impression of verisimilitude. If you know the city being described, being able to picture the specific corner makes it easier for you to create a scene in your own mind, whether or not it is exactly like the scene that the speaker experienced.

In filling in a scene based on details, listeners do some of the work of making meaning in the conversation. If they do this successfully, the result is a feeling of involvement in the conversation and with the person telling the details.

CONCLUSION

Those who study literary works such as novels, stories, and poems often analyze the language used. Among the linguistic elements that have been analyzed in literature are repetition, reported speech, and the use of imagery. These same linguistic elements are also basic to everyday conversation. By looking at transcripts of conversation for repetition, dialogue, and details, you can begin to see the seeds of literary language in the language of daily talk. Seeing the patterns of these linguistic elements also helps you appreciate the poetic power of words in conversation and how they bring us together in a community of talk.

NOTES

The material in this chapter comes from my book *Talking Voices: Repetition, Dialogue, and Imagery in Conversational Discourse* (Cambridge University Press, 1989). The introductory section is similar to my article " 'Oh Talking Voice That Is So Sweet': The Poetic Nature of Conversation" that appeared in the journal *Social Research*, Vol. 65, No. 3 (Fall 1998), pp. 631–651.

1. Mathabane (pronounced motta-BAH-nay) was a guest on *The Diane Rehm Show*, WAMU-FM, Washington, DC, August 28, 1989, on the publication of his book *Kaffir Boy in America*.

2. I have broken up the transcript into lines not to imply that it is really poetry but to re-create the chunking of words into breath groups that occurs naturally when people talk. Spoken language does not come out in long undifferentiated blocks, like a paragraph in writing, but rather in short spurts that are visually represented by lines in poetry. Other transcription conventions:

.	Period shows sentence-final falling intonation
?	Question mark shows sentence-final rising intonation
,	Comma shows clause-final intonation ("more to come")

/?/   Question mark in slashes shows inaudible utterance
-               Hyphen shows abrupt cutting off of breath
...   Three unspaced dots show half second pause
..   Two unspaced dots show less than half-second pause
Underline   shows emphatic stress.

3. Notice the repetition of the line "There'd be no blood," which does not add any new meaning but rather adds emphasis.

V

On Dictionaries and Grammars

WHO WROTE YOUR DICTIONARY? DEMYSTIFYING THE CONTENTS AND CONSTRUCTION OF DICTIONARIES

Sylvia Shaw

WHO WROTE YOUR DICTIONARY?

Although most people possess a dictionary and refer to it when they want to find out how a word is spelled, settle a dispute about what a word means, or decide whether a word belongs to a language or not, it is unlikely that they will know who wrote it. It is also unusual for people to question the validity of information found in a dictionary or think it strange that some of the words they use in everyday conversations are not actually included.

Of course, your dictionary was probably written by a group of lexicographers on a large project, headed by an eminent editor. The reason why people do not question the information that they find in a dictionary is that it is perceived as being an extremely authoritative source of information about a particular language. If you asked someone why they believed the information contained in a dictionary, they would probably only be able to answer something like "because it's a dictionary!" However, a dictionary is a type of text, and (like any other text), it is constructed by a person or group of people, by a process of construction, for a particular purpose and readership. It is only by asking simple questions such as what is "the dictionary"? what is (and is not) contained within it? and how is it made? that these publications can be demystified and their contents assessed. This chapter considers some of the questions that people do not normally think to ask about dictionaries and their construction.

WHAT IS "THE DICTIONARY"?

When most people think of a dictionary, they think of the kind of dictionary that they use most frequently. For many people this is a *native-*

speaker dictionary. Some examples of English-language native-speaker dictionaries are the *Oxford English Dictionary* (*OED*) (Simpson and Weiner 1989) and *Merriam-Webster's Collegiate Dictionary* (Mish 1995). These dictionaries are for people whose first language is English, and they are intended to be guides to standard or correct spelling, pronunciation, and meaning. When "the dictionary" is referred to, it is normally this type of dictionary that is meant. It is a dictionary with a long tradition. Samuel Johnson published his *A Dictionary of the English Language* in 1755, the first edition of Noah Webster's *American Dictionary of the English Language* was published in 1828, and the first edition of the *OED* was published in 1888.

These general-purpose native-speaker dictionaries of the English language originally had overtly prescriptive aims, which means that they tried to inform people about how they should (and should not) use language. Only words that were deemed to be "correct" and to belong to the standard varieties of the language were included. They validated their claims about what was or was not "correct" English by collecting citations from what were thought to be the most prestigious writers of the times. As described below, citations are now taken from a much greater range of sources, and modern dictionaries aim to include many different varieties of English. However, even today, much of the authority that these dictionaries have is due to their long historical tradition and their declared aims of representing the "correct" version of the English language.

Another common type of dictionary is the *bilingual dictionary*, which is used by students of a second language. These dictionaries have the vocabulary of one language with definitions in another language, often followed by a second section that reverses the two languages. These dictionaries rely on translation of the meanings of the words into one language from another being carried out accurately, and when there are a range of equivalent translations for a word or meaning the learner must select the correct one.

A type of dictionary aimed specifically at advanced learners of English is known as the *monolingual learners' dictionary*. This type of dictionary works on the principle that when learners of English as a second language have reached a level of ability where they are fairly competent in English, it is not a good idea for them to translate "back" into their first language to find the meaning of a word. It helps their linguistic acquisition of the "new" language if they remain in that language, even when they are finding out what new words mean. For this reason, the definitions of all the words in this type of dictionary are in English (unlike the bilingual dictionary), and are constructed using a "simple" or basic vocabulary so that they are easy to understand. The aim of this type of dictionary is to be as useful and informative as possible to students learning English, rather than to represent "correct" English. This type of dictionary is therefore not prescriptive, but aims to be descriptive and, in particular, to describe what actually happens in a language in a way that is helpful for learners, rather than to prescribe how users should use the language.

Other types of specialist dictionaries include dictionaries of particular aspects of the language such as dictionaries of new words, phrasal verbs, or idioms. There are also dictionaries of medical terms, philosophy, and probably every other academic discipline, as well as dictionaries for many popular hobbies and activities. In each case these are books that loosely follow the format of a general-purpose native-speaker dictionary in that they are alphabetically organized and provide definitions for individual words or phrases.

So when someone refers to "the dictionary," he or she is usually referring to one of many different types of dictionary, namely, the general-purpose native-speaker dictionary of a particular language (such as the *OED* or *Merriam-Webster's Collegiate Dictionary*). We now turn to consider exactly what type of information is contained within this sort of dictionary by contrasting it with a monolingual learners' dictionary.

WHAT IS IN THE DICTIONARY?

It is commonly thought that "the dictionary" represents the totality of "the language" that it describes. However, there is much about "the language" that is not presented in dictionaries. As mentioned earlier, the information that is presented in dictionaries is linked to the purpose of the dictionary and the needs of the users, rather than objectively describing every aspect of the language. In order to show the high degree of selectivity about what is included in a dictionary, one can compare two types of dictionaries, a general-purpose native-speaker dictionary of English, *Merriam-Webster's Collegiate Dictionary* (10th edition; Mish 1995), and a monolingual learners' dictionary for learners of the English language, the *Longman Dictionary of Contemporary English* (3rd edition; Summers 1995).

One of the main differences between these dictionaries is that *Merriam-Webster's Collegiate Dictionary* is intended to show the variety of English known as American English, whereas the *Longman Dictionary of Contemporary English* (*LDOCE3*) is intended to describe both British English and American English. Apart from this central difference, a number of other differences exist between the dictionaries. The following example shows the first part of the entry for the word *confound* in *Merriam-Webster's Collegiate Dictionary*:

> **confound** \[pronunciation]\vt [ME, fr. MF *confondre*, fr. L *confundere* to pour together, confuse, fr. *com-* + *fundere* to pour] **1 a** *archaic*: to bring to ruin: DESTROY **b**: BAFFLE, FRUSTRATE **2** *obs*: CONSUME, WASTE (adapted from Mish 1995, 242)

After showing the pronunciation of the word (which is not shown in the extract given here) and informing the reader that the word is a transitive verb by the label "vt," the entry gives some etymological detail. The etymology of a word refers to its origin and history. In this entry, the letters "ME" and "MF" stand for Middle English and Middle French, respectively, and this information gives an indication of the earliest usage and origin of the word. Information about the derivation of the word from Latin origins is given. In addition to the etymology of the word, the entry gives a number of senses of the word. The first sense is marked *archaic*, showing that this use is old-fashioned. The definitions are short and rely on synonyms or word equivalents, which are shown in small capitals. One of the senses is marked *obs*, which stands for "obsolete" and shows that this sense is no longer used in contemporary English.

In comparison, the entry for the word *confound* in *LDOCE3* is quite different:

> **confound** \[pronunciation]\ *v* [T]   **1** to confuse and surprise people by being unexpected: *His amazing recovery confounded the medical specialists*   **2** *formal* to defeat an enemy, plan, etc   **3** If a problem etc confounds you, you cannot understand it or solve it: *Her question completely confounded me.*
> (adapted from Summers 1995, 286)

This entry does not contain etymological information, and the definitions are written with "simple" vocabulary. Each of the senses gives an example of a way in which the word is typically used. *LDOCE3* gives a total of four senses for the word *confound*, while *Merriam-Webster's Collegiate Dictionary* gives six senses plus a number of subsenses. The point of comparing these two dictionaries is not to suggest that one of them is more "correct" or somehow a "better" description of the English language. What it shows is that a native-speaker dictionary such as *Merriam-Webster's* gives an extremely detailed account of particular aspects of a word, such as etymological information, and "obsolete" senses. This type of detail is not necessary or helpful to an advanced learner of English, so *LDOCE3* gives only the most central senses of the word, does not give synonyms as definitions, and presents the definitions and examples in vocabulary that will be easy to understand.

As mentioned earlier, native-speaker dictionaries like *Merriam-Webster's* are intended to represent a standard version of a language. In doing so, they do not include many of the informal words we use in speech because these are not considered to be part of that standard. In particular, these dictionaries do not include words or meanings in spoken language that have interactional functions in conversation (such as the meanings of *sure* shown in the next paragraph), or very informal words and phrases such as *never mind* or *wotcha* (which means "hello" in British English). These types of dictionaries are very much biased toward written language rather than spoken language, although spoken language probably accounts for over 90 percent of total language production.

Traditionally, some linguists have tended to perceive written language and spoken language as dichotomies, with one medium having supremacy over the other (Biber 1988, 6). Some prescriptive grammarians have thought that written language is "better" or more correct than spoken language and have viewed spoken language as being haphazard and full of "errors" (Cheepen and Managhan 1990, 2). It is certainly true that spoken language is more informal than written language and contains what many people would call slang or colloquial expressions, yet *LDOCE3* attempts to describe spoken language as well as written language because it is useful for advanced learners of the English language to be able to understand and produce all types of English, from formal written styles to informal conversational styles. For example, *LDOCE3* gives a number of senses for the word *sure* that only occur in spoken language:

3 *Spoken especially AmE* used to say 'yes' to someone: *"Can you give me a ride to work tomorrow?" "Sure."*

4 *AmE Spoken* used as a way of replying to someone when they thank you: *"Thanks for your help Karen." "Sure."*

5 *AmE informal* used to emphasise a statement: *Mom's sure gonna be mad when she gets home.* (Summers 1995, 1449)

These spoken senses of the word *sure* are included in the dictionary because information about conversational English may help learners attain a higher degree of fluency in the language. These senses are not given in *Merriam-Webster's Collegiate Dictionary*. There is a usage note under the entry, but the note only mentions the sense of *sure* to emphasize what is said, and compares the use of *sure* and *surely* (Mish 1995, 1185).

Spoken language can be a rich source of data for the lexicographer, especially to gain information about new words or *neologisms*. These new words typically originate in spoken language or the print media and are gradually absorbed into the rest of the language until they become included into native-speaker dictionaries. Some new words arise because a new object or concept has been created that needs a name, such as *e-mail*. Other neologisms include words that already exist but whose meanings change with time, such as the meaning of the word *bad* changing from meaning "very negative" to meaning "good" when used by children and adolescents in London. In order to identify new words, lexicographers can read publications such as youth-oriented magazines, newspapers, and specialist magazines for business or computing. Any words that are not already defined in the dictionary can be considered for inclusion. The difficulty with deciding whether to include a new word or sense of a word is that some words are ephemeral or transitory. These words only exist in the language for a particular period of time and then are no longer used. An example of this is the word *yuppie*. This is a slightly derogatory word that means a "young, urban professional." It was used especially of young adults in the mid-to-late 1980s who were extremely ambitious and motivated by economic gain. A lexicographer writing a dictionary at that time would have found many citations of this word in the print media and on television and so might have included the word in the dictionary. The lexicographer would have had no way of knowing that the use of the word *yuppie* would not extend into the 1990s, and the word would in the future be associated with the ethos of individual achievement and economic boom thought to characterize the 1980s. In terms of the dictionary, the inclusion of transitory words such as *yuppie* would make the dictionary appear dated after a very short period of time. In the same way, the omission of neologisms can also make a dictionary appear out-of-date: *Merriam-Webster's Collegiate Dictionary* does not contain an entry for *stalking* (the criminal activity), but only includes a definition of the general meaning at the entry for *stalk*. This omission makes the publication appear dated, as the concept and activity of "stalking" is a 1990s phenomenon, involving the creation of new criminal legislation to combat "stalkers," and is the focus of much debate in the media. These are important considerations because revising dictionaries and making new editions of dictionaries is an extremely expensive process and may only happen at intervals of five or more years. Therefore, it is important that the information within the dictionary appears to be "up-to-date" for as long as possible.

The fact that neologisms often arise in spoken language brings up another problem for dictionary makers in including spoken language in dictionaries. This is associated with the transitory nature of speech itself. As soon as someone utters a neologism or phrase in spoken language, it disappears. The sounds of speech need to be recorded in some way to allow lexicographers to analyze and refer to them. In order to record and analyze a conversation, a researcher would need to record the conversation on audiotape and then make a written interpretation of the sounds of speech in the form of a transcription. Compared to the ease with which written material can be collected and analyzed, the analysis of spoken language is much more lengthy, time-consuming, and expensive. These practical considerations have not helped to increase the balance of spoken-language data to written-language data incorporated into dictionaries.

HOW IS THE DICTIONARY MADE?

There are a number of tools available to the lexicographer in order to help analyze exactly what a word means, determine what part of speech it best belongs to, and arrive at accurate definitions. The first source of evidence about word meaning is the intuition of the lexicographer; if his or her first language is English, the lexicographer will have accurate and reliable knowledge about most words in the English language. However, this type of knowledge must be supplemented by other sources of evidence because an individual's knowledge of the language may be somewhat idiosyncratic, and he or she will not know about all the words in the language.

Traditionally, since Samuel Johnson's *Dictionary* (1755), hand-gathered citations have been used to analyze word meaning. Johnson's citations were all examples taken from English literature, so his dictionary reflected written rather than spoken English. Over time, the range of text types that citations were drawn from increased dramatically until the sources included popular magazines and newspapers.

In the mid-1980s, the process of collecting and examining citations by hand was revolutionized by the advent of large-scale computerized corpora. These databases replaced the traditional citations and consisted of millions of words of written and spoken English. The size of these corpora, together with the fact that information could be extracted from them very quickly, allowed the incorporation of many different text types in one computerized database. Some linguists claim that the largest corpora (of 100 million words or more) are so vast and cover such a diverse range of written and spoken text types that what is found within them is representative of what is actually in the language. Therefore, if a word is not very frequent in the corpus, lexicographers can deduce that the word is not very frequent in the language itself. However, this is a contentious claim, and it is more accurate to conclude that the data within dictionaries represent the citations and corpora that were used to compile them, rather than an absolute or objective view of the totality of a language.

WHAT IS *NOT* IN THE DICTIONARY?

The reliance of dictionaries on particular databases or citation indexes is an important factor in considering what may be left out of them. When new editions of dictionaries are written, they are not normally constructed anew, but simply updated or modernized. Much of the text remains unchanged from one decade to the next, relying on the original analysis of a word based on old citations. In this way it is also possible for dictionaries to carry historical prejudices that are perpetuated by collecting material for citation selectively.

The *OED* was first published in 1888 and mainly relied on citations from literature for information about the meanings of different words. Modern editions have shifted emphasis toward American sources and periodicals but have continued to neglect citations from works by women and workers and writing from other English-speaking countries (Willinsky 1994). It has been noted that "clearly the Oxford English Dictionary is no simple record of the English Language 'as she is spoke'. It is a selective representation reflecting certain elusive ideas about the nature of the English Language and its people" (Willinsky 1994, 13).

The reliance of publications like the *OED* on literary citations meant that other types of written language were not deemed suitable for evidence of word meaning. A number of researchers have pointed out that people employed in clerical jobs, such as scribes and clerks, played an important role in the initial development of standards for written British English in the fifteenth century (Willinsky 1994, 178):

> The truth of the matter is that *written* literature (poems, plays, tales, sermons, treatises) bulked as small in the lives of most people in the fifteenth century as they do now. . . . The sort of writing most likely to carry a sense of national authority would be bureaucratic (licenses, records, etc.), legal (inheritance, transfer of property), or business (bills, agreements, instructions). (Fisher 1977 894)

Many common types of written language were omitted from the dictionary, and literary works were privileged when inclusion in the citation indexes was considered.

Some studies have shown, for example, that the wording of definitions in the *OED* has been detrimental to women, both by defining characteristics associated with women in a negative way and by the social stereotyping of women in roles limited to appearance and domestic roles (Fournier and Russell 1992, 19). There is also an imbalance toward male authors in the works collected in the *OED* citation index. Female authors, even prolific writers, have been altogether omitted. Even though female authors historically were much less common than male authors, women's contribution to publishing and the language "appears to be the dictionary's most notable omission." It is also noted that

> this exclusion has its roots in the general regard of the masculine hold over artistic creation, philosophical speculation, scientific inquiry, political theory and so on. But even in areas in which women came to dominate publishing activity, such as with the eighteenth century novel, their work was to be overshadowed in literature courses and dictionary citations by a few male writers. (Willinsky 1994, 184)

The construction of the *OED* also omitted written language of the working classes. Although such publications as the pamphlet "The Poor Man's Plea against the Extravagant Price of Corn" (1699) and the *Mechanics Magazine* (1823–71) were included in the citation indexes, many publications, including working-class newspapers, were omitted (Willinsky 1994, 182). The circulation of these newspapers was large, and certainly the genre of written language represented in these papers reflected the norms of written language for a majority of the population.

Recently, there have been attempts to reintroduce instances of over-looked citations from different historical periods and from different social classes into the *OED* citation indexes (Schäfer 1989). Some writers have also attempted to reauthorize women's participation in language with publications such as *A Feminist Dictionary* (Kramarae and Treichler 1985), which, for example, includes as one of the definitions for the word *home* the sense "most women's place of work" (Cameron 1985, 115).

The omission of particular types of writing such as journalese, as well as the omission of writing by specific groups in society such as women and workers, can be pinpointed and traced in the history of a dictionary such as the *OED*. Although there have been attempts to reintroduce some of these overlooked works, the consequences of their omission upon the standardization and development of English are likely to be profound and to a large extent irrevocable.

CONCLUSION

Dictionaries are for many people an everyday guide to word meaning and usage. General-purpose native-speaker dictionaries are one of many types of dictionary that seek to describe the standard variety of a language. In doing so, the dictionary is a publication that not only reflects but also helps to promote the very standard it describes. Dictionaries cannot reflect the entirety of "the language" and have traditionally concentrated on written rather than spoken language, as well as omitting citations of written language from a number of sources. It is only by analyzing the processes of dictionary construction and by attempting to answer such questions as "Who wrote the dictionary?" that the selectivity of the information represented in these publications can be revealed.

REFERENCES

Biber, Douglas. 1988. *Variation across speech and writing.* Cambridge: Cambridge University Press.

Cameron, Deborah. 1985. *Feminism and linguistic theory.* London: Macmillan.

Cheepen, Christine, and J. Monaghan. 1990. *Spoken English: A practical guide.* London: Pinter.

Fisher, John. 1977. Chancery and the emergence of Standard Written English in the fifteenth century. *Speculum* 52: 870–99.

Fournier, Hannah S., and Delbert W. Russell. 1992. A study of sex role stereotyping in the Oxford English Dictionary 2E. *Computers and the Humanities* 26, 13–20.

Johnson, Samuel. 1755. *A Dictionary of the English language.*

Kramarae, Cheris, and Paula Treichler. 1985. *A feminist dictionary*. Boston: Pandora.

Mish, Frederick C., ed. 1995. *Merriam-Webster's Collegiate Dictionary*. 10th ed. Springfield, MA: Merriam-Webster.

Schäfer, Jürgen. 1989. *Early modern English lexicography: Additions and corrections to the OED*. Vol. 2. Oxford: Oxford University Press.

Simpson, J. A., and Weiner, E. S. C. eds. 1989. *The Oxford English dictionary*. 2nd ed. Oxford: Oxford University Press.

Summers, Della, ed. 1995. *Longman dictionary of contemporary English*. 3rd ed. Harlow: Longman.

Willinsky, John. 1994. *Empire of words: The reign of the OED*. Princeton, NJ: Princeton University Press.

FURTHER READING

Dictionary

Jackson, Howard. 1988. *Words and their meaning*. Harlow: Longman.

Corpora

Aijmer, K., and B. Altenberg, eds. 1991. *English corpus linguistics*. Harlow: Longman.

McEnery, Tony, and Andrew Wilson. 1996. *Corpus Linguistics*. Edinburgh: Edinburgh University Press.

Feminist Lexicography

Mills, Jane. 1991. *Womanwords: A vocabulary of culture and patriarchal society*. London: Virago.

ONLINE RESOURCES FOR GRAMMAR TEACHING AND LEARNING: THE INTERNET GRAMMAR OF ENGLISH

Bas Aarts, Gerald Nelson, and Justin Buckley

The question of how to teach grammar to high-school students and undergraduate students has exercized many linguists and teachers over time and continues to be the focus of much interest. Traditional teaching tools often fail to fulfill students' needs for a variety of reasons. One of these concerns the fact that grammar is often perceived to be a dry and boring topic. Another drawback of traditional grammar is that it is frequently explained by making heavy use of notional concepts. Thus, for example, under a notional definition nouns are traditionally said to be words that denote the names of people, places, or things, verbs are words that express actions, and so on. In modern approaches to grammar teaching the methodology is different. Here emphasis is placed on defining terms by making reference to the order of the elements of the language being described, for example, how particular words or word classes are arranged with regard to each other. In other words, modern grammar relies much less on meaning in defining particular grammatical terms; instead it regards *distribution* as being of paramount importance. Thus, instead of defining nouns as being words that refer to people, places, and so on, modern grammar additionally characterizes them distributionally by noting that, for example, they are a word class that displays a number contrast. What this means is that nouns can occur in the singular form (*cat*) or in the plural form (*cats*). We return to this issue later.

We believe that the problems with regard to the traditional teaching of grammar signaled in the preceding paragraph can be overcome, and we have written a new type of grammar of English, not in book form, but on the World Wide Web. We call it the Internet Grammar of English (IGE).

IGE is a fully fledged networked resource for grammar teaching, available to everyone with Internet access.[1]

WHAT IS IGE?

The Internet Grammar of English is a description of the grammar of the English language and a tool to study English grammar interactively using a computer. We have aimed it primarily at undergraduate university students, but students in the final year of high school will also benefit. The course is not designed for learners of English whose mother tongue is not English, but again, these users are naturally not excluded from using IGE, nor is the general public. Typically, we expect you as a user of IGE to have some notion of what grammar is about, but your knowledge might be a little patchy and hazy. From our point of view, what this means is that we expect that you have heard terms such as *noun, verb,* and *adjective* before, but you may not be able to specify exactly what these terms mean. Similarly, you might know what the notion of word class refers to, but have no idea what criteria classify one word as an adjective, another as an adverb, and so on. In this chapter we will take a closer look at IGE and show you some of its characteristics. It would be ideal if you log on to the IGE site while you read this chapter. The address is *http://www.ucl.ac.uk/ internet-grammar/.*

OUTLINE AND GENERAL CHARACTERISTICS OF IGE

When you log on to IGE, (or load the CD-ROM), you are connected to IGE's Home Page, shown in figure 18.1. Please take a moment to see what this page and the screen shots that follow contain. Note that this page is the hub of the IGE site from which you will be able to access any part of the grammar, whether for the first time or after returning, having taken a break from studying. The screen divides naturally into two parts, with navigation tools, such as the Contents, Glossary, Index, and Search buttons on the left, and the main component, notably the entry point to the grammar (the "Click here to start" button), on the right. In the sections that follow we will look at each of the components of IGE in turn, as well as the "add-on" features such as the Exercises, which are embedded in the topic pages. We start with a description of the course in general.

The course is designed in such a way as to guide you through a predefined path in the grammar. IGE starts with a description of the smallest elements, words, and then moves on to phrases, clauses, and sentences. After dealing with this "bottom-up" approach (sometimes referred to as a "rank scale") we then move on to a discussion of grammatical functions such as subject, direct object, adjunct, and so on. A very important part of the grammar is an explanation of how exactly form and function relate to

Figure 18.1
The Internet Grammar of English Home Page

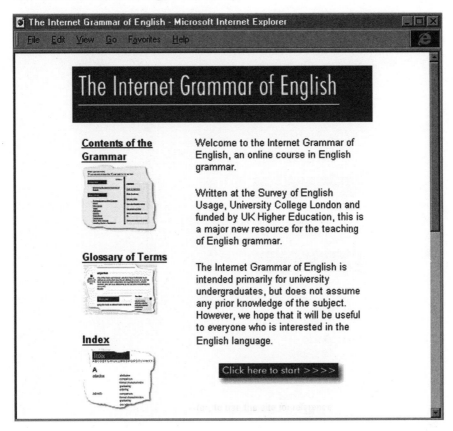

each other. If you click on the Contents button on the left you are taken to the screen shown in figure 18.2.

SOME EXAMPLES

The best way to illustrate the workings of IGE is by looking at a few examples of topic pages. We will start by presenting a page from the part of the grammar that deals with word classes (figure 18.3). This screen shot shows the first page of a total of five pages dealing with nouns. The way we have written the grammar is to start with a general introductory section that characterizes nouns. This is what is shown in the screen shot. As you can see, we start off defining nouns in the traditional way, as "naming words," but we quickly move away from this definition, as linguists now

Figure 18.2
IGE's Contents Page

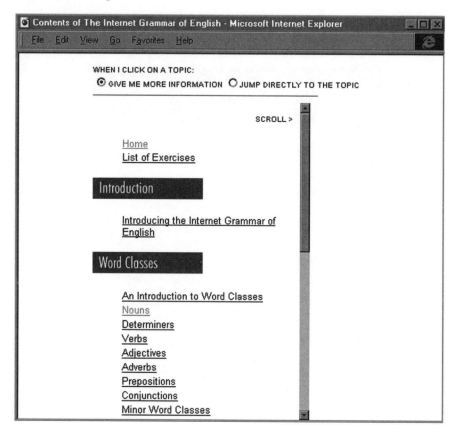

generally regard this definition as inadequate: it is easy to think of many nouns that do not name people, places, or things at all, such as *love, happiness*, and *endurance*. It is much better to define nouns by discussing the way they behave in sentences, that is, the way they are *distributed*. For example, we can say that nouns can take plural *-s* endings, as we saw earlier, or they can be preceded by words like *the*, or can be positioned in the blank slot of the sequence "My ——— phoned me this morning." Furthermore, nouns are embedded in larger units called *phrases*. Examples are *an interesting person* or *that tedious film about a sinking ship*, and we call such stretches of words, where the noun is the principal element, *Noun Phrases*. Figure 18.4 shows an excerpt from the IGE page on Noun Phrases.

The World Wide Web has enabled us to use the latest technology to teach grammar in a novel way. We believe that among the most exciting

Figure 18.3
IGE's First Page on Nouns

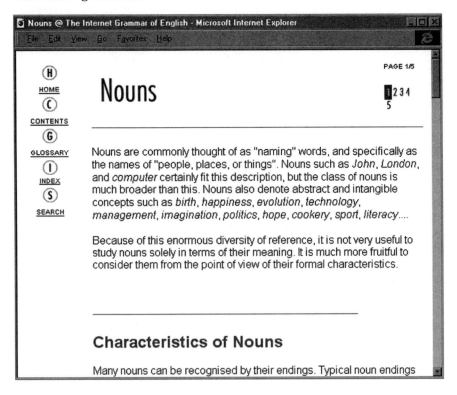

types of pages in IGE are those involving animation. The use of animation allows us to use moving images on screen to build sentences, construct trees, activate demos, and so on. For example, we can show how a particular sentence is structured by slowly putting together its components on screen, or show how a so-called *active* sentence like "My sister bought this CD" is related to its *passive* counterpart "This CD was bought by my sister." By using animation you will get a much better feel for the structure of sentences, their building blocks, and how they are related. This is a major advantage of IGE over traditional approaches to grammar.[2]

IGE'S COVERAGE OF ENGLISH GRAMMAR

You may be wondering how much of English grammar IGE actually covers. Naturally, we have aimed to cover at least the basics of any topic in the grammar of English. What we mean by this is that we have tried to give the user enough information so that he or she can identify the elements

Figure 18.4
Beginning of IGE's Section on Noun Phrases

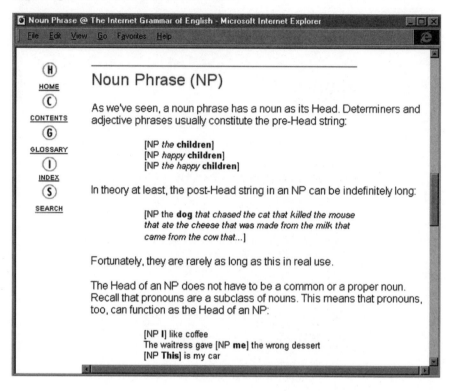

of language, say, nouns and their associated Noun Phrases, and knows where these elements occur in sentence structure. In addition, we have striven to make clear how these elements *function* in sentences. For example, in a sentence like "My brother left the house," we like you to know that *my brother* is a Noun Phrase that functions as the subject. While the basics of grammar are absolutely crucial, in many cases we have been much more ambitious in taking users beyond the core grammar of English. This is why IGE discusses topics that are less central, but nevertheless of interest for the initiated user. Let us briefly illustrate this point by looking at English auxiliary verbs. Auxiliary verbs are "helping verbs" that occur before other verbs to express a certain meaning. In the sentence "Mary can come to the party," the main verb is *come*, and this verb is preceded by an auxiliary verb, namely, *can*. In isolation this sentence is actually ambiguous and expresses either that "Mary is able to come to the party" or that "Mary is permitted to come to the party." The meanings "ability" and "permission" are, as it were, added on to the meaning of the main verb *come*, hence

Figure 18.5
Excerpt from the IGE Page for Auxiliary Verbs

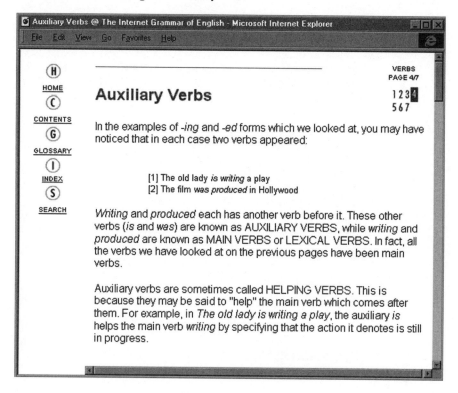

"helping verb." Consider now the screen shot from the page for auxiliary verbs in figure 18.5. This page deals with a more detailed characterization of the notion of auxiliary verb and extends the initial definition of auxiliaries as helping verbs. The terminology used is slightly more technical.

THE EXERCISES

No learning process is complete without practice and revision. We believe that doing exercises consolidates the knowledge you have acquired and is absolutely essential when learning grammar. We also believe that doing exercises need not be a chore. It should be *fun*. There is no need for the stuffy kind of "pattern repetition" exercises that were used during the 1970s and 1980s. These exercises involved students learning patterns by heart. The underlying philosophy was that if you repeat a certain pattern or structure often enough, you will eventually master it. This method was especially popular in the teaching of foreign languages. We believe that you

Figure 18.6
Example of an Exercise on Verbs

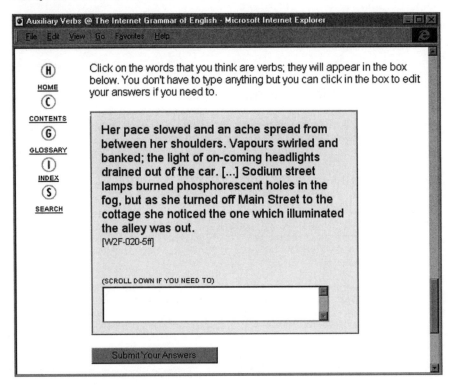

are much more likely to learn the material you have been asked to study if it is linked to your world and interests, and if the material is enjoyable to study and use. As a young and dynamic medium, the World Wide Web allows for new and exciting ways of designing different types of exercises. IGE makes full and creative use of these new possibilities. Each section of IGE has a generous set of exercises appended to it that we hope will be stimulating and a pleasure to do. The exercises in IGE are exercises with a difference. Not only do they require you to do something, you can get immediate feedback. Let us become a little more concrete and take a look at some examples of exercises.

Figure 18.6 shows an exercise from IGE's section on verbs. Here you are prompted to click on the main verbs in the sentences displayed, which then appear in the box below the paragraph. To check your answers, you can then click on the "Submit Your Answers" button at the end of the page. The correct items then appear on the screen, allowing you to compare these with your own responses. You are always given feedback to your responses,

Figure 18.7
Example of an Exercise on Adjectives

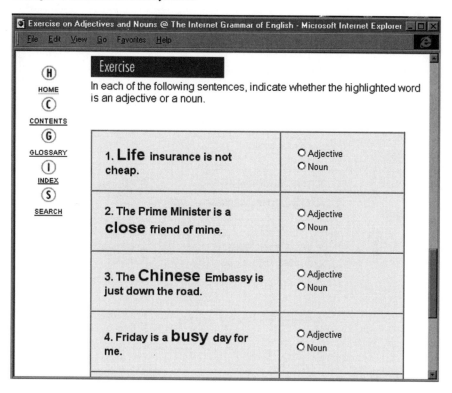

so that if your answers were wrong, you can find out exactly *why* they were wrong, as we will show in the next example, this time from the adjectives section (figure 18.7). This exercise asks you to identify the word class of the highlighted words. The correct answers are displayed on screen when the "Submit Your Answers" button is clicked (figure 18.8). Again, you can verify which answers you got right, and which you got wrong. The exercise is then reviewed, explaining the correct answers, as is shown in figure 18.9.

We feel that feedback of this type is an important part of any learning process. It enables you as a learner to assess the knowledge you have acquired and stimulates you to improve it. Naturally, exercises can also be done independently from the text, for example, when reviewing for an examination.

Exercises are interspersed within the text. There are two main reasons for this. The first is that it allows you to keep track of your own progress as you study the grammar. If you get answers wrong in the exercises, you

Figure 18.8
Answers to the Exercise on Adjectives

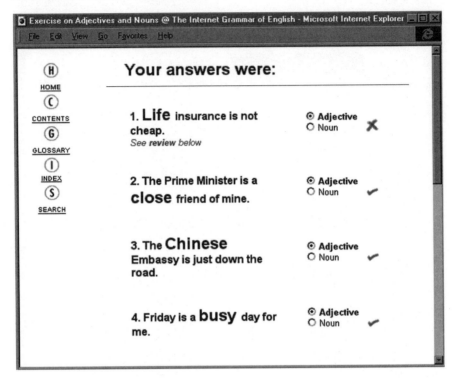

can go back to the text to review before proceeding to more difficult material. Second, we believe that in-text exercises break up the text and introduce an element of interactivity, which should result in you, as a user, feeling that you are involved in the learning process. Rather than being a vessel into which knowledge is poured, you are prompted to contribute to your own learning process.

NAVIGATION TOOLS IN IGE

Naturally, you will need to have access to the navigation tools, such as the Glossary, the Index, and so on. These are important aids when reading through a page. For example, if you have forgotten what the meaning of a particular term is, you can consult the Glossary, which is a list of grammatical terms used in IGE with their definitions. It can be regarded as a "plug-in," in that it can be opened into the main text, consulted, and then

Figure 18.9
Review of the Exercise on Adjectives

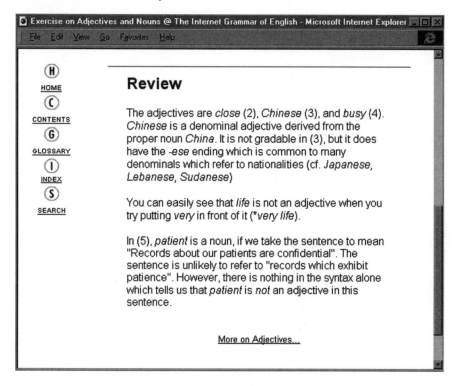

closed, at which point you return to the text you were studying. It thus works in much the same way as the glossary in a book, with one important user-friendly difference. As can be seen in figure 18.10, it is possible to open a menu of "See Also" terms, which can consecutively be consulted. However, unlike in a book, where you need a book marker or your fingers to keep tabs on other pages where "See Also" terms appear, in IGE, with the help of this menu, access to "See Also" terms is instant.

The Index is like a traditional index in that it consists of a list of words that users may want to look up in the grammar. Naturally, they are hypertext links that allow immediate access.

The Contents page (see figure 18.2) gives users an overview of the IGE site and affords immediate access to a particular part of the grammar. It is thus especially useful if you have taken a break from studying IGE, and if you want to start from where you last stopped studying. Each term on the left-hand side of the page is clickable. For example, if the user clicks on

Figure 18.10
Excerpt from IGE's Glossary

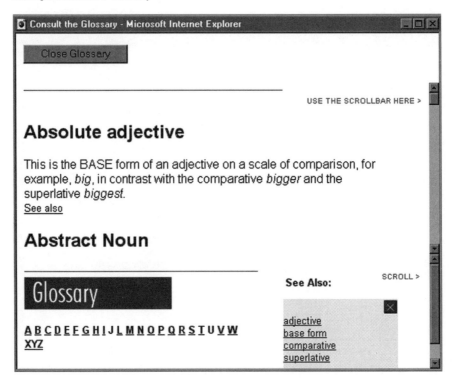

"nouns," the menu for this word class appears on the right, yielding a further set of choices. The Search facility allows users to create a list of all the pages where a particular term occurs.

REAL LANGUAGE EXAMPLES

Linguists in the past have been criticized for making use of made-up, and hence often unnatural, examples when teaching English and other languages. A phrase book that teaches learners how to say in French, "My great-grandfather was a mechanical engineer in the armed forces," somehow has its priorities wrong. The trend of using made-up examples is in the process of slowly being reversed. For example, there is now a family of dictionaries and learning books for the English language under the name *Cobuild* that pays particular attention to the fact that learners need to look at real English. As far as possible, IGE too uses real language, more specifically material from the British component of the International Corpus of English (ICE). A corpus is a collection of real language collected with a number of possible research and pedagogical goals in mind. One such goal is furnishing examples for grammars like IGE. For a much more detailed discussion of the ICE project, see Nelson and Aarts (1999).

IGE AND LEARNING

What is the best way to use IGE? As noted at the beginning of this chapter, traditional grammar teaching has often been marred by the idea that grammar is dry and boring. We believe that the fact that grammar is often viewed in this way has nothing to do with the nature of grammar, but has very much to do with the way it is taught. Given the opportunities offered by the World Wide Web, it is now possible to teach and learn grammar in a stimulating, creative, interactive, and enjoyable way. How can this be done using IGE? There are a number of possibilities, some of which we outline here.

First of all, IGE can be studied by anyone at home or in college on his or her own. Because the exercises are interactive, IGE is ideal for those who do not attend a taught course in grammar. For the students studying grammar in this way, IGE provides a system of guided learning in which feedback is delivered at regular intervals.

Second, IGE can be used as a main teaching text in small groups of students in a computer cluster room. In this setup the teacher will be on hand to answer any queries students may have. A major advantage of using IGE in this way is that the students can learn at their own speed. Naturally, students can also work in groups, ideally consisting of two students. In our experience this has the advantage that problems, but also insights, are shared, thus making the study of grammar less daunting and more fun. Answers to exercises can be compared and discussed. Students will learn from each other's understanding of the material being offered.

Third, IGE can be used as a backup for traditional teaching. Students attend "regular" classes on grammar and are then directed to IGE for review and to do the exercises. It is possible for teachers to answer questions submitted to them via e-mail.

AVAILABILITY

The Internet Grammar of English is available to everyone worldwide, currently at no cost. However, as all users of the Web know, downloading pages can take a frustratingly long time. We have therefore also decided to release IGE on CD-ROM. The major advantage of this is speed of access (and, where there is a charge for local telephone calls, a reduction of the costs for logging in). We also plan to add more exercises to the CD-ROM.

Schools, colleges, and universities can network their copy, allowing large groups of students to access the software at the same time.[3]

NOTES

1. The Internet Grammar of English forms part of the W3-Corpora project, co-ordinated at the University of Essex (*http://clwww.essex.ac.uk/w3c/*), and is funded by the Joint Information Systems Committee, grant number JTAP-2/247. The URL for IGE is *http://www.ucl.ac.uk/internet-grammar/*.

2. Naturally, it is not possible to show animation on paper. An example in IGE is shown on the following IGE page: *http://www.ucl.ac.uk/internet-grammar/function/active.htm*. You will need to use at least a version 4 browser: Netscape Communicator or Internet Explorer 4.

3. Further details on the IGE CD-ROM are available from the Survey of English Usage at *http://www.ucl.ac.uk/english-usage/*.

REFERENCE

Nelson, Gerald, and Bas Aarts. 1999. Investigating English around the world: The International Corpus of English. *The workings of language*, ed. by Rebecca S. Wheeler, 107–115. Westport, CT: Praeger.

INDEX

About the Editor and Contributors

BAS AARTS is Senior Lecturer in English Language and Director of the Survey of English Usage at University College London. He has published books and articles on English syntax, both from a descriptive and theoretical point of view, including *Small Clauses in English: The Nonverbal Types* (1992) and *The Verb in Contemporary English: Theory and Description* (edited with Charles F. Meyer, 1995). His most recent publication is *English Syntax and Argumentation* (1997). With David Denison and Richard Hogg at the University of Manchester, he edits the journal *English Language and Linguistics*, founded in 1991. He has lectured at a number of foreign universities.

EDWIN BATTISTELLA is Professor and Head of the Division of Humanities at Wayne State College in Nebraska. He received a Ph.D. in linguistics from the City University of New York in 1981. He has taught in New York City, Birmingham, Alabama, and the Czech Republic and has worked as a Visiting Scientist at the Thomas J. Watson Research Center.

JUSTIN BUCKLEY is a Research Assistant in the Survey of English Usage at University College London, where he has worked for a number of years on the International Corpus of English project. He is the Web page designer on the Internet Grammar of English project.

JEANNINE M. DONNA has taught at Middlebury College and the University of North Carolina at Chapel Hill; she is currently Associate Professor of English in the Ph.D. Program in Rhetoric and Linguistics at Indiana University of Pennsylvania, where she also serves as a teacher and Coordinator for the English as a Second Language (ESL) Program. Her areas of interest, in addition to grammar and teacher training, include psycholinguistics, second-language acquisition, syntax, and Persian language and literature.

SUZETTE HADEN ELGIN holds a doctorate in linguistics from the University of California at San Diego and is Associate Professor Emeritus (retired), Department of Linguistics, San Diego State University. Her dissertation was on Navajo syntax; her specialty is applied linguistics. She is founder and director of the Ozark Center for Language Studies (near Huntsville, Arkansas), a virtual business that offers a complete line of products and services in verbal self-defense. She writes and publishes the *Linguistics and Science Fiction* newsletter, now in its seventeenth year. She has published two linguistics textbooks (one coauthored) and twelve science fiction novels and is the author of the Gentle Art of Verbal Self-Defense series. She maintains a regular schedule of seminars and speaking engagements, as well as a private practice as a communications consultant. She is married, mother of five, grandmother of ten and had a book on grandmothering published in September 1998.

SUSAN K. HECK teaches composition at Arizona State University, where she is also currently engaged in full-time doctoral study. Her areas of research include second-language writing, teaching in the computer-mediated classroom, and teaching English as a second language.

RICHARD HUDSON is Professor of Linguistics at University College London, where he was in the Department of Linguistics when it was founded by Michael Halliday. Since those days he has had a keen interest in school-level language teaching, but he also teaches syntax and sociolinguistics, and his research is in syntactic theory. His most relevant books are *Sociolinguistics* (2nd edition, 1996), *Teaching Grammar* (1992), and *English Grammar* (1998).

PATRICIA L. MacGREGOR-MENDOZA received her Ph.D. from the University of Illinois at Urbana-Champaign in 1996. She is an Assistant Professor in the Department of Languages and Linguistics at New Mexico State University, where she teaches courses in Spanish and linguistics and is the head of the linguistics component. Her research interests include examining the relationship between language and school. She has forthcoming articles on the history of attitudes toward Spanish in the United States and the current language use and attitudes of bilingual teachers in the Southwest.

JOHN MYHILL is an Associate Professor in the English Department at the University of Haifa. His research has centered upon sociolinguistics, particularly Black English, and text analysis; he is the author of *Typological Discourse Analysis* (1992).

GERALD NELSON is a Research Fellow at the Survey of English Usage, University College London, where he has been responsible for the British component of the International Corpus of English since the start of the project. His research interests include corpus linguistics and English syntax, on which he has published widely. He is the author of the Internet Grammar of English.

ANCA M. NEMOIANU received a Ph.D. in Applied Linguistics from the University of California at Berkeley and teaches linguistics to nonlinguistics students at the Catholic University of America in Washington, D.C., where she also directs the ESL program. She has published on various issues in developmental linguistics, but her more recent interests concern the pedagogical challenges of teaching linguistics to English education majors and graduate students of English literature.

TODD OAKLEY received his Ph.D. in English Language and Literature in 1995 from the University of Maryland, College Park, and is currently Assistant Professor of English and Director of Composition at Case Western Reserve University. His dissertation focused on the relationship between cognitive linguistics and argumentation theory. His current research interests include mental imagery in linguistic and iconic systems, conceptual blending and integration, evolutionary theories of meaning, writing pedagogy, and prose style. His influences include classical and modern rhetorical theory and cognitive science. He has published articles in *Rhetoric Society Quarterly* and *Cognitive Linguistics*.

VICTOR RASKIN is Professor of English and Linguistics at Purdue University, where he also chairs the Interdepartmental Program in Linguistics. Educated at Moscow State University in Moscow in what was then the USSR (B.A., 1964; M.A., 1966; Ph.D., 1970, all in linguistics), he taught there until his emigration to Israel in 1973, where he taught both at the Hebrew University of Jerusalem and at Tel-Aviv University until his move to Purdue in 1978. He has been a visiting professor at the University of Michigan and a visiting speaker at many Soviet, Israeli, British, Dutch, Belgian, Canadian, Italian, and U.S. universities and research centers. He has published 16 books and over 200 articles in linguistic and semantic theory, linguistic applications, computational linguistics, the linguistics of humor, and other related areas. He has been Editor-in-Chief of *Humor: International Journal of Humor Research* since its founding in 1987.

SYLVIA SHAW is a Lecturer in Communication Studies at Middlesex University, London. Her current research project concerns gender, language, and political debates in the British House of Commons. Before starting at Middlesex, Shaw worked as a lexicographer for Longman Dictionaries, where she also undertook research into the incorporation of spoken-language data into dictionaries using computerized spoken-language corpora.

NICHOLAS SOBIN received his Ph.D. in linguistics from the University of Texas at Austin and is currently Professor of English at the University of Arkansas at Little Rock. He has been a visiting professor in linguistics at the University of Iowa and a visiting scholar in linguistics at the Massachusetts Institute of Technology and at Harvard University. His research has covered a variety of areas, including syntax and syntactic theory, language variation, and second-language acquisition. His work has appeared in major journals, including *Linguistic Inquiry* and *Natural Language and Linguistic Theory*.

DEBORAH TANNEN is on the faculty of the Department of Linguistics at Georgetown University, where she is one of only four faculty members who hold the distinguished rank of University Professor. She has been Mc-Graw Distinguished Lecturer at Princeton University and was a fellow at the Center for Advanced Study in the Behavioral Sciences in Stanford, California, following a term in residence at the Institute for Advanced Study in Princeton, New Jersey. She has published sixteen books and over seventy articles on such topics as spoken and written language, doctor-patient communication, cross-cultural communication, modern Greek discourse, the poetics of everyday conversation, and the relationship between conversational and literary discourse. Among her books are *Talking Voices, Gender and Discourse*, and *Conversational Style*. She received her Ph.D. in linguistics from the University of California at Berkeley.

ELIZABETH CLOSS TRAUGOTT received a Ph.D. in English linguistics at the University of California at Berkeley in 1964 and has been Professor of Linguistics and English at Stanford University since 1977. She has done research in linguistics and literature, historical syntax, semantics, grammaticalization, discourse analysis, and sociohistorical linguistics. Her current research focuses on language change, particularly lexicalization of pragmatic implicatures, and subjectification. Her publications include *A History of English Syntax* (1972), *Linguistics for Students of Literature* (with Mary L. Pratt, 1980), *On Conditionals* (coedited, 1986), and *Grammaticalization* (with Paul Hopper, 1993). She is writing a book on regularity in semantic change with Richard Dasher. She has been a Fellow at the Center for Advanced Study in the Behavioral Sciences and a Guggenheim Fellow.

DAVID B. UMBACH received his Ph.D. in English linguistics from Purdue University. He is currently an Assistant Professor in the Department of English at Drake University, having previously taught at Idaho State University. His research interests center on discourse analysis and critical linguistics.

GAIL BRENDEL VIECHNICKI is a Ph.D. candidate in linguistics at The University of Chicago. Her interests include evidentiality, epistemology, hedging, and spoken and written academic discourse. Her publications include "An Empirical Analysis of Participant Intentions: Discourse in a Graduate Seminar," University of Chicago M.A. thesis, published in *Language and Communication* (May 1997); "Theory and Data in Discourse Analysis" (coedited with E. M. Jones) in a special issue of *Language and Communication* (May 1997); and "Professional Intimacy: The Consultant-Student Relationship," *Writing Lab Newsletter*, Purdue University (1994). In addition, she has taught composition for the last four years in The University of Chicago's writing program, the Little Red Schoolhouse, as well as at DeVry Institute of Technology, Robert Morris College, and Loyola University of Chicago.

REBECCA S. WHEELER is Assistant Professor of English at Christopher Newport University, in Virginia, where she teaches grammar, linguistics, writing and fiction. In the environment of an undergraduate English department, she has become interested in helping unbind the negative associations grammar holds for many people. The current volume offers an alternative vision of grammar, inviting students to become sleuths as they explore and probe the language data of their everyday world. Her research interests have centered on the nature of meaning in language, ambiguity, polysemy, and the interface between syntax and semantics. Recent publications include *The Workings of Language: From Prescriptions to Perspectives* (Praeger, 1999); "Home Speech as Springboard to School Speech: Oakland's Commendable Work on Ebonics" (in Rebecca S. Wheeler, ed., *The Workings of Language*, Praeger, 1999); "Will the Real Search Verbs Please Stand Up?" (1996); " 'Understand' in Conceptual Semantics" (1995); and "Beyond 'Try to Find': The Syntax and Semantics of 'Search' and 'Analyze' " (1995). Wheeler, who received her Ph.D. in linguistics from The University of Chicago in 1989, has been appointed to the Undergraduate Program Advisory Committee of the Linguistic Society of America.

WALT WOLFRAM is the William C. Friday Distinguished Professor at North Carolina State University. Over the past three decades, he has pioneered research in a wide range of vernacular varieties of English. At the same time, he has been vitally involved in the dissemination of information about language diversity to the American public. Recent books include *American English: Dialects and Variation* (with Natalie Schilling-Estes) and *Dialects in the School and Community* (with Carolyn Adger and Donna Christian).

ISBN 0-275-96055-2

HARDCOVER BAR CODE